MICHAEL CAMPBELL
Rookie on Tour

To Al
All the best
Michael
Campbell

MICHAEL CAMPBELL

Rookie on Tour

Russell Gray

Hodder Moa Beckett

ACKNOWLEDGEMENTS

Rookie on Tour could not have been written without the the co-operation of Michael and Julie Campbell. It wasn't always convenient, but Michael and Julie gave up their time on brief visits to New Zealand during breaks in their tournament schedule when they would probably have preferred to be out enjoying themselves. There were also many telephone conversations from distant locations which were not only informative but enjoyable.

The project would also have been impossible but for the help provided by Thomas and Maria Campbell and their daughter Michelle. They welcomed me into their home and the scrapbooks Thomas has kept were invaluable.

Mal Tongue, Max Cunningham and Stephen Scahill were a wonderful source of information. I am grateful not only to them but to other friends and associates of Michael who went out of their way to help, as well as to my proof-reader who not only found any mistakes but also made valuable suggestions.

Russell Gray

ISBN 1-86958-298-5

© Michael Campbell/Russell Gray 1996

Published in 1996 by Hodder Moa Beckett Publishers Limited
[a member of the Hodder Headline Group]
4 Whetu Place, Mairangi Bay, Auckland, New Zealand

Cover photos: (Front) Allsport, Tim Matthews; (Back) Allsport, Stephen Munday
Photos: Unless credited otherwise, photos have been supplied by the
Campbell Family Collection or by Michael and Julie Campbell.

Typeset by Mills Typeset Ltd, Auckland

Printed by Wright & Carman (NZ) Ltd, Upper Hutt

Contents

"Michael Campbell is one of those sports people who come along once every decade. Michael manages to combine an easygoing attitude to life with a fierce dedication to succeed.

I believe he will be a dominant force in the world of golf for many years to come."

Greg Norman

Foreword

How much Michael Campbell has achieved in a relatively short time in golf was brought home to me when I went to Augusta for the US Masters.

Every golf magazine I picked up in America contained feature articles on Michael. During his rookie years he has been a marvellous ambassador for New Zealand through his performances on the golf course and his demeanour away from it.

From the time I first met Michael there were never any doubts in my mind that he could go to the top in golf if that was what he wanted. That hasn't changed. Technically he is up there with the best.

What has impressed me just as much as his golfing exploits is the way he has developed as a person.

Michael is the type of person who can enhance people's lives without touching them. The simplicity of his performances shines through in golf and he has the type of smile which could melt an iceberg.

He has come to terms with so much in such a short period of time and has been able to fit himself into all types of environment. Whether in Titahi Bay or Augusta, Georgia, Michael has been himself. The common touch which endeared him to his peers during his early days in golf hasn't left him. He can still laugh at himself and he is trying hard not to forget his roots which are as a New Zealander and a Maori.

Since he began playing Michael has wanted people to judge him as Michael Campbell the man just as much as Michael Campbell the golfer. I believe he has passed that test.

Like most of us, Michael had his dreams. Unlike most of us he has been able to realise his. I know he is proud of what he has done but it hasn't happened by accident.

In all sports the only path to success is through hard work. Michael might make what is a technically difficult game look so simple, but he has worked hard to get where he is. It has been a privilege to work with such a talented young man for whom I feel the best is yet to come.

Mal Tongue
May 1996

Introduction

It would be satisfying to be able to say that upon first setting eyes on Michael Campbell I immediately realised that here was a golfing star of the future, someone who would go to the very top of the game.

That wasn't the case. The Michael Campbell I watched ten years ago was a pleasant young man who loved playing golf. He had an abundance of talent and there were parts of his game which stood him apart from his peers; but he was raw – very raw.

The swing which these days is drawing rave reviews from top players and commentators alike was still inside Michael Campbell, waiting to emerge. It was released and refined by coach Mal Tongue, an Englishman who found his niche in the game of golf 12,000 miles from home, light years away from the mining job he could easily have ended up with in his native Nottingham.

I have the feeling that Michael Campbell would still have become a professional golfer, such was his desire to play the game for a living, had Tongue not stepped into his life. Whether he would have made the impact he has in such a short time is another matter.

During those early days Michael Campbell, like every young sportsman, had dreams. One day he was going to play in the British Open, and win it, he would tell you. Even at that stage no one laughed at such lofty ambition.

Over the years it has been a pleasure to watch Michael Campbell on the golf course, to work with and, occasionally, socialise with him away from it.

MICHAEL CAMPBELL

No home-grown golfer has captured the New Zealand public's imagination as Michael Campbell has. His immediate professional predecessors, Frank Nobilo, Greg Turner and Grant Waite, are known, liked and respected, but Campbell has the X factor which makes him that little bit different.

In his rapid rise up the world rankings, from playing alongside his mates in the Wellington team to pairing up with players the calibre of Greg Norman, Ernie Els, Nick Price and Jack Nicklaus, Michael Campbell hasn't changed. He is still the easy-going, smiling person who one day early in his amateur career approached me with the comment, "Hey, what was that rubbish you wrote this morning. I didn't play that badly did I?"

Told that, in my humble view, he had indeed played that badly, Campbell grinned and said, "Make sure you're watching today. It is going to be a lot different." It was, and he went on to finish second in that particular tournament.

More than once over the years Campbell suggested that one day we would write a book together about his exploits. When the publishers asked me to write *Rookie on Tour* I was only too happy to take up the challenge.

I have endeavoured to describe Michael Campbell's life and his time as a golf rookie through my own experiences, his words, and the eyes of those who know him best. It is something I have enjoyed doing.

Russell Gray
May 1996

1
Hitting Home

L adies and gentlemen, on the tee, at nine under par – Michael
Campbell, New Zealand." Those packed into the stand which
looks out across the first and 18th fairways of St Andrews Old
Course on the final day of the 1995 British Open, many of whom had
been sitting there for hours, welcomed the New Zealander with warm
applause. The two players about to finish their round on the adjacent
18th green took time out from surveying their putts to watch the action.

Italian Costantino Rocca, who was starting the final round in
second place two strokes behind Campbell, had just played his tee shot
and now stood watching as Campbell went through his pre-shot
routine.

Rocca looked almost uninterested as he stood with arms folded
– but he was interested all right. Over the past few months the Italian
and New Zealander had got to know each other well at European
tournaments and Campbell was the man Rocca felt he had to beat if
he was to win his first Major championship.

The applause which had acknowledged Rocca's drive died away
and all eyes turned to Campbell. Most of the gallery were getting their
first look at the 26-year-old from New Zealand in the flesh, though they
would have noticed him in contention on television in recent times.

There were plenty of New Zealanders among those waiting
expectantly for Campbell to play his first shot, many patriotically
wearing the silver fern. For some the day was extra special.

Thomas Campbell had to keep telling himself that he really was at St Andrews and that his son, a rookie on the European Tour, was leading the biggest golf tournament in the world by two shots with just 18 holes to play.

Michael's fiancee Julie Wendel, an honorary Kiwi despite hailing from Sydney, looked cool and assured, though butterflies were dancing around in her stomach.

Coach Mal Tongue, an Englishman who had just become a New Zealand citizen, could have been forgiven had he allowed himself a quiet smile after predicting that Campbell could compete with the best in the world but, as usual, Tongue was too nervous for such a luxury.

Neil Munro, then a coach, had helped Campbell early in his career. At St Andrews his role was as a tour leader, responsible for many of the New Zealanders who were at the Open, though tour duties were taking second place for Munro on this day, as he cast his mind back to the raw product he had helped, in a small way, to mould into such an exciting player.

There were only two New Zealand media representatives watching proceedings. I was one of them, along with NZPA's Simon England, and it was hard to be objective while waiting for the last pair to hit off. For ten years I had watched Campbell blossom from a useful junior to a player capable of footing it with the best golfers in the world. During that time we had often talked about his ambitions and winning the Open was the one he talked about most. The first Open I covered for *The Dominion* newspaper was at St Andrews in 1990 and when I got back to Wellington Campbell was full of questions. What was the town like? Was the course what it was cracked up to be? How did it feel to be watching such great players in the flesh? Who did I talk to? What did they say?

It was the same each time I arrived back from an Open. Michael wanted to know everything about it and the conversations always finished the same way with him telling me, "One day I'll play in the Open at St Andrews and win it."

In New Zealand it was 1.45am Monday. Lights were being switched on in living rooms throughout the country, and cups of tea made before people, some of whom had never watched golf before, settled down in front of television sets hoping to see a New Zealander win the British Open for only the second time.

It had been so different when New Zealand's greatest golfing son,

Bob Charles, had won the 1963 Open at Royal Lytham and St Anne's. When Charles was writing himself into history New Zealanders heard about it on radio or in the following day's newspapers.

Nowhere was the tension greater, not even among those watching on course, than at the Titahi Bay Golf Club where more than a hundred members had gathered in the clubhouse to watch the youngster who ten years earlier, as a 16-year-old playing off a six handicap, had set their course record of 62.

Michael's mother Maria was in the front row. Maria knew how edgy her son was feeling. She had spoken to him for half an hour before he left for the course and had sensed how nervous he was. Michael's sister Michelle was at home recovering from the birth, the previous day, of her second child – a boy about to be named after his uncle Mike, making sure neither would ever forget the moment. Or perhaps Michelle was just making sure Michael senior would never forget his nephew's birthday.

The welcome on course for Campbell had seemed much louder and warmer than it had been for Rocca, and why not? Twenty-four hours earlier Campbell had thrilled the 40,000 at the course, and millions watching on television, with a round of golf which would long be remembered, and a shot which will be talked about as long as the Open is contested.

A third-round seven under par 65 in conditions which had the world's best golfers struggling meant Campbell had announced his arrival on the world stage in dramatic fashion. No longer was he merely a well-performed rookie on the European tour. That day he played the shot of a lifetime on the infamous 17th, the dreaded Road Hole, and emerged with arms spread wide from the bunker which had once cost Japan's Tommy Nakajima the Open title. On his face was a beaming smile which captivated all those who saw it.

In modern times Jack Nicklaus, twice, Seve Ballesteros and Nick Faldo – all great champions – have won the Open at St Andrews, and those three giants of the game would have fallen over one another to have claimed the shot Campbell played from tight against the face of that bunker.

As Campbell had surveyed his options, playing partner Brett Ogle, a tall, easy-going Australian who has been playing in Australasia, Europe and the United States since turning professional in 1986, watched with interest. While he might have envied Campbell his place on the leaderboard with 19 holes and a bit to play he was delighted not to be in the situation the Kiwi now found himself.

The only way out of the bunker for Campbell, Ogle thought, was backwards. Campbell's caddy Max Cunningham thought likewise. Campbell disagreed. So far as he was concerned he couldn't go backwards or sideways, there just wasn't room to swing the club. As he paced back and forth considering his options, Campbell must have begun to feel there was no apparent exit from one of the game's enduring nightmares. At least no shot you would find in the coaching manuals.

It was then that Campbell showed why players such as Greg Norman were predicting such a big future for him. He hit the ball vertically on to the lip of the bunker and it rolled down to within 18 inches of the hole, from where he completed one of the unlikliest pars imaginable.

Ogle summed it up: "I didn't think he could get it out but he played a truly great shot. You have to hand it to him. It was one of the most amazing golf shots I have seen. He went to hell and came out alive."

A par on the last, though Campbell was kicking himself for not making birdie, completed his 65 and he was looking ahead to the last round, 18 holes with the eyes of the world focussed on him.

Since arriving in St Andrews on the Sunday, Campbell had been soaking up the atmosphere all week and was delighted at his father being able to share the experience with him. It was hard to tell who was enjoying it the most with Campbell senior wide-eyed as he was introduced to players he had only read about and watched on television.

"Dad had a ball all week. He was like a kid in a candy store as he did things he or I could never have imagined happening to us. Not only was it the first time he had been to an Open, but it was at St Andrews.

"The most relaxed times during Open week are the practice days. It is on those days that spectators can get close to the players. Autographs and photographs are sought as you walk from a green to the next tee. People get the chance to exchange a quick word with players like Greg Norman. Sometimes it was hard to take in the fact that I was one of the players rather than a spectator. It wasn't long ago that I would have happily settled for being on the outside of the ropes looking in, just to get a taste of the atmosphere at an Open. I would have been the first to ask Norman for an autograph as well.

"Dad and Mal were able to walk down the fairway with the players on practice days and Dad loved every moment, specially when he got to caddy for me. Max had to nip to the toilet so Dad insisted on taking over the bag. There he was striding down the fairway with this huge bag over his shoulder – how times had changed from when I used to caddy for him at Titahi Bay. It was a good job his bag was never that big or I wouldn't have been able to pull the trundler.

"On the first practice day I played with Craig Parry, Ian Baker-Finch, David Frost and Robert Allenby. After the round my elbow was a little tender so I headed off to the physiotherapist's trailer for treatment and found myself next to Greg Norman, who was having his back worked on. Greg suggested we play together the following day and said he would fix up another couple of guys – who turned out to be Raymond Floyd and Nick Price.

"I introduced Dad to them. 'Greg, this is my father Tom.' 'Honoured to meet you Mr Norman,' he said. 'Ray . . .'. 'Pleased to meet you Mr Floyd'. 'Nick . . .'. By this time Dad was so tongue-tied he replied 'Pleased to meet you Mal.' He was so embarrassed, but Nick told him not to worry as it happens all the time. As it turned out Greg didn't play much that day because of his back but that didn't make it any less special for Dad.

"I got so much enjoyment out of Dad being at St Andrews. He couldn't believe how my lifestyle had changed, how much had happened in the first seven months of the year. Sometimes I couldn't believe it myself. I would sit back and reflect on everything. It was hard to come to terms with a lot of things that had happened. The days, the tournaments, the travel had all gone by in a bit of a blur but it had all been fun.

"Dad doesn't show his emotions much. He has always been one who keeps his feelings to himself but that week it all came out. It was so nice to see that side of Dad. I hadn't see it for a long time."

Thomas Campbell might have been overawed but the week was an amazing experience for Michael Campbell as well. There were high expectations of him because of the way he had performed on the European tour during the first six months of 1995. There was also self-imposed pressure. This was his third attempt at the Open. In 1993 at Royal St George's he didn't get a start after failing to get through pre-qualifying, a situation for which he only had himself to blame. The following year he sailed through pre-qualifying, went on to perform creditably over the first two rounds but not quite well enough to make the cut.

Both situations annoyed Campbell. A proud young man who had left amateur golf on a high, he had tasted success early in his professional career and didn't like it when he let himself down. Some players go through their entire careers without getting a start in a Major championship and would have settled happily for two starts in succession whatever the outcome. For Campbell it isn't enough. He enters golf tournaments to win and Major championships are no different to any other event. Inevitably he puts more pressure on himself than others put on him. The public expects plenty from their sporting heroes, but Campbell expects just as much as they do. That is the way Mal Tongue has insisted he be. If he didn't set high standards and demand results from every shot then Tongue wouldn't be in his corner.

It all led to a pressure-packed week and when Campbell arrived in St Andrews the tension increased as he looked in awe at the famous old clubhouse. There is a special feeling about St Andrews during Open week. A quiet town most of the time, St Andrews bursts into life when it hosts a golf tournament and never more so than when it is the Open, that most alluring of championships.

Halls of residence at the famous old university are filled with folk talking golf rather than academia. Rooms in which the midnight oil normally burns for the purposes of study are taken over by golf enthusiasts, many of whom will play on some of the wonderful courses within easy reach of St Andrews at first light, and head back to the Old Course to watch their heroes later in the day. At night a few beers in one of the packed bars will bring sleep easily before the cycle begins again. Scores Hotel, a pitching wedge from the locker room, is a focal point for golf fans of all nationalities. During Open week they congregate to discuss the day's play and as the night wears on the overflow happily drink their pints of beer or sip wine on the pavement till long after darkness has fallen around eleven o'clock.

Nowhere in the world can the fans get closer to their golfing heroes than at St Andrews. They hang over the temporary barriers which stand within yards of the locker room door from early morning till the last player has left the course which, apart from Saturday and Sunday, can be well after 10pm.

It was through those fans that Michael had to find a path when he arrived four days before the championship was due to start. Some pushing autograph books in front of him, or asking for any spare balls as souvenirs, knew of him. To those people he was the New Zealand lad who had been going so well on the European Tour lately, though there were others who thought he might be Tiger Woods or Robert Gomez. By the time the championship was over they would all know it was Michael Campbell.

Michael Campbell has always been a bit of a showman. Big crowds normally don't intimidate him. Rather they bring the best out. This was an atmosphere he knew he was going to enjoy, but to do that he had to perform.

"It was nerve wracking stuff. Not only was it the British Open, but it was at St Andrews where golf was born. My first tee shot in the opening round went 100 yards left of where it should have gone and into the burn. I almost missed the widest fairway in golf, that's how nervous I was.

"I was totally overwhelmed by the whole atmosphere, the history behind St Andrews and the Open itself. I didn't think it was possible to feel more nervous and unsure than I did before that first shot on Thursday."

There had been no hint of what was to come with Campbell shooting one under par 71s in his first two rounds, though he was particularly pleased to be under par in his second round which was played in strong winds. The round took five and a half hours and the conditions got worse by the minute, but the tougher they got the tougher Campbell became mentally, something he put down to coming from Wellington where wind and cold were no strangers.

Going into the third round Campbell trailed the leading trio of Brad Faxon, Katsuyoshi Tomori and John Daly by four and there was a host of top players between him and the top three, including United States Open champion Corey Pavin and his predecessor Ernie Els.

Birdies at the third and fifth holes moved Campbell up the leaderboard and the smallish gallery following him noticed that those ahead of him at the start of the day were not going that well in the early stages of their rounds. By the time Campbell reached the turn at four under for the day and six under for the tournament, after birdies on the seventh and ninth holes, he had moved into third place.

While he was playing the 10th and 11th he moved into second spot with pars and when he sank a birdie putt on the 12th green he went to the top of the leaderboard for the first time. It was a moment Campbell will treasure for the rest of his life, no matter how many tournaments he wins, on whatever the tour. The thrill he got from seeing his name move ahead of the best field in world golf gave him a huge thrill.

That was the moment when the camaraderie which is prevalent in golf came the fore.

"As we moved to the next tee Brett Ogle put his arm round my shoulders and told me to just keep playing my game, not to worry about anyone else and to ignore the gallery, whatever their reaction.

"I birdied the 13th and 14th holes and Brett said, 'Isn't this fun?' I replied, 'Yes, it's great fun.' I'll always be grateful for the way Brett was that day. He was so supportive. The difference between golf and, say, rugby, is that in rugby Aussies and Kiwis would be punching each other, whereas in golf here was an Aussie making sure his Kiwi mate kept a good run going.

"After we'd signed our cards Brett said, 'Tell you what Cambo, you kicked our arses last night in rugby [the All Blacks had beaten the Wallabies in a Bledisloe Cup match] and you've kicked our arses at golf today.' "

As Campbell made his way towards the clubhouse the galleries began flocking to him. Reporters arrived to chart his progress over the final holes and those who knew little or nothing of him, particularly the Americans, wanted to know everything about him. Did he play rugby? Could he have been an All Black? He used to play softball? Didn't know you played softball in New Zealand.

While those on the periphery were clamouring to know more about the dark, handsome young man who was striding down the fairways with a smile on his face, Campbell was having a ball. Always the showman, he lapped up the attention and while the birdies had dried up he was still making pars and staying well clear of the field. At one point he led by five. He was never going to keep such an advantage with so many talented golfers playing on the course behind him but he was still ahead by two after late charges from Costantino Rocca and Steve Elkington.

The gallery following Campbell was huge by the time he hit his driver off the 17th tee and they had no way of knowing that his drive had stopped in an old divot.

"The wind was blowing right to left and the ball was above my feet which would encourage the hook. That's what happened and the ball ended up in the bunker.

"My heart dropped when I saw where it was. Max and I talked about it for what seemed a long time. I said, 'Look, I can't go left or right or backwards.' We had a bit of an argument. I told him I couldn't go backwards as he suggested because I wouldn't be able to get the club up fast enough for the lip. By that time I had made my mind up and played *that* shot. I couldn't see what was happening because of the bunker wall, but the crowd's reaction told me something good was happening. When I got out of the bunker and did my little pose I thought 'someone is smiling on me'.

"But that was the shot of a lifetime. If I go in with a thousand balls I would never play it the same again. Actually I tried it at the Dunhill Cup later in the year. I couldn't resist. I put it back in the same position and couldn't get the ball out. A number of times the ball went up and down again to land in my footprint. Imagine if I hadn't got the bounce I did that Saturday. It could have been in my footprint and I might have made eight or nine. I can imagine how Nakajima felt; there is such a fine line between what is seen as brilliance and disaster. On a golf course you have to take the good with the bad and this was good.

"As we drove home after that round everyone was in shock. There were four of us in the car – Julie, Mal, Owen Williams [a friend and sponsor] and myself. It was a 45-minute drive and there was absolute silence. Not a word. Anyone who knows the four of us would find that hard to believe but that's how it was.

"It didn't change when we got to the house. Everyone was looking at each other but saying nothing. It was weird. I'd just had the round of my life. We should have all been on top of the world but we couldn't take in what had happened.

"I eventually broke the ice by saying, 'Look guys, let's say something here' but it didn't really make much difference. Here I was, only thirteen years after first starting playing golf, leading the Open and none of us could talk about it. It was almost like wasting the moment.

"Mal and Owen went out for dinner to give Julie and myself a bit of time to ourselves but even over dinner with Julie it was quiet. We were awestruck.

"When you dream about things – and I had dreamt of this moment ever since I had first swung a club while caddying for Dad at Titahi Bay they never seem the same when it actually happens. It is hard to accept that what you have always fantasised about is coming true.

"When I was about to win the Open in my dreams, the night before the final round definitely wasn't spent playing computer games, but that was my preparation for the big day.

"When Mal got back from the restaurant about 9.30 he got out his portable computer and I spent the next few hours playing solitaire and minesweeper. It must have been the kid in me coming out, but at the time it was heaven sent because it took my mind off golf. All I could think about was beating the computer.

"I had to come back to the real world eventually though and at about two o'clock thought I had better get some sleep. That was easier said than done. For the next couple of hours I tried everything but sleep just wouldn't come. My mind was going crazy. I was thinking about all sorts of things. I was getting too far ahead of myself, thinking of the consequences.

"If I win the British Open my world ranking will change dramatically, financially I will be made . . . and so on. I can't recall them all because I was trying not to think about such things at the time but there must have been thirty or forty things going round in my head.

"I began to get frightened and in the end I was frightened to win it. I knew if I won the Open it would change my life, our lives. The lives of people around me. Family and friends. My relationship with Julie."

Sleep eventually came for Campbell around four in the morning but by eight he was awake again. Did he dream during those four hours? "Yes. I dreamt I won."

On Sunday morning the house was just as quiet as it had been Saturday night as they tried to come to terms with what had happened.

"It was hard to comprehend. I couldn't come to terms with the fact that little Michael Campbell from Titahi Bay, population 20,000, who started playing golf on a course where there are fences round the greens and sheep shit everywhere, was leading the Open."

Being the leader and not teeing off till 2.45 meant all morning being spent waiting around the house. There was more time than normal to kill because Campbell had decided to mark the moment by going to the course in a helicopter, which was another first for his father.

Whether Campbell would go down that road again only time will tell, but perhaps he could learn from Nick Faldo. When Faldo was leading the Open in 1990 and '92 he was either on the putting green practising or keeping himself occupied.

There was still ninety minutes to his tee time when Campbell arrived on course and headed into the locker room. Waiting for him was caddy Max Cunningham, who had been preparing in his own way and had been at work on the course while his player was still sleeping.

At first light Max was out checking yardages and pin placements so that the Campbell-Cunningham team knew exactly what to expect. He was as well prepared as could be. A caddy can't control the weather, however, and during the morning there were no obvious signs of the gale force winds which would whip up when the leaders were out on the course.

I met Max by chance outside a St Andrews newsagents around 9am and we discussed prospects for the day. Max told me that he had a plan for the dreaded 17th should Michael have a couple of shots to spare going into the hole on which so many Open aspirations have foundered. Sadly, he never had chance to put it into operation. When they reached that point Michael was trying to catch John Daly rather than setting the pace himself.

Max Cunningham isn't the type to get carried away. He wouldn't have lasted with the level-headed Scotsman Sandy Lyle had he been. That Sunday morning, though, he appeared quietly confident and when we parted I hoped he would be smiling later in the day.

In the locker room, Max told Michael there were a few faxes in his locker. He proved to be the master of understatement. When Michael opened the locker the faxes tumbled out over the floor.

"There were hundreds and hundreds of them, from all parts of New Zealand. From people I didn't know, from friends and family . . . everyone. I was overwhelmed and couldn't resist sitting down for a few minutes to read some of them.

"I must have spent more than half an hour reading them and hardly seemed to have made a dent in the pile when Max said that it was time to warm up. I didn't want to stop and kept telling him one more, one more. Another five minutes must have passed when he said, 'Come on Cambo, time's getting tight you've got to go now.' I still couldn't drag myself away till Max demanded we go to the practice fairway.

"I know the people who sent the faxes wanted to help me and they did. Okay, I didn't win the Open but they inspired me to play well, and despite the way the day panned out I believe I did play well and didn't let myself or anyone else down."

Eventually Max got him down to the practice fairway and it was there, away from the crowds, family, friends and supporters that the fact that he was leading the Open finally hit home.

"I remember looking around the practice ground which had been a hive of activity all week and it was completely empty. Rocca had just left and everyone else was on the course playing. It was then that I thought, 'Wow, this is real after all.' It gave me a warm, fuzzy feeling and I headed back to the practice green for a few putts feeling good."

I watched Campbell in those last few minutes before he headed for the tee and he looked completely in control, though the jaunty wave and smile he had greeted people with the day before was missing. There was a seriousness about him which had been absent during the rest of the week; only natural given the position he was in. Inside his heart was beating faster and louder by the second.

"It started beating faster because there was only five minutes to go, then four minutes, three . . . and when it was time to head to the tee I thought it was beating so loudly other people would be able to hear it."

As he was escorted to the tee Campbell was aware of silver ferns all around him. It seemed everyone who wished him luck was wearing the fern. After telling Rocca to play well and watching him hit off Campbell heard his own name called and as the crowd roared a welcome his heart started beating so fast it began hurting and just teeing the ball up became more difficult than playing a shot.

"I almost fainted as I bent over to put the tee in the ground. It was a terrible, terrifying moment. Even now I can't really explain how

I felt. I was frightened, really frightened. I was frightened of winning, I was frightened of losing.

"Eventually I settled myself and hit a bad shot left. I thought the ball had gone into the burn as it had on the first day and I said to myself, 'Please don't do this Michael. Don't make a mess of it.' "

Taking a deep breath, Campbell set off in search of his ball and breathed a huge sigh of relief when he saw it had stopped five or so yards from the burn. Had it gone in a shot would have been dropped, but as on the first day he escaped with a par.

The warning signs were already there, however. There was a tenseness about Campbell which hadn't been seen before at the tournament. Watching television in Sydney was Campbell's sports psychologist Michael Martin who told him later that he was too intense and too dark on himself. The key to the previous day's brilliant round, according to Martin, was his relaxed jovial attitude.

On the second tee Campbell remonstrated with a photographer, which was totally out of character. "That last day brought something out of me you don't normally see. The real, mean side of Michael Campbell. I began to get picky about people moving, photographers taking pictures while I was swinging. I was so tense. It wasn't me."

Despite the conditions being horrendous with a gale-force wind and rain squalls, Campbell safely negotiated the first four holes and when he did drop a shot at the par-five fifth he felt cheated. Caught in two minds over his second shot when drips of water fell on his ball while addressing it, he thought about pulling away but decided to hit the shot and it finished up so far right it was on the adjacent New Course. When Campbell punched an eight-iron to the green I began to formulate an intro in my mind about the golfer who won the Open playing two courses in the same round. It seemed like a simple two putt and that was why Campbell felt cheated at taking three.

"For my first putt the wind was blowing right to left and helping me. In those circumstances you leave yourself a foot on the right-hand side, but as I hit it a gust of wind came down and that's why I left it six feet short. On my second putt if there was no wind it was straight, but there was a right to left breeze, quite strong, so I aimed about four inches right of the hole. I hit it exactly as I wanted but the wind stopped and it went straight."

Going into the last six holes Campbell was two shots behind

Daly. He had chances to catch up but, unlike the previous day, the ball wouldn't drop. On the 18th tee Campbell had the amazing thought that if he holed his drive, and remember this was a 354-yard par-four, he would win the Open. He drove the green but pulled the shot a little and was left with a 50-foot uphill putt to tie with Daly. He left it short and slightly left, but before that had the wonderful sensation of walking up the 18th fairway to a standing ovation.

It is something which stays with a player for life, a hair-raising sensation only a fortunate few ever get to experience. Ian Baker-Finch, the 1991 champion, will always regret that he never got the chance to, as he put it, smell the roses during his walk from Royal Birkdale's 18th tee towards the packed stands. Baker-Finch was too busy trying to stay on his feet as the gallery swelled on to the fairway along with the final group. At one point the man about to be crowned champion was knocked over.

"That walk with around 40,000 people standing and cheering, at St Andrews of all places, was fantastic, a dream, something which happens in Boys' Own stories. I suppose it is like an All Black playing in a World Cup final. It gave me goose bumps on goose bumps. I knew Dad was out there somewhere and that he would be proud of me. That meant so much to me. When I talked to him afterward he had the same mixed emotions as I had. Happy to be so close, but sad I had missed out.

"It would have been nice to win, but I gave Dad the thrill of his life. It was my little payback to him and to Mal as well. Mal had been helping me for seven years and I know how proud he was that day."

When Michael Campbell left St Andrews it was as he had played, with style. A friend, JP McManus, flew him back to London in his private jet along with Julie and his father. The rumour was, and no one was denying it, that JP McManus had £10,000 each way on Michael to win the Open at odds of 80 to 1. At a quarter the odds for a place, the Irishman made a nice little profit from the Kiwi's third-equal if that was true.

As Michael, his father and Julie jetted back to London in luxury it must have seemed a far cry from when he used to leave the Titahi Bay course on a bike.

Early days . . .

Michael's first haka, four-years-old.

With close cousin Shiran Cunningham at Titahi Bay Beach.

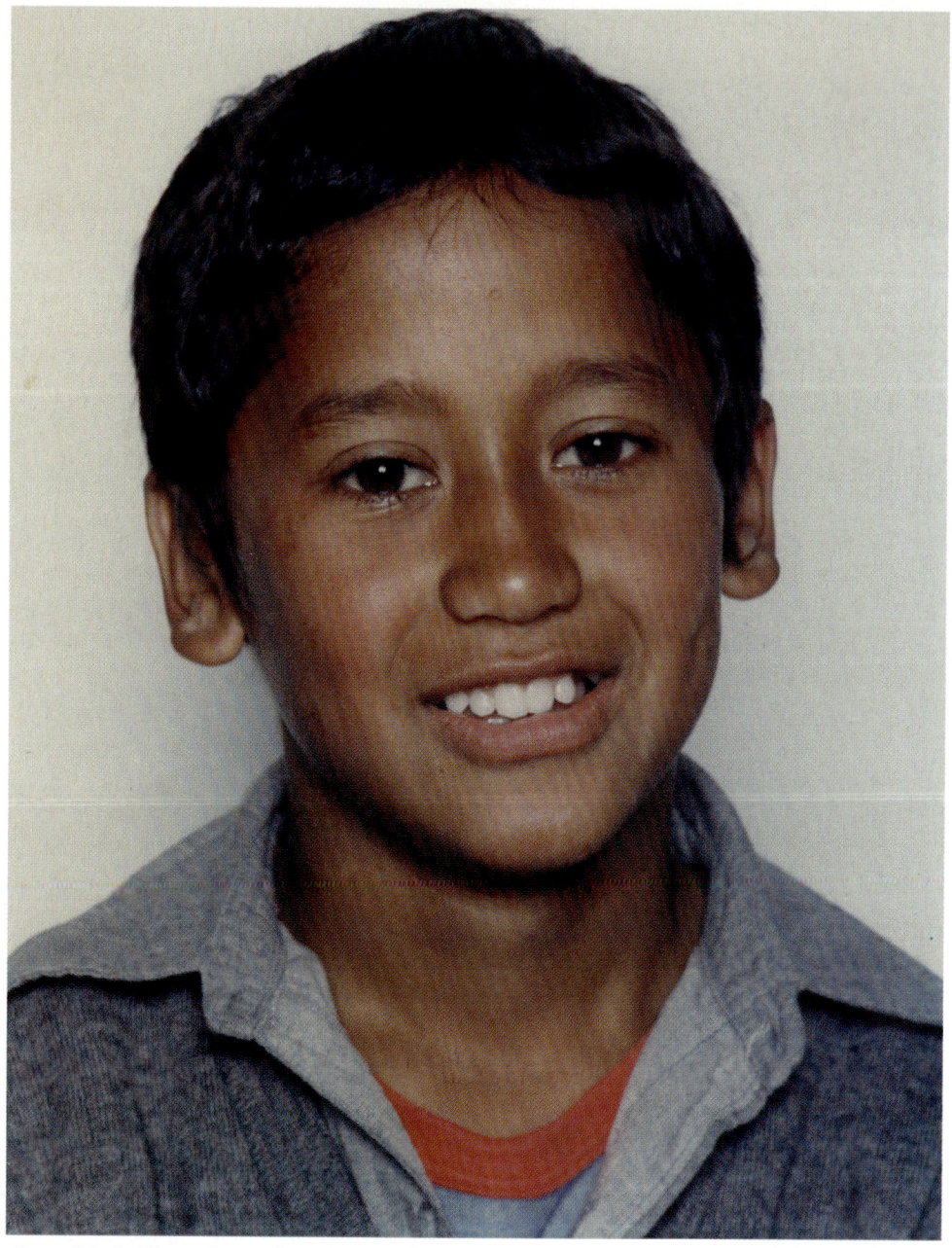

Sister Michelle used to sell Michael's photos to girls at school. Eleven years old, Titahi Bay Intermediate.

Michael, front row left, and his all-conquering junior softball team. Next to Michael is Jason Farrow who went on to represent New Zealand at the World Series.

Local club trophies proudly displayed at home.

Michael (Jackson), Kirstina Smith and Fred Omeri at the Senior Formal at Mana College.

2

A Golfing
Talent

On Michael Campbell's first day at college, along with the rest of
the class he had to stand and say who he was, where he came
from and what he was going to become when he grew up.

His classmates were predictable. They wanted to be policemen,
lawyers, doctors, nurses or firemen, which was understandable for a
bunch of kids from a predominantly working class area. They were
good, steady career options. Get into one of those jobs and their future
families would do well. When it was Campbell's turn he calmly stated
he was Michael Campbell, originally from Hawera and now from
Titahi Bay, and that he would be a golf professional. As he looked
around the classroom he couldn't understand why everyone was
laughing at him.

"They thought golf was for old men. They just didn't
understand. They obviously hadn't watched the top players on
television, or felt the satisfaction that comes from playing a good golf
shot. Everyone who plays golf, whether they are a weekend golfer who
will never improve because they can't play enough, or Nick Faldo on
the way to winning the British Open, knows that wonderful feeling
when the ball does just what you wanted it to do. I hadn't had that
feeling too often by that time, but when I did it was something to
savour and I would lie in bed that night reliving the moment over and
over.

"The other kids were welcome to pursue whatever careers they
wanted, but I knew what I was going to be. The only problem really

was that I didn't know how to go about becoming a professional golfer.

"I was 13 at the time and dreamt of playing golf for a living. What could be better than doing something you loved, and getting loads of money for it. At that time I didn't think about having to beat 143 other guys every week if I was going to win tournaments and earn all that money which seemed to be available. I had no idea what path or direction would have to be taken to turn my dreams into reality. No idea at all. I just wanted to go out there and be a pro golfer. When you are 13 you think it just happens because you want it to."

Michael Campbell was born in Hawera on February 23, 1969, and moved to Wellington with his family when his father Thomas got a job transfer with the Post Office. Michael was four years old and his sister Michelle two. They were a normal working-class family living in Titahi Bay . . . not far from a fledgling golf course.

Since making a name for himself in golf Michael Campbell has often admitted he is a showman at heart, liking nothing better than a big gallery to perform in front of. His love of the spotlight probably goes back to the days when he and Michelle put on concerts for the neighbours in the lounge of the Campbell home.

"Our cousins from Patea often came down to stay with us and we would put on shows for the neighbours," Michelle remembers. "We all took part. Grease was the show then and we used to sing songs from it, dance and do skits. Michael was pretty good.

"Because I was the youngest I would get locked out of my room while the girls rehearsed. The boys would use Michael's room to get it right.

"It was great fun and I know Michael used to enjoy it just as much as any of us."

It was soon after the Campbell family arrived in Titahi Bay that young Michael found himself on the local golf course, caddying for his father. He had just turned five and the trundler and bag he was pulling was bigger than him, but there were never any complaints. Why should there be when there was a mince pie as a reward at the end of the round? If it happened to rain he would get a milkshake as well. While going round the course, which wasn't easy terrain for a five-year-old kid who had a trundler in tow, with his father, Campbell would get out a club and ball and have a hit himself. It would be nice to say that as soon as he got a club in his hand it was obvious here was a potential champion in the making. That wasn't the case but, to be fair to Michael, he might have shown promise earlier than he did had he been playing with the right clubs. Thomas Campbell is left-handed and consequently his son had to play that way if he wanted to have a hit.

Golf wasn't the only sporting interest young Campbell had. Softball and rugby also figured high on the agenda and, like all young New Zealand boys, his ambition was to become an All Black. His mother Maria wasn't too keen on him continuing in rugby when he started arriving home with sprig marks down his back, but he carried on and was good enough to represent the Western Bays area of Wellington at halfback and hooker in the under-16 side.

Softball was his sport in summer. In that code he played for Western Bays at under-14 and under-15 level. The Titahi Bay softball team Campbell played for was pretty useful and were unbeaten for three years. Also in that side was Jason Farrow, who went on to play in a World Series for New Zealand.

Whatever sport Michael tried he soon became proficient at. His father remembers taking him to the squash club and it wasn't long before son was beating dad. It was the same when a table tennis table was installed in the basement of the family home. "Michael soon had me jumping all over the room trying to return the ball to him. He would chase me round the room with the ball, laughing his head off all the time. It was apparent that he was one of those kids to whom sport just comes naturally."

If sport did come naturally to Michael Campbell, it was because it was in his genes. The Campbell family is rich in sporting blood. Michael Campbell's first cousin is former All Black Steven Pokere, the son of Thomas Campbell's brother Bill.

There were 14 children in the Campbell family and two, Bill and sister Ani, were adopted out. Not only did Bill produce Steven Pokere, but Ani had two sons who went on to play senior rugby for the champion Petone club in Wellington.

In those early years in Titahi Bay, Thomas Campbell still had golf to himself, though not for long.

"By the time I was around nine Dad had got down to a nine or ten handicap and I wanted to start playing as well. I loved being out on the golf course with him and when we got home we would carry on playing in the back garden. I was playing left-handed because there was no choice. Dad was a left-hander and his were the only clubs we had. I didn't care though. I was just happy playing.

"For six months I whacked balls around the lawn left-handed. We always seemed to be having new windows put in and I'm surprised Mum didn't stop me. I couldn't have blamed her either if she had banned me from playing in the lounge, but she didn't. Quite the opposite, in fact. While I must have been driving her mad she was still so supportive of what I wanted to do. The way Mum and Dad and Michelle were behind me all the way through has had a lot of influence on what I am doing today.

"All of a sudden, and don't ask me why, I decided I should be playing right-handed. Why such a decision should come at that time is hard to work out. After all, if you take into account all the time I had been knocking a golf ball around while caddying for Dad, I had been playing left-handed for about four years.

"Dad realised though that I was right-handed in everything else. So he got me a part set made up of a three-wood, six-iron, wedge and a putter."

Michael found that first set of clubs in the garden shed while we were working on this book, and spent the rest of the afternoon caressing the rusted irons as if they were a brand new set of clubs.

"If Dad hadn't played golf and asked me to go to the club with him I'm sure I would never have taken the game up. It was his influence which started me off and I will always be grateful to him for that.

"I would caddy for him in the morning and we would go round in circles. Titahi Bay was a nine hole course and we would go round three times. At times we were almost running so he could get in as much golf as possible. That is how much Dad loves the game and it must have rubbed off on me.

"While Dad was playing and I was caddying I would also be looking for golf balls and tees at the same time. It was a disappointing day if Dad didn't score well and I didn't arrive home with a few balls and tees. About the only thing I didn't find was clubs, but they would have had to be handed in so that would have been no fun.

"I was playing rugby in the winter and softball in the summer on Saturdays. Sundays were for golf. I would still caddy for Dad in the morning and then muck around by myself after the round because I didn't have a handicap and couldn't get out on the course on my own.

"I would watch guys teeing off while I was practising – if that was what you could call what I was doing then – and wish I was going with them. Eventually it came time for my first competition round, a traumatic event which even now brings shivers.

"I was twelve years old and on a 34 handicap. Imagine a twelve-year-old on the first tee in his first golf tournament. I bet there are a lot of people reading this who are now thinking back to how they felt playing in their first competition or pro-am, and most of them would have been a lot older than twelve. I was petrified and it showed with my first swing in competitive golf. I missed the ball completely. After two more swats with my six-iron – there wasn't a lot of choice about which club to use with my half set – the ball was still sitting on the tee. I just couldn't wait to get out of there. Thankfully connection was made with my fourth swing but it went straight into a hazard. I think I made 12 on that first hole.

"In its way it was just as nerve-wracking as teeing off in the British Open. At least I made contact in the Open."

At this time Campbell was saving up for some new clubs. He had a paper round and worked in a local fish and chip shop where he operated the spud machine, turning potatoes into chips. After six months he had got down to a 20 handicap and his father said he would help him get some new clubs if he broke 90. It wasn't long before he was out shopping for new clubs and golf was gradually taking over his life, becoming almost an obsession.

"As soon as school finished at three o'clock I would race home, get changed and head for the golf course. Every minute of daylight was spent either practising or going round the golf course. I got a little chopper bike to get me there quicker. A few minutes saved meant an extra hole or a few more six irons on the practice ground. I would do my homework when it got dark, well sometimes, but I was totally hooked on golf. When I wasn't playing the game I was thinking about it, imagining how I would play this shot or that shot.

"There were three or four of us who hung around together at the golf course. Dean and Shane Robinson lived between our house and the golf course and I would call for them on the way. When you got to the course you didn't just tee off. There was the serious business of who you were going to be for that day's round. One would be Seve Ballesteros, another Jack Nicklaus. I was Greg Norman whenever they would let me. Greg and Seve have always been my heroes. We would pretend we were those guys by trying to swing as we thought they did. Obviously we were nothing like them but we thought we were.

"Once our competition was over I would head to the practice area and search for balls. I would use anything I found whether it was round or oval. I didn't care; the more golf balls I had to hit the better."

By the time Michael reached 14 his father had begun to think his son might just be a little better than average as a golfer. Thomas Campbell decided a coach should have a look at the youngster so took him to Dennis Sullivan at the Hutt Club. A year later Thomas Campbell knew he was right.

"I was managing Titahi Bay's Watt Cup team and was seeing golfers at other clubs," Thomas Campbell remembers. "Even though they had all been playing a lot longer than Michael they weren't any better than him. I remember vividly one day at Miramar. He was on the tee and took a mighty swing. I thought, 'That is better than Seve's swing', though he was bending his back in those days rather than rotating."

Campbell was now being coached not only by Sullivan but at times by Neil Munro as well, and his handicap began to drop quickly. At 16, while on a six handicap, he shot a course record 62 at Titahi Bay, a mark which still stands, and won the club championship for the first time. The 62, carded under a local rule of no placing, was made up of an eagle, five birdies, a bogey and 11 pars. At that time there was a proposal before club members to change the layout of the holes to make the terrain less demanding. After his round Campbell described the course as "Okay as it is."

"Everything was happening very quickly and I was picked for the Wellington boys team. I knew then that, hard as it was going to be, it was time to leave the Titahi Bay nest. I loved those early days at Titahi Bay, and really my heart is still there, but I knew if I stayed I would never reach my potential. I had learnt all I could at Titahi Bay and now needed a more challenging course to play on if I was going to improve my game."

His father also realised that his son had to move on and saw Manor Park, just over the hill in the Hutt Valley, as the right type of course for him. Campbell senior paved the way for the move by speaking at length to Kevin Lord, then club captain at Manor Park. Lord agreed to take Michael under his wing and see how he went.

Little did Lord realise at the time how much publicity Campbell would eventually bring the Manor Park club.

"Manor Park is a good course and Dad bought me a car so I could get there. It wasn't that far because my record was 17 minutes from the house into the car park, but then I was always keen to get to a golf course. Playing on a better course made me a better player almost immediately and I was soon in the Manor Park team which meant I got to play on the best courses in Wellington.

"At the time I was a cocky little bugger. When you are young and think you are going to make it, you want to tell people how good you are. When you actually make it then you don't need to tell anyone because you have proved you can do it. I must have been a pain at times when I first got to Manor Park but every step I was taking was positive, another rung up the ladder I had set my heart on climbing. It meant stepping up each time, from Wellington Juniors to Wellington Seniors, to New Zealand juniors, to New Zealand seniors. I got there eventually but there were a few close shaves along the way when I almost fell off the ladder. Thankfully there was usually someone with my best interests at heart, even if I didn't think so at the time, holding it steady."

Thomas Campbell was now definitely beginning to harbour thoughts that Michael might eventually earn a living from golf but his conservative background meant he wasn't going to let his son take any chances with his future. Thomas and Maria Campbell were willing to back Michael all the way, to give him every possible chance of realising his dream, but they wanted a safety net in place in case it didn't work out as they all hoped.

Telecom had been a good employer to Thomas Campbell so it was only natural that Michael should start his working life with the same company as a trainee technician.

Campbell settled into his apprenticeship and continued playing all his sports, but gradually golf became more and more important – rugby and softball were beginning to get in the way of practice.

At work, where Campbell had a good boss who was generous in making sure he had time off to get to tournaments, he was thinking more about golf shots than fixing faults in telephone exchanges.

Thomas Campbell could see how restless Michael was becoming and rang Dennis Sullivan for advice on how the possibility of eventually playing professionally should be approached. After the call he made notes: 1, Michael should finish his technician's certificate and then attempt to qualify to play on the Australia-New Zealand circuit; or, 2, begin a three-year apprenticeship as a professional and be prepared to do another two years after that. Those were the sensible routes to take.

"I'm pleased I saw the Telecom apprenticeship through but towards the end of my time I have to admit that I was skiving off a bit because of golf. I was struggling with my game at that point and was having trouble breaking 80 because I was working with Mal Tongue on changing my swing.

"My job with Telecom involved going round Wellington fixing faults in telephone exchanges. It was perfect. I had a pager on my belt and a car to get around in. I would arrive at work, get my pager and car keys and nip down to the car park to switch my clubs from my car to the company one before shooting off to the nearest field and start hitting balls till I got paged.

"I was always being asked where I'd been and would come up with all the excuses in the world. I must have been very inventive, but they knew. One day my boss called me in to his office and asked whether my heart was in a career with Telecom or golf. I told him the answer was obvious and he said in that case I shouldn't be there. I agreed. I didn't want to be there. Two months later I resigned and went to play golf full time."

In 1988, while working for Telecom, Campbell asked the company for $3000 sponsorship to help him play golf. They turned him down because "the corporation has decided to concentrate its sponsorship activities into specific areas where there is significant public acknowledgement for Telecom relative to the investment". They gave him $300 as a grant in recognition of his talents and achievements.

Telecom might not have been prepared to back Michael Campbell, but the Campbell family were prepared to invest in their son. They were sure he had what it takes to make the grade as a professional, but, just in case, they began putting money aside to help him if it took a long time to make the breakthrough. In October 1995 Thomas Campbell felt it was safe to spend that money on a new car for himself!

Michael Campbell's golfing talents were recognised outside Titahi Bay and Wellington by the time he was 16. He was included in the New Zealand junior squad and attended coaching schools where he came under the guidance of New Zealand's Australian-based coach Alex Mercer. During those schools Campbell met up with Philip Tataurangi, who was going to become a close friend and fierce rival.

"I wasn't used to anything as regimented as those schools. They were gruelling weeks when I sometimes wondered what we were all doing there. Running the school at Trentham Camp was a former Army guy called Graeme Cooke and I remember his first speech to us as if it was yesterday. 'Hello everyone. My name is Graeme Cooke, but you call me God.' Cookie would wake us at 5.30 every morning for a run. We would have breakfast, practice from nine till five, and then play nine holes to finish the day off. We were just kids but Cookie realised how important discipline was if we were going to do anything with our lives, especially in golf.

"Some of the guys I remember from those camps are Phil Tataurangi, Paul Devenport, Craig Perks, Matthew Lane, Michael Long and Elliott Boult – so they must have worked."

Acquitting himself well at the schools and posting good scores in tournaments led to selection in a national team and March 3, 1988, is a red letter day in the Michael Campbell story. It was on that day he got a passport for the first time so he could go to Australia with the New Zealand under-21 side.

"That was a great day, but I was also apprehensive, having not been out of New Zealand on my own. There had been one trip overseas with the family when I was 10, but I honestly don't remember anything about it. This was different. I had been chosen to represent New Zealand. When you are told for the first time that you are going to play for your country it is a very special feeling. I wanted to tell everyone I had been picked even though I had taken a bit longer than others to make the team. Most of the guys being chosen for the under-21 side were 16 or 17. I was old at 19 but that didn't matter to me.

"The team was Michael Long, Tony Christie, Grant Moorhead, Steven Alker, Lyndon Cron and myself. I think we finished fourth at the inter-state competition in Bundberry, Perth. I know we won the tournament for New Zealand for the first time in about 20 years the following year in Launceston, Tasmania. The only change in the team was Phil Tataurangi coming in for Lyndon Cron."

New Zealand amateur golf was on the verge of a golden era in which Campbell was to play a starring role.

3

Amateur Years

When New Zealand Golf Association executive director Grant Clements in 1986 unveiled a paper titled *In Search of Success*, Michael Campbell was just taking the first step on a ladder he hoped one day would take him to the top of the golfing world by being picked for the Wellington junior team.

While they weren't exactly growing on trees, a few extremely promising young golfers were beginning to emerge in New Zealand at that time. Others besides Clements were aware of the new era which appeared to be dawning on the country's golf courses, but it was Clements who had the foresight to plan for the future, to leave nothing to chance. The young golfers who were causing so much optimism were the ones who would benefit from his vision.

In Search of Success was Clements' blueprint for the future. Its goal was for New Zealand to win the world teams' championship, the Eisenhower Trophy, in 1992. There must have been a temptation for Clements to talk of producing a British Open or US Masters champion. That, he said, was unrealistic at the time. Winning the world amateur title was an achievable goal if everything was done correctly.

There were doubters, even among the higher echelons of the Golf Association but, thankfully for New Zealand golf, there were enough believers to enable Clements' plans to be put in place.

It was from Clements' paper that the Titleist training squads and camps were born. Players would be chosen for the New Zealand under-

21 team and embraced into the squad. Neil Woodbury, now president of the NZGA, and Roger Brennand, who successfully managed the 1992 Eisenhower team, regularly took junior teams to Australia. Eventually those teams became so successful in the inter-state competitions that the invitations to compete stopped arriving. Why keep inviting guests to your party if they were going to take home the presents?

There were some who thought it demeaning that New Zealand should have to enter a national under-21 team in another country's domestic championship, but Clements wasn't proud. He saw overseas competition early in a player's career as a stepping stone to the future.

It was during the training camps that firm friendships were forged among the young players who attended. It was only natural that they should become close, for they were there with a common goal and would spend a week together hitting golf balls during the day and discussing their dreams at night. When it came to international competition on foreign soil those young men, despite their tremendous talent, found themselves under enormous pressure, totally different to what they had experienced on the domestic scene where they were competing among familiar faces. That was when they would turn to their friends, fellow squad members, for support. There was always someone to lean on when the going got really tough, a mate ready with words of encouragement after a bad day or congratulations if things had gone well. One day a player would be providing support, the next receiving it. They were a close-knit bunch who fed off the success of others in the group, rivals who were healthily jealous of their friends' achievements. When one of their number won a tournament it made the rest all the more determined that they would be the one lifting the trophy next time.

It was at a coaching school run by Alex Mercer that Michael Campbell and Philip Tataurangi roomed together for the first time. Despite the difference in age – Michael was 16, Philip 14 – they hit it off from the start.

"We just clicked immediately. I think probably because we were both Maori – there were 26 in the squad but only four were Maori – we became closer to each other than with the rest of the guys. We felt completely comfortable in each other's company.

"While we became close friends Phil and myself were real rivals from the beginning. Rivalry was something we didn't talk about. We knew it was there, there was no need to bring it up. There was jealousy when the other won something but there is nothing wrong with that. It is a healthy situation in sport.

"It wasn't just Phil and myself who were competing against each other. For two or three years there was a group of guys around 21 or 22 who between them won every amateur golf tournament in New Zealand. We got into each other's slipstream and that dragged us along. Early on I was jealous of their success and that made me want to succeed even more.

"You can be rivals and still enjoy the moment when something good happens to the other guy. When Phil got in New Zealand's team for the 1988 Eisenhower I was thrilled for him. At 16 he was the youngest player to represent New Zealand at a world championship. I really wanted him to do well because above everything else he was my friend. I had worked alongside him on the practice fairway and I wasn't surprised that he played so well in Sweden and was New Zealand's best performer.

"When he came back from Sweden he was still on a high after having a great time. He had lots of photographs and shared his experiences with me. That was something he didn't have to do but he did, which was nice. That is how we've always been. I liked nothing better than beating Phil, and I'm sure he felt the same way when he came out on top in our duels, but I was delighted that he had done so well in Sweden.

"Phil had worked so hard to make that team, he deserved to be chosen. If he hadn't played well I would have been disappointed but listening to him talk about the tournament only made me more determined to play for New Zealand at an Eisenhower Trophy.

"We were both in the running for the 1990 Eisenhower team for the tournament which was played in Christchurch. There was a long series of trials, which were gruelling in themselves, and at the end of them we both missed out. I wasn't too disappointed when not named in the team because I wasn't playing well. In fact, I suppose I'd almost resigned myself to not getting in. It was at a time when I was changing my swing and wasn't able to put the numbers on the board consistently, whereas those who got in the team were scoring well most of the time.

"Phil wasn't going well either but for different reasons. His father Te Roi, who he was very close to, had just passed away. For an 18-year-old to go through that was terrible. Phil's Mum and Dad had supported him just as my mother and father were behind me, and his suffering made me appreciate my parents and the fact that they were still there for me even more.

"After his Dad died we talked more and more. Phil was very emotional and from that point on we were closer than ever. I hope I was able to help him in some small way to get through the pain he was suffering and my Mum and Dad were there for him as well if he needed them."

The competition between Campbell and Tataurangi became more obvious in the latter stages of their amateur careers, especially when they were battling for individual honours at the 1992 Eisenhower, but for two years Michael Campbell had another scrap on his hands closer to home with the arrival in Wellington of Stephen Scahill from Bay of Plenty.

Scahill, as did Campbell, turned professional following New Zealand's Eisenhower Trophy success, and while he hasn't made the immediate impact Campbell did there is little doubt Scahill will one day make his mark in the game.

For more than two years the pair were almost inseparable because of golf. They practised side by side at the Manor Park club under the watchful eye of Mal Tongue, and travelled throughout New Zealand together to compete in tournaments.

"Stephen Scahill made me a better player. When he was regularly kicking my butt in 1991 and '92 it made me practise harder and play harder because of the success he was having. As was the case with Philip and myself at the early schools he dragged me along with him. Now I've overtaken him I hope I can do the same for him.

"Steve is a fine player who just needs a breakthrough to set him on a roll. I got a break in Dubai and Manila at the start of 1995. That is what he needs and when the break comes, which it will, you will see just how good Stephen Scahill is.

"We used to travel together throughout New Zealand by car. When you are in situations like that you really get to know someone. It is easy to fall out and fly off the handle, especially when two people are as different in their outlooks on life as we were then. That it didn't happen shows that in our way we needed each other. When we first began spending a lot of time together Steve was very selfish, almost arrogant. But he was very professional.

"I was the opposite, happy go lucky and not very professional whatsoever. Being together so much meant the different qualities we possessed rubbed off on each other. He helped me become more professional, while I helped him to be more relaxed and less intense."

Despite the intense rivalry, a firm friendship developed. Such is the bond between the pair it was no surprise that Scahill was best man at Campbell's wedding.

Scahill recalls those days when they were competing so fiercely. "There's no doubt we learnt a lot from each other. Michael would tell me that the key was to have a balanced life, one that is well-rounded with interests other than golf. It is a philosophy he has always had and it has rubbed off on me.

"From my point I would tell him that he was going to be in this game for a long time, that he should look after himself healthwise and view it as a long-term thing. Michael used to treat everything on a day-to-day basis. He would be doing well today so would not worry about tomorrow. He would never organise himself for the next tournament or plan ahead. That is an area in which he has changed completely, but he has done it without losing the relaxed attitude which is so important to the way he plays."

Scahill describes the Campbell he first met as an accident waiting to happen. He was always going to be a world-class player. It was just a matter of when.

"The first time I met him was at a coaching school at Trentham when we were 17. He was impressive even then; he hit the ball so well. He was one of those guys who always flushes it. It might have sometimes been off line but it would always come off the middle of the club. He got better and better once he met Mal and refined his technique but he has always had the potential to be a great player."

There were times during their days together with Manor Park, Wellington and New Zealand teams when Scahill found Campbell something of an enigma. Where some players get above themselves when they find success, according to Scahill Campbell was the opposite.

"When Michael wasn't playing well, when he was struggling to get his game together, he could be cocky and arrogant. He went through a phase where he became very self-centred. The strange thing is that when he is playing well and winning things he goes the other way. He becomes more generous and thoughtful and gives his time to more people. It is weird.

"It is as if he felt the need to tell people how good he was going to be because he wasn't doing as well as he wanted to at that particular time. Now that he is playing brilliantly and getting great results there is no need to say anything. The results speak for themselves. He is still confident but he keeps it inside and doesn't need to shout about it."

During those days when the young guns of the Titleist squad were carving up New Zealand's tournaments, Campbell was the life and soul of the group, always fun to be with.

"I loved Michael's company right from the start. If you were with Michael you knew you would have a good time, a bit of a laugh and be able to forget the day's events if you had had a tough time on the course. He was brilliant for that. Being around Michael was great therapy.

"I have never known Michael to suffer from worrying about anything. Certainly not golf. I have never seen him walk off the course and panic about the way things had gone as I might have done. Once he was in the car driving home golf went out the window. He would go back the next day and just start again. There would be no sitting down trying to analyse why things hadn't gone well, there were other things in life to do and enjoy besides golf. He is a lot more casual than most top sportsmen. He has found out what works for him."

When Campbell was, as he puts it, getting his butt kicked by Scahill during 1991 and '92 he had only himself to blame. He was the one who asked Scahill to move from Bay of Plenty to Wellington in mid-1990 and smoothed the path for him.

"I think Michael felt at the time that he wasn't being challenged enough in Wellington. He knew I was playing well because we were having some great battles in tournaments. People think I went down to Wellington for the sole reason of being coached by Mal Tongue, but Michael was the one who instigated the move, not me. He rang to ask if I would like to move. When I said I was interested, he was back on the telephone a week later telling me he had arranged for me to join the club with no membership fee, had got me a part-time job as a greenkeeper at the course and had found me a place to live right by the course. And this is a guy I'm saying wasn't organised!"

Scahill's switch had the desired effect. Within weeks of his arrival in Wellington the pair were vying for the No 1 spot in the Manor Park team and it was to be the same in the Wellington and New Zealand teams, though there were some ups and downs along the way.

It was in 1987 as an 18-year-old that Campbell began to emerge from the virtual obscurity of the Wellington inter-club competition, where he was playing an important role in the Manor Park team. The inter-club was providing valuable experience but he was ready to cut his teeth on bigger tournaments.

At the start of the year Campbell achieved his first goal, a place in the Wellington senior team to contest the Southland Invitational strokeplay event on Invercargill's Otatara course. He performed well enough to stay in contention for a spot in the side for the premier amateur teams' event on the New Zealand golfing calendar, the inter-provincial championship.

Anyone living outside Wellington has probably never heard of the Shandon Open but it was his performance in that tournament, played on the beautiful tree-lined course nestled alongside the Hutt River, which persuaded the Wellington selectors that Campbell was ready for a place in the province's team for the national inter-provincial.

Campbell finished equal first in the Shandon Open with Cliff Moore, a 41-year-old former Wellington representative playing on his home course. It wasn't just the fact that Campbell shared the spoils with Moore, who knew the Shandon course like the back of his hand, which impressed the selectors. The way he earned his share of the top spot was just as important. After starting the last round one shot behind Moore, Campbell had challenged throughout the final round till he dropped four shots between the 10th and 15th holes to trail Moore, who parred the last three holes, by three shots. For one so young, in golfing terms as well as age, Campbell showed remarkable maturity, and superb ball-striking, to birdie his last three holes to tie.

While others lavished praise on Campbell for his brilliant finish, Michael himself was thinking more about an eagle putt he had missed on the par-five 17th rather than his tee-shot to two feet on the par-three 18th. Had he sunk that putt on 17, as he felt he should have, he would have won outright, he said.

The Shandon Open was in August. The following month Michael Campbell scored his biggest success by winning the New Zealand under-21 title on Dunedin's St Clair course.

Dunedin is the butt of endless jokes about its weather, but the conditions competitors in the national under-21 tournament had to contend with that year weren't funny. The wind howled, the rain lashed down and there was even a flurry of snow at one point during the last round. A final round 70 put Campbell level with Michael Long, later to become an adversary on the Australia-New Zealand professional tour, and the pair would have preferred to be in the clubhouse rather than heading off to the tee for a sudden-death playoff. Mercifully, for Campbell anyway, the playoff went only one hole with Campbell making birdie to Long's par.

The newly crowned national under-21 champion then set his sights on the Lawnmaster Classic, in its third year and rapidly becoming one of the most prestigious amateur events in the country. In later years it would become a New Zealand trial played solely at the Manawatu Golf Club's Hokowhitu course. In 1987 the first two rounds were played at Feilding with the third and fourth rounds at the Palmerston North Golf Club.

Campbell took a real liking to Palmerston North and his final round four under par 69 served further notice that here was a player to keep an eye on. At the time Campbell wasn't known as a good putter around Wellington – a flashy putter he called himself – but at Palmerston North he won the Lawnmaster around the greens, needing only ten putts on the last nine holes.

The Wellington team in which Campbell made his inter-provincial debut at number four in Whangarei in November 1987 was far from the calibre of the sides Wellington would produce during the 1990s as the province began to dominate New Zealand golf. Representative teams still went into tournaments in a hit-and-miss fashion.

Wellington was finding it hard to break into the top echelon when Campbell made his debut and in Whangarei didn't make the semi-finals. There was encouragement for Campbell, though, with his wins including a three and two success over New Zealand representative Glen Goldfinch. Beating higher-rated opponents was important for Campbell. It gave him a benchmark to work against and a win over Goldfinch told him he was still going forward.

When the inter-provincial championships were played the following year Campbell wasn't in the Wellington team, though it had nothing to do with a lack of form. His golfing star was still rising but there were other things on his mind. While the Wellington players were treading the fairways of the Christchurch Golf Club's Shirley course, Campbell was sitting in the classroom wrestling with the intricacies of his Telecom technician's exams.

While Campbell won the Taranaki Classic in 1988, retained his Lawnmaster title and was chosen to represent New Zealand at the Australian inter-state championship, he was still very much a weekend golfer full of potential, unable to spend enough time working on his game. After winning his second Lawnmaster, Campbell said he was rapt to retain the title, particularly as he knew he wasn't playing enough through having to work during the day and study for his exams at night.

Despite those restraints a wider golfing world was starting to open up for Michael Campbell. He was one of eight amateurs invited to play in the Air New Zealand Shell Open at Titirangi in December 1988 and he had the time of his young life as he took his place among the professionals.

That week in Auckland it was hard to wipe the smile off Michael's face. I remember talking to him on the first day and he couldn't wait to tell me he had bumped into Australian star Rodger Davis who the previous week had won a cool half million dollars. He had wished Davis luck for the tournament, he said, and the Australian had reciprocated. Out on the course he seemed to be spending as much time looking at other players as he did thinking about his game. At one point he couldn't resist pointing out that two-times United States Open winner Hale Irwin was on the next fairway. He was in seventh heaven, not knowing what he was going to do next but determined to enjoy every moment.

Going into the tournament Campbell said he didn't have any big ideas, rather he was grateful to be there for the experience he would gain. While he was talking like that, typically he was determined not to let down himself or those close to him. Three amateurs were guaranteed entry into the final two rounds but Campbell didn't need that concession. He made the cut with rounds of 75 and 71, six over par, finished second-best amateur, and his appetite was whetted.

The New Zealand Open at Paraparaumu Beach the following week was won by Australia's Ian Stanley from compatriot Mike Clayton and American Corey Pavin, who was seeking his third New Zealand Open title. The trivia question being asked around Wellington the following week was who made the most birdies at the New Zealand Open? It wasn't any of the first three placegetters, or any of the professionals in fact. It was amateur Michael Campbell.

Campbell's scorecards for the 72-hole tournament contained 16 birdies and two eagles. The fact that Campbell finished eight over par on 292 suggests that the 19-year-old may also have won the prize for the fewest pars. It was becoming obvious though that Michael Campbell had the temperament for professional golf. How many of the professionals in the field would have been able to shrug off the disaster which befell Campbell on the par-four 11th hole during the third round at Paraparaumu? On the 11th Campbell ran up a catastrophic 11, which would have made even a weekend hacker blush. The three birdies he posted over the final seven holes says he didn't let it get to him.

The adventures at the 11th hole meant for the second week running Campbell had to settle for second-best amateur in a professional tournament. He was three strokes adrift of Tataurangi after four rounds and could justifiably point to the 11th hole as the cause.

Professional tournaments seemed to bring the best out in young Campbell even when he was playing for nothing, as he showed when beginning the 1989 Air New Zealand Shell Open in dramatic fashion with two birdies and an eagle in the first five holes. On Titirangi's sixth green Campbell was putting for an eagle which would have taken him to six under for the tournament and to the top of the leader board. The eagle putt didn't drop but he happily settled for birdie and an early second placing. It was an exciting time but Campbell couldn't keep the momentum going. He dropped nine shots in 12 holes and had to settle for a 74 which left him well off the pace and he went on to miss the cut after the second round.

Campbell's comments at the time were that he got too excited about the way he had begun but that the experience of being under pressure would stand him in good stead in the future.

New Zealand's top amateurs all had one goal in mind during 1989 – to make the Eisenhower team for the 1990 world teams event in Christchurch. As part of a long selection process the national selectors named a nine-man squad at the conclusion of the inter-provincial championships on Hastings' Bridge Pa course and Campbell was in it.

Wellington were starting to make their mark on the national scene as they finished third. Campbell had four wins, two halves and a loss from his seven matches at the tournament, including beating Philip Tataurangi in another close encounter between the two great rivals. The Hastings tournament also produced Campbell's first hole in one, with a six-iron at the 149-metre fourth hole. An ace, whatever the circumstances, is a once-in-a-lifetime experience for most golfers. Even professionals remember them fondly but Campbell has no recollection of that shot. He was surprised to be told that when he got the hole in one he was three down in a match against Aorangi's Charlie Alexander which had started at the 10th hole. That shot not only turned the match around and enabled Campbell to come out with a half, it also set the tournament alight for him and he went unbeaten from that point.

Realistically Michael Campbell didn't have much chance of making the 1990 Eisenhower team. He had forced his way into the squad too late in the piece, and in the lead-up to the October tournament his game went off the boil. Tataurangi was well in contention for selection. The best performed New Zealander at the world event in Sweden two years earlier, Tataurangi looked a certainty but the death of his father knocked him off stride. Tataurangi missed out and Campbell felt for his friend and rival.

The 1990 New Zealand team of Steven Alker, Michael Long, Grant Moorhead and Brent Paterson almost ruined Grant Clements' script. He had headed one section of his *In Search of Success* paper "Why Not the Eisenhower in 1992?" The 1990 side finished equal second with a United States team which included Phil Mickelson, but 13 strokes behind a classy Sweden represented by Mathia Gronberg, Gabriel Hjerstedt, Klas Eriksson and Per Nyman.

Campbell says he knew deep in his heart that he wasn't going to make the New Zealand team for the 1990 world event but that didn't stop him trying.

Wellington won the Tower inter-provincial championship in 1990, the province's first national title since 1977. That the drought was broken was due in no small part to Campbell and his new teammate Stephen Scahill, with the latter being named player of the tournament after winning all his eight matches.

As the curtain came down on 1990 Michael Campbell couldn't have anticipated what the next 12 months would bring. There would be further successes, though they would be tempered by a loss of form which at times had him wondering whether he could play the game as he wanted. There was even a point where he felt like throwing his clubs away.

4
The
Eisenhower

Whatever happens in their lives as the years roll by, Michael Campbell, Philip Tataurangi, Stephen Scahill and Grant Moorhead are inexorably linked through the events of October 4, 1992.

The fabulous four, as they became known in the New Zealand media, earned a place in New Zealand sporting folklore that day when they beat the best amateur golfers the world could offer to win the Eisenhower Trophy in Vancouver. New Zealand has played in every Eisenhower Trophy event since the first at St Andrews in 1958. They have often been in contention and twice finished second, beaten 12 strokes by the United States at Madrid in 1970, and 13 strokes behind Sweden at Christchurch in 1990.

Campbell, Tataurangi, Scahill and Moorhead. Names which rolled off Kiwi golf followers' tongues so easily in the weeks following their remarkable victory and, usually, in that order. If it was an Auckland or northern newspaper or radio station writing or talking about the quartet, then Tataurangi's name would probably precede Campbell's. Further south, Campbell would be named first, but Scahill and Moorhead always followed in their wake.

It wasn't a deliberate slight on Scahill and Moorhead, merely the fact that Campbell and Tataurangi captured the imagination, even though the other two had cemented their places in the team well before Campbell and Tataurangi. Eighteen months out from the Eisenhower, Campbell was playing in what was effectively New

Zealand's second string side in the Clare Higson under-23 competition against Australia, while Scahill and Moorhead were members of the top team contesting the Sloan Morpeth trophy against an Australian side which included Robert Allenby and Stuart Appleby.

Tataurangi left his run even later than Campbell. As the countdown to Vancouver progressed Tony Christie looked like joining Campbell, Scahill and Moorhead in the team until Tataurangi produced a string of results that made it impossible for the selectors to leave him out.

During the final months of preparation the New Zealand team became a close-knit unit, and much was made of the fact that team unity played an important part in New Zealand winning the Eisenhower for the first time. Under the surface, though, there was some tension even if it was barely noticeable.

Afterwards Grant Moorhead was quoted in *Sport Monthly* as saying the Eisenhower had been hijacked by the Maoris. It was a statement which took Michael Campbell by surprise.

"That might have been Grant's opinion but I think it is pretty harsh. The fact that Philip and myself came first and second on the individual standings meant we inevitably stole the limelight somewhat, but it is something neither of us set out to do.

"Actually we were a little embarrassed by all the attention. So far as I was concerned it was a team effort, though I remember feeling there was a little bit of animosity between myself, Grant and Stephen. I just put it down to the way the media handled it rather than there being anything between us.

"We had no control whatsoever about the way the team was portrayed in the media. It is a shame, but it is just one of those things that happen. Phil and myself happened to play really well that week but without the other guys' scores we wouldn't have won the Eisenhower. I still say it was a team effort and I didn't care in what order the team was written."

Stephen Scahill, one of those perceived to have been slighted, agrees with his teammate that it was inevitable Campbell and Tataurangi would be in the spotlight more than their mates because of the way they performed, not because they were Maori.

"Maori people tend to be more open with their feelings and there were quite a few of them in Vancouver supporting the team,"

Scahill says. "It was unavoidable that Michael and Philip got the headlines because of the way they played that week. I've never held a grudge against anyone because of it. Nothing like that concerns me. I went there justifiably as a member of the team, did my job well, and we came away with the trophy.

"Any praise that was heaped on individuals rather than the team as a whole didn't matter. Phil was first and Michael second after four rounds of strokeplay against the best amateur golfers in the world. People were going to talk about them more after that. We all played well, and everyone contributed, but those two guys played their pants off and for that week were the best two amateurs in the world. They deserved all the accolades they got.

"Whatever happens to any of us in the future it is something we can look back on as a very special episode in our lives. It was an experience between the four of us which will always be there."

The foundations for the magical moments in Vancouver, a city so like Christchurch that the Kiwis felt at home from the moment they arrived, were laid straight after the 1990 tournament.

Campbell's path into the team after the disappointment of missing out in 1990, though he admits he didn't deserve to make that side, began in 1991, a year in which he resigned his job with Telecom and became basically a full-time golfer.

"I had been working with Mal Tongue for about six months and, even though he says I always flush the ball, there was a point where I felt I could hardly hit it never mind flush it.

"It was at a time when I was still working for Telecom and fitting in practice at the end of the day – or while I was waiting for my pager to bleep. It meant that I was tired when I began practising and I wasn't getting enough time working with Mal.

"The Eisenhower team seemed a world away at one point in 1991 when I was going through a patch where breaking 80 began to seem an impossible task. I remember three tournaments in a row, the Wellington, Canterbury and Auckland strokeplay events, where I really struggled and the target became to get below 80. At the Auckland tournament I think I shot 84, 86, 81, 83.

"I was completely demoralised. Had anyone told me then that I would be playing professionally a couple of years later they would have been committed. I didn't know what to do and was a very confused young man. There came a point where I really wanted to chuck my clubs away. If it hadn't been for Mal Tongue I probably would have."

Those practising and playing with Campbell knew he was going through a difficult period, though not from Campbell himself. As always he kept his worries and fears inside and got on with the job.

"He would never let on that things weren't going right," Stephen Scahill says. "It was obvious he was struggling with his game and I was playing particularly well at that time. That must have made it doubly hard for him but he never showed any signs of jealousy towards me or anyone else. Michael would congratulate me on playing well but would never whinge in my ear that he was playing crap. At no time did he bail me up and cry on my shoulder. If he was going to talk to anyone it would be Mal. Talking to him would get it out of his system. But to his mates, never."

Despite Campbell's despair the form loss was only temporary and he was soon performing well again. Top five placings in tournaments among his peers became the norm, and the breakthrough he had been seeking arrived at the Waikato strokeplay event where he finished on six under par to take the title from a strong field.

With his confidence restored, Campbell in September headed to the Australian amateur championships in Perth where he and Stephen Scahill combined to finish third in the foursomes, six shots behind the New South Wales pairing of Lester Peterson and Wayne Stewart. While he didn't set the Lake Karinyup course on fire in the strokeplay, Campbell qualified for the matchplay competition – the winner of which is the Australian champion – only for his tournament to be ended abruptly through appendicitis.

"It was a nightmare and at the time I wondered what I had done to deserve such a fate when things were going so well. It was something I won't ever forget and even thinking about it now I can feel the pain.

"On the morning of the first round of matchplay I woke up around 6.30 with terrible stomach ache and thought it was caused by something I had eaten. They got me some medicine which seemed to help for a while but by the time I arrived at the course it was getting worse and worse.

"When you have set your heart on doing well in a tournament like the Australian amateur the last thing you want to do is pull out. I convinced myself that the pain would disappear once I got out on the course. Unfortunately, it got even worse. Steven Alker hadn't qualified for the matchplay and was caddying for me. The pain became so bad that I couldn't bend down and Steven had to line up the putts for me. Eventually it got to the point where I couldn't see the ball properly and told our manager Roger Brennand what was happening.

"Roger told me to stop straight away and I was soon on my way to hospital where they removed my appendix later in the day. I was feeling really sorry for myself. There I was moaning and groaning about my bad luck while all around me were people who might never walk or who had lost a limb.

"It quickly changed my attitude. I stopped complaining about my bad luck. I began to appreciate that I would soon be playing golf again and that these people would never have that pleasure. So I was going to miss a couple of tournaments. So what? I hadn't spent time in hospital before and that night opened my eyes. It made me realise how much more there is to life."

Having his appendix removed meant Campbell had to pull out of the New Zealand team which contested the Pacific Teams' event following the Australian amateur, but he was chosen to play in November's Asian Pacific championship in the Philippines along with Stephen Scahill, Steven Alker and Grant Moorhead as the side began to take shape. Manila, like Perth, didn't provide pleasant memories.

"We all got food poisoning and were really sick. It seemed worse than the appendicitis, which was still fresh in my mind. We had diarrhoea, stomach cramps and were dehydrated. It wasn't that we had been careless. We were staying at a lovely hotel, the Manila Pavilion, but it hadn't made any difference. When we got back to New Zealand the night before the Tower tournament at Timaru we were all still feeling weak but it was great to be home.

"What I had seen and experienced in Manila made me realise just how lucky we are in New Zealand. While parts of Manila are fine, such as the area where the golf course was situated, there are other parts which are very third world and you wouldn't want to live anywhere near them.

"Seeing young kids, almost babies some of them, living on the streets, under bridges, by railway lines and even on traffic islands came as a shock.

"These days playing as a professional I don't get as much chance as I would like to explore the places we visit, but in my amateur days when I was playing for New Zealand we used to get the odd day off and take the chance to have a look around. Manila left a lasting impression for all the wrong reasons."

Sandwiched between Perth and Manila, and much more palatable so far as Michael Campbell was concerned, was the 1991 Air New Zealand Shell Open at Titirangi. It was won by American John Morse, the 1990 Australian Open champion, but in many ways the tournament belonged as much to Campbell as it did to Morse, certainly in the eyes of New Zealanders. And why not? Here was a young amateur finishing fourth, the leading New Zealander, in a top professional event. It was the best performance by a Kiwi amateur in a professional event since Bob Charles won the 1954 New Zealand Open.

"That was a great week. I loved every moment of it. Mixing with players such as Chip Beck, who had become only the second person in golfing history to shoot 59 not long before he came to Auckland, was a fantastic experience. I tied for fourth with Chip and to finish on the same score as Mr 59 was a big thrill.

"There were times when I felt like a little boy amongst a field of men because they were names I had only read about, but once on the course I didn't feel inferior. I was playing well going into the tournament and had learnt a lot from the time two years earlier when I had started with a bang and then fallen away.

"I had been five under after six holes in that tournament when I looked at the leaderboard and saw my name near the top. It blew my mind. Two years on I had matured a lot and when I saw it up there again I knew I deserved to be there because of the way I was playing. Just before I teed off in the last round someone mentioned to me that I could be the top amateur and remember telling them 'Never mind top amateur; I want to be the top New Zealander, professionals included.'

"It wasn't only a great experience for me. My family shared in it. My dad was caddying for me and Mum was watching along with other members of the family. I don't know how much of my rounds Mum saw, though, because she would get too tense watching me and wander off to look at other players.

"Having them there gave me a feeling of security. You can have all the friends in the world, but there is nothing like having your family around you."

It was at the Air New Zealand Shell Open that a more mature Michael Campbell was displayed. Over the previous twelve months he had had a haircut, discarded his earring and lost a stone and a half in weight. Looking and feeling different played a part.

"I got up to fifteen and a half stone without realising it. One night I saw myself on television and didn't like what I was looking at. I realised that night that if I wanted to make it as a golf professional then I had to do something about it.

"The weight wasn't going to disappear as easily as it had gone on so the only way was to work hard. I pumped weights, did circuit training and aerobics at the gym and gradually it came off.

"It meant that most days I would practise from nine till five, then go to the gym from 6.30 till 8. People don't realise how hard you have to work to keep in trim for top level golf. They see you tee off and say you are a natural, which is far from the truth.

"I did have some natural ability and flair but that only takes you so far. At the time I knew I had to make sacrifices even though it was hard when I would see my mates going off for a drink.

"After some gentle persuasion, particularly from Vic Pirihi who runs the Maori Golf Foundation, I also tidied myself up in other areas. The foundation helped people like myself get to amateur tournaments throughout New Zealand. We would all stay together, which was terrific fun, and Vic was like a father to us.

"I had never paid too much attention to my appearance on the golf course. I just enjoyed getting out there and playing. Whatever I was wearing at the time seemed fine to me. It was also trendy to wear an earring and I thought I looked cool with one. As for long hair . . . going to have it cut was a nuisance and loads of people wore their hair long – though I suppose I stood out a bit on the golf course where people do tend to be more conservative.

"I got a letter from Vic Pirihi which was short, sharp and to the point. Basically it said lose some weight, lose the earring and lose the hair or you are out of the squad.

"Being a stubborn little so and so I wasn't going to roll over and do as I was told, but after three or four conversations over the telephone with Vic I did as he asked. He was just as stubborn as me and that's probably why we got on during those years. It is the same with Mal Tongue. We are both stubborn as hell."

That New Zealand was going to play a major role in deciding where the Eisenhower Trophy would reside for the following two years became obvious as 1992 turned into one long celebration, not only for New Zealand golf, but also Michael Campbell. It was a fabulous year for the New Zealanders who gave the Australians a bitter pill to swallow as they regularly plundered Australia's treasured golfing trophies.

Michael Campbell became the first New Zealander to win the New South Wales championship by beating Philip Tataurangi in the final. If that wasn't enough for the young Maori from Titahi Bay he wrote another piece of golfing history by taking the Australian amateur title to New Zealand for the first time.

For good measure, Philip Tataurangi and Grant Moorhead won the Australian foursomes, Tataurangi took the New South Wales strokeplay title, with Campbell the runner-up, while Moorhead and Stephen Scahill won the Riversdale Cup. As a team New Zealand won the Australian inter-state championships. They also beat Australia in the Sloan Morpeth competition by a resounding 12-6.

The Australians began to take notice of Campbell when he won the State title at the Mollymook Golf Club on New South Wales' south coast. The New Zealander showed stamina as well as talent as he played 168 holes during the five rounds of match play, and the Kiwis' domination was evident in that Campbell had to beat Tataurangi, who was his roommate, in the championship final.

Winning in New South Wales was a fine achievement for Michael Campbell, though that success paled in significance when he shocked the Aussies by becoming the first New Zealander to win the Australian amateur championship in its 99-year history.

The grounding and overseas experience provided over the preceding years by the New Zealand Golf Association paid off for Campbell when he beat West Australian Jarrod Moseley four and three in the final at Royal Adelaide. *Australian Golf News* called Moseley "a fresh-faced and almost innocent 19-year-old blond headed kid from Perth" while describing Campbell as a "23-year-old veteran".

Moseley agreed with those descriptions saying "it was very exciting but I was overawed, especially on the second 18 with the cameras around. I'm not used to that. It tightens you up, you lose the edge."

In contrast for Campbell, who the previous year had been playing in front of huge galleries while in contention at the Air New Zealand Shell Open, it was little more than an afternoon stroll.

"It did make a difference. I'd played in front of big galleries whereas it was completely new to Jarrod. When you get into a situation like that it is worth a few holes to the experienced guy and, compared to Jarrod, I really was experienced. That stood me in good stead when I found myself three down after 17 holes. I was able to turn it around and while he was probably worrying during lunch about the afternoon round I put on my walkman and listened to some boogie music from C & C Music Factory while practising my putting.

"My New Zealand teammates also helped by giving me a few tips about the way I was putting and it went from there. When the match finished on the 15th green it was hard to comprehend what I had achieved.

"I was overwhelmed. To be the first Kiwi to win the Australian amateur, and being a Maori, was a very proud moment. When I settled down and was able to think about what had happened I think the most satisfying thing was that I had been able to give something back to New Zealand golf for what it had done for me."

Ironically, caddying for Michael Campbell on the day he had the biggest individual win of his amateur career was Richard Lee, who earlier in the year had denied Campbell the other title he desperately wanted – the New Zealand amateur champion – by beating him in the final.

The Australian amateur win gave Campbell a place in the Australian Open field and, more importantly for his future, a two-year exemption from having to qualify for the Australia-New Zealand PGA tour. It meant he could switch to the professional ranks when he was ready rather than be tied to the dates of the qualifying school.

With those things on his mind, and the Eisenhower tournament on the horizon, there was little time for Campbell to sit back and savour the moment of Royal Adelaide. Gearing up to Vancouver was the next step and no one was more confident of a New Zealand success than the newly crowned Australian champion.

With a record 49 teams assembled in Vancouver for the world championships, the tournament was staged on two courses, at Marine

Drive Golf Club and Capilano Golf and Country Club. It was difficult for teams to know exactly where they stood with two players on each course over the first two days, but after 36 holes it was the Kiwis who were making the pace at 12 under par and three clear of favourites the United States, with Australia third a stroke back and hosts Canada a distant fourth. Michael Campbell, with rounds of 67 and 66 was the leading individual, one shot ahead of Philip Tataurangi.

The third day belonged to American David Duval, who fired nine birdies in his 65 and was left lamenting what might have been had he not also had a triple bogey on his card. Thanks to Duval, and Allen Doyle's 68, the Americans overhauled New Zealand to finish two shots ahead in what had become a two-team race.

The final day tension was electric as the David and Goliath of world golf prepared to slug it out. Goliath got the first big blows in and while it is difficult to pinpoint the difference in shots at precise moments, the Americans were looking good at around five strokes ahead with nine holes to play.

It was then that the experience the Kiwis had of playing under pressure, all those overseas tournaments they had competed in, began to tell. Over the final nine holes New Zealand was a collective two under par, the Americans eleven over. During the run in the Americans became ruffled as they posted bogeys while watching their opponents make pars and birdies. David Duval, the golden boy of American golf, seemed to be feeling it the most as his playing partner, Campbell, found out.

"Things got a bit testy at the 16th hole, a par three. David had just gone bogey, double bogey, bogey while I had two birdies and a par to catch up six shots in three holes.

"On the 16th I was so nervous that I topped my tee shot along the ground and into the bunker, while David hit a two-iron to about 10 feet. I blasted out of the bunker to 12 feet and as I was marking my ball noticed it had a cut, a little smile, on the cover.

"I showed David the smile and asked if I could replace the ball. He said he couldn't see anything wrong. I said, 'Excuse me?' but he repeated that he couldn't see any mark. I had never experienced anything like that before. I was so flustered I didn't know what to say so I just put the ball down again and knocked it in the hole for par. He missed his birdie putt so we both made three.

"I said, 'That's justice for you' and walked off to the next tee. We didn't shake hands after the 18 holes, which was another first for me, but his version of the story is probably different to mine.

"It wasn't till the USPGA in 1995 that I saw David again. He said hello and congratulated me on the way I had played in the British Open and I reciprocated because he had been playing well on the United States circuit. There was a bit of small talk and he asked me for a practice round the next day. I said sure, but I didn't turn up.

"That wasn't nice of me, but what happened during that last round at Capilano isn't the sort of thing you expect to come up against in golf. Perhaps the occasion was getting to him. His teammates were falling by the wayside with bogeys and double bogeys while the Kiwis were making birdies and pars. They probably thought they had the title sewn up and we took it off them.

"By the time Phil knocked the final putt in on the 18th we knew we were the world champions. What a feeling!

"There were around 70 New Zealand supporters at the tournament and round the 18th green at Capilano on the last day everyone was hugging each other. They were coming up to us with tears in their eyes, thanking us for what we had done. Thanking us! We wanted to thank them just as much. Many were family and friends without whom we wouldn't have been where we were. They had travelled so far to be with us, to encourage us when things were getting tight, to enjoy the moment when we were going well. I think the supporters suffered more from nerves than we did at times.

"When it was all over and the prizegiving was about to start all the teams lined up in a semi-circle with the hierarchy of world golf in front of us. They announced the tie for third place between France and Australia. Then the runners up, the United States.

"I couldn't believe the roar that went up when they announced 'First place and Eisenhower Trophy winners, New Zealand'. The New Zealand supporters were the loudest but they were helped by the Canadians who got behind us once their team was out of contention. The feeling between Canadians and Americans is a bit the same as between Kiwis and Aussies.

"We had been practising the haka and while the speeches were on Phil and myself went over it again with Stephen and Grant. When our manager Roger Brennand had finished his acceptance speech Phil

At the beginning . . .

Michael's first appearance for Wellington at the inter-provincial championships in Whangarei (1987).
Back row: Michael Campbell, Martin Pettigrew, Lance Phelps, Stuart Thompson, John Sanders.
Front Row: Neil Munro (coach), Basil Jacobs (manager) Murray McDonald.

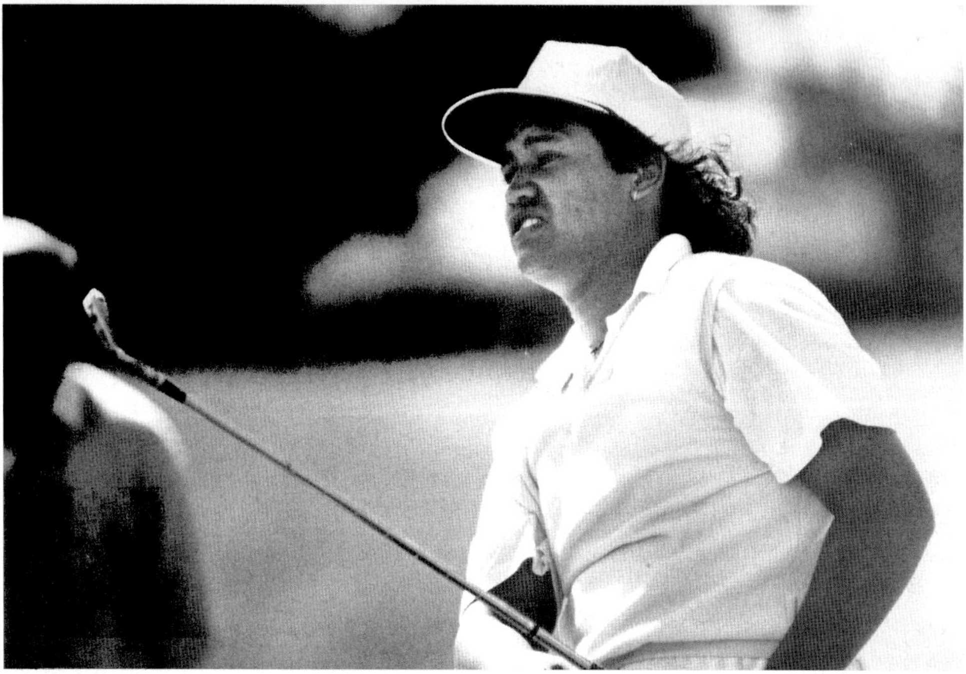

THE DOMINION

Michael during his early amateur days with Wellington, before he began to work on his fitness.

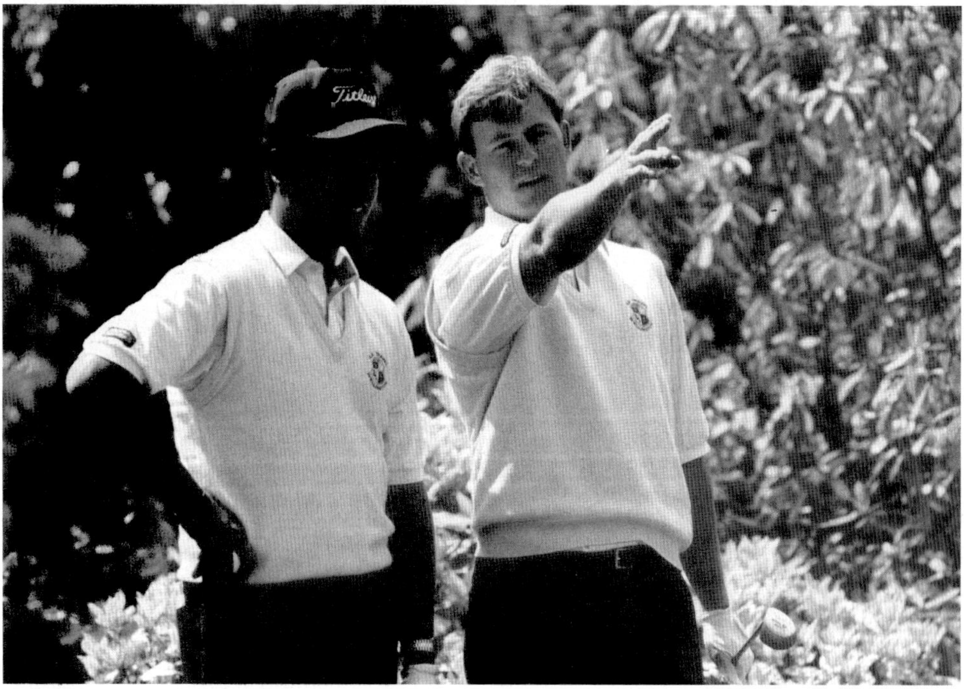

MAL TONGUE

Michael and Stephen Scahill discuss tactics during a foursomes match for Wellington.

All mine! Michael with his trophy in 1992 after becoming the first New Zealander to win the Australian amateur championship at Royal Adelaide.

Michael lines up a putt during the 1992 Eisenhower Trophy world teams' championship tournament in Vancouver.

The Kiwis thrill the crowd with a haka during the closing ceremony of the Eisenhower Trophy tournament in Vancouver.

Michael with the Eisenhower Trophy.

went to the microphone and explained what a haka was, that it was a challenge to the next guys in two years' time. Then we did it with all the Kiwi supporters joining in. It was a very special feeling and I think it received the biggest cheer of the week.

"The flag lowering was really emotional and when they played God Defend New Zealand I couldn't hold the tears back any longer. I realised that this was the last time I would be representing my country as an amateur and who knew what might happen in the future.

"Since then I have played for New Zealand as a professional and it is still a great feeling. Every time you wear the silver fern is special, but that day was different. I had grown up with these guys. We had been through so much together. Ups and downs, good times and bad. We had been there to support each other when someone had a problem.

"It was so different when I first played for New Zealand at the Dunhill Cup qualifying in Taiwan in 1993 as a pro with Frank Nobilo and Greg Turner. I didn't know them at all. I was the new kid on the block and these guys had been around a long time. They were strangers to me. I didn't feel part of the team. While I had spoken to them before it had really been mainly small talk so I found it hard to relate to them.

"It has become more comfortable for me as I've got to know Greg and Frank better but it was strange at first.

"Whatever happens to me while playing for New Zealand in the future will never replace the feelings of that day in Vancouver.

"Once the ceremony was over we went to get changed and we were the last team to arrive at the banquet. By that time we had got a grip on our emotions, but they started to spill over again when we walked into the room and the hundreds of people who were present stood as one and applauded us.

"I looked at the other guys and even now when I close my eyes I can see the looks on their faces. It is something which will always stay with me."

5

TURNING PROFESSIONAL

Some people make golf look a ridiculously easy game. They are envied by the vast majority who play a sport which can be the most frustrating pastime imaginable, even to those who have excelled in other codes which rely on hand-eye co-ordination.

Michael Campbell is one of those who can play the game seemingly without effort. It appears to be the most natural thing in the world as he guides the ball round a golf course as if on a piece of string, or hits shot after shot unerringly down the practice fairway each one landing within feet of the previous ones.

Most of us who battle with the intricacies of golf would give anything to be able to hit the ball even half as well as he does, but then so would some of those who play the game for a living.

Those who practise alongside him must often shake their heads in wonderment at just how simple Campbell makes the game appear. Coach Mal Tongue says he used to feel for those who shared the practice facilities with Campbell during his amateur days.

"It comes so easily to him," said Tongue. "When he was going through a bad patch off the course where he couldn't be bothered turning up as early as the others, he would wander down to the practice ground at about 10 o'clock, chuck his practice balls down, light a fag, spend five minutes talking, and then make one swing and hit the type of shot those around him had been striving for since they arrived. I saw one or two shake their head in disbelief, but Michael wouldn't notice. That was the shot he wanted, why wouldn't it happen?"

Michael Campbell will tell you that his golfing ability isn't all down to a God-given gift, even though after a practice session where he has hardly hit a ball off line he will turn to his coach, look up at the sky and joke "Why me Lord?"

He has got a gift. No one could have hit a ball as Michael did from the start without being blessed, but the gift has to be used and there have been times during his career, short as it has been to this point, when he has been in danger of wasting it. Thankfully those moments have been few, with Campbell quickly realising what he would be throwing away.

Campbell could have been forgiven for getting a little carried away with himself as his amateur career drew to a close. In a short space of time he had followed up his New South Wales state championship success by becoming the Australian champion, and then helping New Zealand win the world teams' title as well as finishing second on the individual rankings at the world championship. Capping it off on his arrival back in Wellington from Vancouver was the news that he had been named Australasian amateur golfer of the year, the first New Zealander to win the award.

That he didn't change says much for his character and to the influence of those close to him, mainly his family, coach Mal Tongue and friends such as Murray McDonald, John Pihema and Grant Duncan, who played alongside him in the Manor Park team.

After the Eisenhower success, and with his two-year Australia-New Zealand PGA tour qualifying exemption in his pocket, it was inevitable Michael Campbell was about to make those who had made fun of his ambitions on that first day at college choke on their laughter.

It was a matter of when, not if, he would turn professional. Campbell's exploits as an amateur had been noticed by potential sponsors and there was no bigger accolade for his achievements than the interest of International Management Group in where his career was heading.

Representing some of the biggest names in world sport, IMG were a major force in turning golf into the multi-million dollar sport it is today through their association with players such as Arnold Palmer and Jack Nicklaus.

The day before Campbell announced his arrival on the world stage at St Andrews with that sensational third-round 65, Palmer had taken a final curtain call on the Old Course. As the grand old man of golf made his way for the last time towards the imposing St Andrews clubhouse, which he had first entered 35 years earlier, people rushed back from all parts of the course to say their farewells to the man who helped change the face of golf.

Those in the stands rose as one to acknowledge the departure of a legend as Palmer ambled up the 18th fairway, after pausing for a moment on the Bridge of Sighs to reflect and say goodbye to the 3000 gathered behind the infamous 17th green.

Behind the 18th green Palmer's fellow professionals had gathered to pay their respects, including Nick Faldo who, some may be surprised to learn, had to swallow hard before he spoke of Palmer, such was the emotion of the moment.

"If it wasn't for Arnie Palmer we would be playing for fifty pounds and changing in a shed on the beach instead of playing for millions," said Faldo as he applauded Palmer's last putt.

It was into that world of million dollar purses that Michael Campbell was stepping and IMG could open doors for fledgling professionals, get them into tournaments which would otherwise be closed. Campbell was flattered that they should consider him worth representing.

"I had been talking to IMG for two months before announcing I was turning professional. It made sense for me to go with them. They had contacts throughout the world and would be able to organise things for me.

"After the Eisenhower everyone wanted to talk to me about my future. There was never any doubt that I would become a professional. That is what I had always wanted to be and what had happened during my amateur days had paved the way.

"It was just a matter of timing and once New Zealand had won the Eisenhower there was nothing left for me to stay amateur for. I had won the Australian championship and got the two-year exemption from qualifying on the Australia-New Zealand tour.

"Just as importantly I had achieved most of the goals I had set myself. When I turned 21 I wrote down a number of goals in golf and made them all, apart from winning the New Zealand amateur championship. I would have loved to win that title but I couldn't wait around for another 12 months to try again.

"It was also the right time to turn professional so far as sponsorship was concerned. Sponsors were coming to me, which is every young sportsman's dream, rather than me having to chase them. Titleist, AMP and Pickering Clothing all wanted to help me, and I was happy to be helped. AMP also helped Stephen Scahill and Mal Tongue which showed they cared about New Zealand golf and not just one player. Because of all those things I had no doubt that the timing was right and so I went for it."

Over the past few years New Zealand's top amateur golfers have been as well looked after as their counterparts in any part of the world. Despite having to work with a modest budget compared to some countries, the New Zealand Golf Association has provided its players with overseas experience second to none. When players have left New Zealand to represent their country they have had nothing to worry about apart from playing golf. Travel and accommodation is all taken care of, as are meals and other expenses.

Having played as an amateur in that environment it can be a rude awakening when a player turns professional and has to fend for himself. No longer do air tickets magically arrive in the post, paid for by someone else. There is no car or bus waiting at the airport in a strange country to take him to the well-appointed hotel which has been checked out to make sure it is suitable.

Instead of picking up his baggage and heading for his organised transport, a young player suddenly has to sort out a taxi, perhaps in a language he has never heard before. When every cent is vital, and that is usually the case when a player quits the amateur ranks, he needs to make sure the taxi driver isn't going to rip him off. Consequently the drive between airport and hotel is often spent with eyes fixed on the taxi's meter, if in fact there is one.

Playing golf on a shoestring isn't conducive to playing well. Where a young amateur international is used to sharing his air-conditioned hotel room with a teammate, during their early days on the circuit many young professionals find themselves sharing a room with exotic creatures such as cockroaches. Air-conditioning is opening the window and having to contend with street noises wafting in on the breeze as others enjoy themselves while he strives for sleep to prepare for the next round of golf, in which how he plays and what he earns may determine whether he can continue to the next tournament.

Even if a newly turned professional has managed to secure some sponsorship, the money can soon disappear if he fails to qualify for tournaments or misses the cut and doesn't pick up a cheque when he does get into the field. The circuit can be a miserable and lonely place if you aren't playing well. It is even more depressing if where the next meal is coming from depends on winning money.

Michael Campbell will be forever grateful that wasn't how he had to start out on the circuit, that he didn't have to worry unduly about money when he set off in the professional world. The sponsorship he received gave him a solid base on which to build and, most importantly, breathing space if he didn't start earning money immediately.

Not that the thought of failure ever crossed Campbell's mind. That isn't his way and he set off for Australia and his first tournament in his usual confident manner, feeling it was only a matter of time before he would win.

Campbell went on record at the start of 1993, and before he had hit a ball as a professional in a tournament, that his first season goal was "to make each cut and finish in the top twenty, or preferably in the top ten".

The moment Michael Campbell had waited for arrived on January 21, 1993, in the Optus Players Championship, on the 6960-yard, par 72 Royal Melbourne course. From being a big fish in the relatively small pool of amateur golf he was about to front up as a minnow in a big pool where his amateur record meant little. There is a genuine comradeship in golf, however, and Campbell was pleasantly surprised when he arrived at the course and realised he wasn't completely unknown after all. Ian Baker-Finch, the 1991 British Open champion, and Peter O'Malley approached him on the practice ground, welcomed him to the tour and wished him all the best for the rest of the year. It was a gesture which was appreciated by the novice and helped to stall what was becoming an attack of the jitters.

Campbell had played his first round of professional golf seemingly hundreds of times before he even left his hotel room. There were different scenarios, some he liked, others he hoped were nightmares which would never become reality.

Reality came when Michael Campbell heard his name called and he stepped on to Royal Melbourne's 10th tee with a bad case of the jitters and visions of his big day turning into a nightmare.

"I thought I had felt nervous before, in Vancouver for instance. But this was something else. Royal Melbourne has such a reputation as one of the toughest courses in the world and it was so scary looking at those bunkers while I was waiting to tee off. I had never felt like that in my life.

"I'll always remember my first shot as a professional. It skimmed through the rough in front of the tee, skidded along the fairway and rolled straight into a bunker!"

That Campbell could blast a four-iron out of the trap, chip on to the green and hole a 20-foot putt for par says much for his attitude.

"The butterflies usually go quickly but that day I was very nervous for the first three holes. I finished up in bunkers on each of them. My short game got me out of trouble and I was happy to be level par by the time I started to settle down on the fourth tee."

Campbell went on to birdie the 14th, 15th and second holes, though after signing for his 69, which included only 26 putts, he began to feel he could have done even better.

"I got too defensive when I got to three under and that isn't the way I play. I started thinking 'If I can shoot 69 in my first round as a pro it would be great'. But I shouldn't have been complaining. Had someone told me when I arrived on course that morning that they'd give me a first round score of 72 or 73, never mind 69, I would have snapped their hand off."

It was a dream first day for the novice pro. After 18 holes he was in equal fourth place, two strokes off the joint leaders, Queenslanders Craig Jones and Tod Power. A second round 71 kept him in contention but a third-round 74 saw him slip down the leaderboard.

"I was quickly learning the difference between amateur and professional golf. I didn't play badly in that third round despite having five bogeys on my card. Not concentrating the whole time cost me. The bogeys weren't through any major bad shots, just lapses in concentration.

"I began to feel a pressure I hadn't experienced before. So many players were attacking the course and carding low scores. It was amazing. I was playing five or six holes in par or one-under and was losing three or four shots because the other guys were burning it up. I wasn't used to that. It was a whole new world. I had known it would be but it doesn't really hit home until things like that start happening."

Campbell showed he had the temperament to compete on the tour by shrugging off the disappointment of Saturday's round to finish as he started, with a 69, for a five under par 283 and equal seventh in the strong field. Campbell's first cheque was for $A8600 but the money wasn't important.

"Of course, I was playing for a living now, but the fact that I finished so high up the list in my first pro tournament meant more than money. I learnt that I could play in that sort of company. I also found out that it was imperative I kept working on my putting. I saw very quickly that the difference between winning tournaments and finishing in the top 10 came down to sinking putts.

"From tee to green that week I held my own, in fact I was probably longer off the tee than those I played with, but I fell behind them on my short game. That is what separates the top guys from the rest. Robert Allenby won the tournament and he was freakish round the greens. That was what won him the golf tournament.

"When I look back at that first tournament it was a brilliant week and a great learning curve. Actually I wondered whether I was going to get to finish the tournament. I had to wait twenty minutes between playing my second to last shot and my last, a one-foot putt, when play was suspended because of a thunderstorm. At that point I just wanted to get it over with.

"During the tournament I played with six different players and they were very kind in what they said about me and my game. They don't have to say that sort of thing because they are competing against you so it's nice when they do. I think the biggest lesson from the tournament was that if you don't make birdies you get left behind. If you make bogeys you go backward pretty quickly."

As he left Melbourne and headed to Perth for the Heineken Classic at The Vines, Campbell tried to put things into perspective. He had done better than he had dared hope at Royal Melbourne. Now it was important to show that he wasn't a one-tournament wonder, that he had the golf game and temperament to compete week in week out with established players.

The Heineken Classic was billed as a shoot-out between a rising star of Australian golf, Robert Allenby, and Greg Norman, the Great White Shark. Norman was never quite able to climb up the leaderboard and eventually tied for 10th place, nine strokes from winner Peter Senior. Allenby, fresh from his win in Melbourne, continued his good form to finish third, four strokes behind Senior and one behind the runner-up, Michael Campbell.

At 7101 yards The Vines Resort course is slightly longer than Royal Melbourne with the same par of 72 and it speaks volumes for Campbell's demeanour so early in his career that he could negotiate it four times without going over par. Three times he was under the card with 70, 69 and 67, while he was level with it in his third round 72.

Campbell was probably unlucky to strike Peter Senior in a mean mood or he may even have won at only his second attempt. Senior, not surprisingly, was miffed that he hardly rated a mention in the Australian media even after opening the tournament with a seven under par 65. It was a round no one got close to equalling throughout the four days as Senior led from start to finish.

"I shot 65 the first day and I led from go to whoa, yet there was very little written about me," Peter Senior said at the time. "It was all Allenby and Norman. After that they talked about every man and his dog being likely to win, but still I didn't get a mention. If I'm leading the tournament I expect a little paragraph somewhere. When I didn't get any credit it made me all the more determined to win it."

After two rounds Campbell was nicely placed on 136, five under, and three strokes behind Senior, who was setting a hot pace. It was in the third round where Senior, who for the second time in three days shot the field's lowest score, made his break. While Senior was carding a 67, Campbell was level with par on 72, seven under for the tournament and in equal fifth place. Between him and Senior were Peter O'Malley, Robert Allenby and Glenn Joyner.

On the last day Campbell charged home in 67 to snatch second place from Allenby. Senior's experience, and broomstick putter, saw him safely through the last 18 holes in 72. Campbell's flying finish took many people by surprise but not the player himself.

"I rang Mal Tongue on the Saturday night and told him I felt something was going to happen for me in the last round. It was difficult to explain but it was there in my mind all night. Everything seemed to be coming together. I was hitting the ball well, my short game was good . . . I just knew it was going to be a good day.

"In the end the last round was one I can look back on and say 'if only', but how many times can you say that, especially in golf. The way I had been feeling going into the round I wasn't too surprised when I started to score well early in the round. After eleven holes I was five under the card and feeling great. I had got to within one shot of Peter and thought if I could just keep going and apply the pressure who knows what might happen.

"On the 12th tee we had a five-minute wait and that is where I lost any chance I had of winning the tournament. The way things panned out Peter would still have won even if I hadn't had a mishap at the 12th, but how he would have reacted had I joined him in the lead we'll never know.

"While I was waiting on the 12th tee all these thoughts started to come into my mind and instead of putting the pressure on Peter it was me who began to feel the tension. When we finally got to play I had a disastrous four putt for double bogey and that was that.

"Even in moments like that I try to find something positive. What really pleased me was that I could put that disappointment – and believe me my stomach dropped after the third putt missed – behind me to bounce back with birdies on the 14th and 15th holes to make sure of second place.

"I was playing with Wayne Grady, a former USPGA champion. Wayne said I had shown character to come back from that body blow on the 12th. He said it would have knocked the stuffing out of players a lot more experienced than me."

A win would have been nice but a $A30,600 cheque was some consolation for coming second and before he left the course Michael Campbell charmed the media, as he was to do often over the next couple of years, with the comment that "this is only my second tournament and I think I could get to like this professional stuff".

New Zealanders were certainly getting to like their new golfing star. For some reason, probably because he was so open and accessible to the media, Michael Campbell was getting far more publicity than Frank Nobilo, Greg Turner and Grant Waite had received early in their professional careers. There was also the fact that he was playing, and in contention, at tournaments close to home, whereas Nobilo turned professional in 1979 and didn't win on the Australia-New Zealand tour till taking out the New South Wales PGA in 1982.

Greg Turner and Grant Waite had served their golfing

apprenticeships at college in the United States, in contrast to Campbell who grew up in front of the public as the profile of golf increased dramatically in New Zealand.

It was something which worried Campbell. His apprehension had nothing to do with self-doubt about his golfing ability, or whether he could compete. He was just concerned that too much would be expected of him too soon.

"I was scared in the period between finishing as an amateur and waiting to start as a pro. Who wouldn't be in that situation? I was confident of footing it with the pros, but people seemed to be expecting an awful lot not only of me, but of Stephen Scahill and Grant Moorhead who had also turned professional after the Eisenhower.

"While you know that you are good enough to succeed it is hard not to think of guys like Steve Conran and Stuart Bouvier, really good amateurs who struggled when they turned pro. I took heart from the fact that top amateurs such as Robert Allenby and Lucas Parsons made the switch successfully.

"When I played in the 1992 Australian Open as an amateur I was in the same group as Robert Allenby for the first two days. A week later Robert, who was still in his rookie year, went out and won the Johnnie Walker Classic at Royal Melbourne.

"I compared myself to him during the two rounds we played together in the Open and the only difference between us was his short game and the way he ground out a score. I saw that every time the pros step on the course their only objective is to post a good score because it is so competitive. It doesn't have to be pretty, the record books don't show how it was achieved.

"At the Australian Open I didn't play badly. I was average and average wasn't good enough to make the cut. Sixty guys were better than me. What was worrying me when I was turning pro was that people in New Zealand seemed to expect me to go out and win a tournament straight away. I said then that if it happened great, but it could also be two, three or four years away.

"As it turned out I started really well and the way I played at Royal Melbourne and The Vines was a real confidence booster. What I didn't realise at the time was that with my next tournament being in New Zealand, the AMP Open at Paraparaumu Beach, I had made things tougher for myself.

"Just before I turned pro I had spent a couple of days with Greg Turner and Frank Nobilo in Dunedin. I was pumping them for information about what was to come and how things should be handled, including whether I should sign up with IMG. They were great and gave me loads of advice, but they also told me how much extra pressure they found themselves under when they played in New Zealand.

"It was, they said, tougher if you had just been playing well overseas. People expected you to perform even better on your home courses. Coming back to New Zealand was hard for Greg and Frank because they usually had to come from Europe and the travelling took a lot out of them. At least I was only coming from Australia.

"I was really looking forward to that week in Paraparaumu and, looking back, I put too much pressure on myself. I didn't want anyone to think I had got above myself because of what had happened over the last two weeks so didn't refuse any requests for interviews from newspapers, television or radio.

"Stephen Scahill and myself were asked to play in pro-ams in Wellington and we didn't want to let anyone down so we said yes. We were saying yes to everything. There was also family and friends to see. I found myself deviating into thinking about things other than golf. I revolved around the media, my family and friends instead of concentrating on golf.

"The end result was that I played badly in the New Zealand Open, a tournament in which I was desperate to do well. You have bad weeks and that week was one of them for me."

After the fairytale start to his pro career Michael Campbell at Paraparaumu Beach experienced the downside of being a high-profile New Zealand sportsman. Some among the galleries who had come to cheer Campbell were quick to criticise the rookie and there were even those who abused him.

I followed Campbell during his second round and could hardly believe my ears as I heard comments, and they were, apparently deliberately, made loud enough and close enough for Campbell to hear, such as "he's not as good as he's cracked up to be". Campbell wasn't playing well, but he didn't deserve that kind of treatment, certainly not from young Maori men who were the offenders. Michael is proud of his heritage. He promotes Maoridom at every opportunity and hopes what he is achieving on the golf course will entice more young Maori into golf.

He sees himself as a role model for those youngsters. During his formative years there were no Maori stars in golf, and hadn't been since Walter Godfrey retired in the 1960s. Jack Nicklaus and Greg Norman were the ones he looked up to. In future there will still be young Maori who will have their imagination captured by players such as Nick Faldo and Fred Couples, but they will have a choice of heroes with one of their own right up there with the best.

After signing for a four-over 75 and sparing himself by one shot the embarrassment of missing the cut, a fate which befell Greg Turner, Campbell admitted he had heard some snide remarks from the gallery. He didn't want to make much of them but the look on his face and the tremor in his voice told you he was hurt by the turnaround. "I had an off day. Perhaps they don't realise everyone can make mistakes," Campbell said at the time.

It defied logic that Michael Campbell, the rookie playing his third tournament, was the warm favourite to win the New Zealand Open, but that was the case according to newspaper and television hype, not to mention the guy in the street who seemed to take it for granted that the young Maori lad only had to tee it up to win after the way he had played the last two weeks.

Certainly he had made a dream start to his professional career in a sport where many a young professional goes for months just trying to make a cut, or even qualify to play in a tournament. Some forget there were 143 other guys, most with far more experience than him, also trying to win.

It was all a bit too much too soon for Michael Campbell. He might have been looking forward to getting to Paraparaumu but by the end of the tournament, in which he earned $587 – barely more than he was getting the previous year for winning microwaves and toasters – for finishing 50th, 17 shots behind winner Peter Fowler, he couldn't wait to get back to Australia and anonymity.

6
Rookie Year
Australasian Tour

T he first few weeks of Michael Campbell's rookie year provided mixed emotions. The elation of making a wonderful start through seventh and second placings in successive tournaments was offset by the disappointment at the way he had performed on home soil in the New Zealand Open and, more so, because of the way that effort had been received.

While he had been forewarned by Greg Turner and Frank Nobilo of the extra pressures he would experience in New Zealand, their words didn't prepare him for the reality of returning home in a blaze of publicity and leaving, as it felt at the time, with his tail between his legs. As Campbell said, everyone has their bad weeks and he just didn't fire as he would have liked during those four days at Paraparaumu Beach.

It was important for Campbell when he returned to Australia to put what had happened in perspective. Once he sat down and analysed the trip it wasn't as bad as he had imagined it to be at the time.

Yes, he had taken on too much in the days leading up to the tournament. No one would have thought any the worse of him had he politely declined the invitations to play in the pro-ams with the explanation that he had to prepare for the New Zealand Open. Yes, he had spent too much time socialising with family and friends when his mind should have been on the job at hand. They would have understood. His family and friends wanted him to do well. If it meant not spending as much time with him as they would have liked, so be it.

Yes, he had wanted to show New Zealanders that he has what it takes to make a career out of golf. Perhaps he tried too hard. If he did, no one could blame him. Michael Campbell has always been a showman and Paraparaumu was a stage on which he wanted to perform to the best of his ability.

Did he really play as badly as some people tried to make out that week? No he didn't. In his first round Campbell was two under the card, a respectable score at a links course such as Paraparaumu Beach with its undulating fairways and variable winds, while in his fourth round he matched par. Sandwiched between were rounds of 75 and 76. Disappointing, but not a disaster. He had shot 74 in his third round at Royal Melbourne before finishing seventh. No one had castigated him for that.

From Paraparaumu Beach and all its distractions Campbell went to Melbourne and the Australian Masters where he tied for 33rd in a strong field. Again there were scores of 76 and 75, in the second and fourth rounds, but at Huntingdale Golf Club Michael Campbell was just another player, not the great local hope.

Campbell could imagine what the reaction would have been had the Australian Masters been at Paraparaumu rather than Huntingdale. After all, he had led the tournament after 26 holes, looking down from the top of the leaderboard at Peter Senior, Greg Norman, Craig Parry, Nick Price, Steve Elkington and a host of other top players.

Then came a disastrous quadruple bogey nine on one hole which sent him sliding ungracefully down the field. It was another learning curve which was much easier to digest away from the glare of a hometown spotlight.

Leading the tournament and dropping away in such fashion hurt Campbell but he made sure he learnt from the experience, bitter though it was. One bad shot had set him on a downward spiral. Instead of taking the mis-hit shot in his stride, as he would learn to do, Campbell allowed himself to become flustered, didn't concentrate on the next couple of shots and the lapses cost him dearly.

It wasn't all bad, however. There was another cheque for $A4062 to bank and there were many young men taking their first steps in a golfing world that is becoming tougher and tougher every year who would have been more than satisfied.

Next stop on the Australia-New Zealand tour was Sydney's Castle Hill Country Club and it was on what is rated by many as Sydney's premier inland course that Campbell truly announced his arrival on the pro scene by winning the 1993 Canon Challenge by three shots in only his fifth start.

There was nothing unusual about the early part of the week as Campbell settled into his routine in Sydney. The days were spent on the practice fairway before moving on to the putting green in late afternoon. It is in such a setting that golfers appear at their most relaxed.

While practising putting they will stop often for a chat. It might be with their coach or a friend they haven't seen since the last visit, or just one of the guys they will be trying to finish ahead of later in the week.

There is a camaraderie among golfers that is missing in team sports. While they compete against each other week in week out throughout the year they share a common bond, knowing what it is like to live out of a suitcase for up to 10 months a year. Laughter is a common sound on the practice green as exploits from the previous night are recalled and embellished.

After the sun has disappeared over the horizon the touring professionals, especially the young, unattached players, will have a few beers together or just enjoy each other's company. It is far better than sitting in a hotel room on your own, and it is during such times that friendships are developed which will last for years despite the intense rivalry of the course where it is every man for himself.

Thursday, the day when the players begin trying each week to earn a living, dawned hot, sunny and calm in Sydney, making conditions on the Castle Hill course conducive to low scoring. Robert Allenby took full advantage to shoot a course record nine-under-par 63. Peter Senior and his broomstick putter was only two shots behind.

Michael Campbell was kicking himself a little on Thursday night. While he had shot 70, two under the card, he knew he could have done better given the good weather and how short the course was playing.

The weather was again kind for Friday's second round, though what started out as a slight north-easterly breeze strengthened during the afternoon, while Campbell was out on the course. Campbell might have got the worst of the day's conditions but he made light of them as he blazed his way round the course. After getting off to a flying start with birdies at three of the first four holes he added four more birdies to his card during a bogey-free round of 65.

Allenby was having one of those days all golfers dread, where nothing would go right for him. When he signed his card there were 12 more shots on it than the previous day, including four putts at the 18th. Peter Senior was again to the fore with a 68 to give him a two shot lead going into the third round. Sharing second place were Michael Campbell and Victoria's Jamie Taylor. Being up with the lead at the halfway mark was a new experience for Campbell and led to a Friday night he will never forget.

"It was a position I hadn't been in before and it took the wind out of me a bit. When I came second at The Vines I had come from off the pace. This was the first time I had been so close to the lead after two rounds and while I tried to make light of it after my round I was very nervous.

"I began to think too much about the situation and what might happen over the next two days. On Thursday night I had rung Mal Tongue because I hadn't been happy with the way I had played that day. The course was there to be taken and I hadn't been able to get the ball close enough to the pin.

"We ironed out a few technical things in my swing over the telephone and I felt a different player on Friday. With the course being shorter than usual most of the greens could be reached with a driver and an eight or nine iron. In that second round I hit my short irons as well as I had ever done.

"I knew I was playing well enough to really do something over the weekend but I had to relax and not let the situation get to me.

"A few friends were going out to dinner and asked me to join them. I was a bit reluctant at first but decided it would do me more good than sitting around worrying. I thought, 'Okay, I'm off at 1.30pm so I'll be all right if I get to bed by 12.30am, have 10 hours solid sleep, up at 10.30am and at the course by 12.30pm.'

"I had it all planned out before we went to dinner. At the time I was partial to a drop, or more, of red wine, especially Wolfblass. It went down a treat that night and before we knew it we had drunk four bottles of red amongst four of us.

"I was really starting to relax by that time. Wondering and worrying about what was going to happen on the golf course was the last thing on my mind. It was my idea to go on to a nightclub, just to have a look and maybe a couple of drinks. By the time I had finished having a look I came out of the club at 4.30am. It was hosing down and I was, you could say, under the weather myself.

"It was one of those nights I got carried away. I wasn't thinking straight. The demon got the better of me. I'm sure subconsciously I was believing that if I drank all this alcohol it would get rid of the tension I'd been feeling when I left the course.

"I had been in front or close to the lead in amateur tournaments but it had felt nothing like this. Everyone wanted to talk to me, either to wish me well for the weekend or to talk about the round I'd just finished.

"On my way home that Saturday morning I was so hungry I bought a pizza to take back to the hotel room and climbed into bed about five after eating it. By eight o'clock I was talking into the big white telephone in the bathroom.

"There was no way I could get back to sleep. Whenever I thought I might drift off I would have to dash to the toilet again. I was sick three more times and as I tried to get myself ready to go to the course I was throwing Disprins down my throat to try and relieve the thumping headache.

"I wear sunglasses all the time now because of being in the sun almost all year round, but that morning they were as much to hide my red eyes as to keep the sun out. When I got to the course I was dehydrated and still had the headache which showed no signs of disappearing, despite everything I had thrown at it.

"There is nothing better than playing golf on a warm summer's day, but I would have given anything for some rain and a cool breeze rather than the blazing sun and 30 degree heat at Castle Hill that Saturday.

"The practice range was a disaster. I began shanking the ball, pulling it, and even topped the ball along the ground with one shot. I couldn't see or feel anything so decided to hell with practice and headed to the locker room to lie down till my name was called for the tee.

"For half an hour I lay there, wishing I was anywhere but getting ready to play what was at that point probably the most important round of golf in my life. For such an important round my preparation consisted of hitting a few balls and having two or three putts. Nick Faldo wouldn't have been impressed by such lack of dedication.

"How I finished up shooting 65 I will never know. I can't really remember the round. It was all a bit of a blur.

"Anyone who has had a night like I had on the Friday knows what a horrible feeling it is when they have to bend down next morning. I almost fell over just putting the ball on the tee.

"The sun and heat didn't help, and neither did the undulating Castle Hill course. Up and down, up and down. I was beginning to feel sea sick. There were so many negative thoughts that day but for some reason a miracle happened and I found myself signing for a 65 and leading the tournament by five shots. I couldn't believe how lucky I was.

"It isn't a preparation I would recommend to anyone. I tried the same formula again later in the year when I was having a frustrating time in Europe. It didn't work so I decided, not unreasonably, that the 65 at Castle Hill must have been a fluke."

Campbell doesn't remember much about his third round at the Canon Challenge so for his benefit it should be recorded that he had four birdies and a bogey on the front nine, before adding four more birdies on the back nine as he had to cope with the added pressures of the lead and a number of would-be challengers. It was also a day when his putter ran hot with only 24 putts on the 18 holes.

At the post-round press conference Campbell was asked how he would spend Saturday night now that he was the tournament leader. "I'll go through the same routine as I have done the last three days. I'll go out tonight and have a couple of drinks until 11 or 12 and just do the same thing really." A little white lie never hurt anyone. What was he supposed to say? That he had got roaring drunk the night before and he was going to do it again!

"Actually, I was so buggered from the night before that I went to bed early on Saturday and had a better night's sleep than I would normally have got when leading a golf tournament."

The Canon was Campbell's fifth professional tournament, but already he had been in or near the lead in four of them at some point, only to falter through inexperience. It was something he was aware of as he prepared for the final round.

"You can't buy experience, but I had been getting closer each time. It was difficult to come to terms with the fact that I was leading by five shots. Had anyone told me I would be in that position in my fifth tournament I would have laughed at them."

Sunday's weather followed the pattern of the previous three days, hot and sunny. This time with a clear head and steady hands Campbell could enjoy playing in conditions he loves.

Starting the final round at 16 under par, Campbell had a five-stroke advantage over Steve Conran, though Peter Senior one stroke further back was probably more of a worry for him than Conran.

Conran, also a former Australian amateur champion, had little more experience than Campbell, despite having turned professional 12 months before the New Zealander. Conran struggled during his first season on the tour, lost his card and had to regain it at qualifying school.

The commentators, most of them veteran playing professionals, seemed to expect Campbell to find the pressure too much even though he was starting with a five-shot cushion.

The doubters had to think again as Campbell all but shut the gate on his pursuers with birdies at the first two holes before swapping a bogey and birdie at the fifth and sixth to turn for home at 18 under the card and six shots clear.

Campbell stumbled momentarily on the back nine with bogeys at the 12th and 13th holes, but when he was staring a third dropped shot in the face after hitting through the green at the 14th he showed something special by producing a superb recovery shot and a six-foot putt for par. That stopped the rot, steadied the nerves, and he parred his way in for 72 and the title by three from Conran.

"It was terrifying on the back nine. I was so relieved to pull through mentally because there was always the chance I could have let it go."

The $A45,000 prize money from the Canon Challenge took Michael Campbell's earnings on the Australia-New Zealand tour to $A88,724 with the end-of-year tournaments to come.

After his win at Castle Hill, Campbell went to Europe where he spent five frustrating and disappointing months having to rely on sponsor's invitations to get into tournaments. They were in short supply, and when the New Zealander returned to the Australia-New

Zealand tour at the Meru Valley Golf Resort in Malaysia in October it
was like starting all over again.

That first tournament back on the tour, the Perak Masters,
didn't provide the type of excitement Campbell had courted at the
Canon Challenge but at least he was playing again. A tie for 20th was
reasonable enough, and had he been able to settle into a routine over
the next few weeks he may have regained the rhythm which propelled
him up the rankings in the first three months of the year.

Before the next Australia-New Zealand event, however,
Campbell was on a plane back to Europe. This time Montpellier,
France, venue for the Volvo European PGA tour qualifying school,
was his destination.

Again Europe wasn't kind to Campbell. According to Mal
Tongue, Campbell had no chance of earning his card to play on the
European tour on that trip. Campbell was, Tongue said, chasing his
tail. His life wasn't balanced, and consequently he was never in the
right frame of mind to play to his potential at the qualifying school
where he finished 81st.

After the disappointment in France it was a dispirited, dejected
young man who headed back to the southern hemisphere wondering
where it had all gone wrong.

Keeping Campbell going at that point was the thought that once
he got back into an environment in which he felt comfortable things
would look up, his game would improve and he would be back on
track. It didn't turn out to be as easy as he thought.

The spark which had made him the star of the show on the
Australia-New Zealand tour at the start of the year was missing, and
he was missing cuts. Three times Campbell headed home before
weekend play commenced. This was something he wasn't used to on
his own patch. While it was disappointing, he could just about accept
missing cuts in Europe. But in Australia, among his mates, that was a
different matter. Pride was at stake.

Eventually, at the 1993 Australian Open, Campbell finally made
a cut. Even then it was a close thing. The cut was set at 148 and, after
rounds of 73 and 75, he just made it.

As if determined to make up for lost time, Campbell cut loose in
the third round with a six-under-par 66 and after a closing 74 he was
happy to settle for a 25th placing.

The following week Campbell tied for 47th in Greg Norman's Holden Classic at The Lakes in Sydney. It wasn't as good as he had hoped for after seeming to get back in the groove at the Australian Open but there were positives to take from that tournament.

In tough conditions on the first day, Campbell shot a three-under 70 to be three strokes behind leader Steve Elkington, before gradually drifting back through the field with rounds of 76, 75, 75 for a four-over 296.

"The first round was encouraging because the three under felt like six under given the conditions. It was nice to play such a round again and coming on top of the 66 at the Australian Open it showed I was steadily getting my game together.

"What was costing me all the time was bad starts. At the Greg Norman I was four over after five holes in the second round, while on Saturday and Sunday I started with a double bogey each time.

"I managed to fight back each time but when you start like that it puts you on the back foot right away. Overall though it was encouraging."

As Michael Campbell left The Lakes he turned his attention to the Air New Zealand Shell Open at The Grange in Auckland. It was there 12 months earlier that he had finished fourth as an amateur and he wanted to perform well again, particularly as his last trip home – to Paraparaumu Beach for the New Zealand Open – had been so disappointing.

There was also the Australia-New Zealand PGA Rookie of the Year title at stake. Campbell was favoured to be the top-earning first year professional after his brilliant start to 1993, but it wasn't clear cut. Other rookies still fancied their chances of heading him off.

Campbell was much more relaxed than 10 months earlier at Paraparaumu. The media spotlight wasn't trained on him as much as it had been prior to the New Zealand Open. American Brad Faxon was the star attraction, and Philip Tataurangi was in the limelight after arriving back from the United States where he had qualified to play on the main US tour in 1994.

An opening round 68 had Campbell three shots behind Brad Faxon who was five under the card. After two rounds six players shared the lead on 137 with Campbell two shots back after a 71. One of the leaders was Australian left-hander Richard Green, who also had his eye on the Rookie of the Year title.

By the end of the third round Green, who had a 65, was sharing the lead with tour battler David McKenzie, who needed a decent cheque to get into the top 60 on the order of merit. Campbell was five shots off the lead.

Green faded with a final round 78 and McKenzie shot 74 as Queensland's Terry Price came through with a 66 to win the tournament by one shot from Michael Campbell, Brad Faxon and Wayne Riley.

The $A17,835 Campbell received guaranteed him the Rookie title and gave him a badly needed shot in the arm after what had been a traumatic year.

The Grange tournament hadn't all been plain sailing for Campbell. On the third day coach Mal Tongue had walked out on him after a disagreement. It wasn't the first time the pair had fallen out. They have different versions of what happened but the end result was the same and it took a few weeks before things returned to normal.

It was the end of a rollercoaster 12 months for Michael Campbell. He finished in seventh place on the Australia-New Zealand PGA order of merit with earnings of $A117,168. He also learnt some harsh lessons in Europe, but showed he had the character to bounce back from adversity.

"It was fantastic to win the Rookie of the Year but I had to make sure I kept it in perspective. I had played well for the first three months of the year and the last couple of months. In the middle it all fell apart.

"I had won a golf tournament in my first year, but I had also made a lot of mistakes, especially off the course. Playing golf for a living wasn't as easy as it appeared during those first two months where everything went right. The fun went out of it when things turned sour in Europe. Finishing second at The Grange gave me the feeling that the good times would come back again if I worked hard enough. It gave me something to build on for 1994."

7

Not Making
the Cut

Thousands of New Zealanders make their way to Britain and Europe every year for the great overseas experience, to sample life and different cultures on the other side of the world.

It is an exciting time for young Kiwis as they get to spread their wings away from the nest, to test their resourcefulness by living on a shoestring budget. Go to any number of pubs throughout London and chances are that one of those behind the bar will be a New Zealander earning money to extend their trip or merely to exist.

In 1993 Michael Campbell was ready for his OE in Europe. A major difference between him and those of his peers who had scrimped and saved to make the trip was his bank balance. While the account wasn't exactly bulging, Campbell's bank statements, thanks to his great start as a pro and the Canon Challenge win in particular, showed a credit far in excess of anything he had seen before.

There was another difference between Campbell and his fellow adventurers. While others would keep in contact with family and friends by letter and telephone, Michael Campbell would do his OE under the scrutiny of the media.

Because of his glittering amateur career, still fresh in the mind, and the way he had played during the first two months of his professional career, Michael Campbell was public property. It wasn't only his family and friends who wanted to know how he was progressing overseas. Those who had followed his exploits in New Zealand and Australia through newspapers and television expected to be informed of what he was doing and how he was going in Europe.

While most would have loved to be in Campbell's situation in having won almost $A90,000 in two months, it was a dangerous period for the young golfer from Titahi Bay. So much had happened so quickly it was hard for him to take everything in.

From being a member of Manor Park's inter-club team, larking about with his mates and enjoying a few beers after matches against people he knew well, Campbell had become an international golfer, had helped New Zealand to its greatest golfing triumph since Bob Charles won the 1963 British Open, turned professional and won around $100,000 – all in 12 months.

When he looks back on his 1993 European experience, Michael Campbell can see clearly where he went wrong. Whether he would change what happened is a different matter. He would have preferred not to suffer the heartache and frustrations of those five months in Europe, but he is convinced that the lessons he learnt during that disappointing time will stand him in good stead in the years ahead.

If he had to go through a bad patch, then that was probably the best time for it to happen. He was young enough to waste five months of his career – for that is what he did – and had the support of the right people to pull him back from potential disaster.

Stepping out from under the protective umbrella of the New Zealand Golf Association to play in Australia wasn't too traumatic. He was close to home, with the prospect of a return to play in the New Zealand Open within a few weeks, as well as still being among people he knew in that many young Australian professionals on the tour had completed their amateur apprenticeships during the same years as Campbell.

Europe was a different matter altogether. Campbell really was going into the unknown. He would be playing among those who had probably never heard of him. Amateur golf doesn't get the same amount of exposure in the northern hemisphere, for instance, that it does in New Zealand. New Zealand's Eisenhower Trophy triumph would have gone virtually unnoticed in England and Europe, whereas it was big news in his home country and Australia, which was rapidly becoming his second home.

Campbell had little choice about where he was to play during the southern hemisphere winter. The Australia-New Zealand tour went into recess during the second week of March and wouldn't recommence till late October. He could have tried his luck in Asia, where openings would have presented themselves after the success in the Canon Challenge, but his managers, IMG, were convinced they could get him starts on the Volvo European tour through sponsor's exemptions. They did, but there was no pattern to his schedule and no way he could plan for tournaments. Campbell would have to hang around hoping to get a start. IMG would ring him on a Monday to say he could play in a tournament starting Thursday. It would be Wednesday before he got to wherever in Europe the tournament was being played and, not being involved with the pro-am, he wouldn't get a chance to play the course till he stood on the first tee on Thursday morning. There were even occasions when he was supposed to be getting a start only for his name to be missing from the starter's sheet when he arrived.

Campbell makes it plain he isn't putting the blame on anyone else for his demise that year in Europe. He pleads, however, that circumstances such as not having a schedule didn't help.

"At the start of 1993 I had set myself the goal of winning a golf tournament and within two months had achieved it. Instead of sitting down and reassessing my goals as I planned – if that is the right word – my trip to Europe, I just let things flow. Consequently, I lost my direction and focus.

"After winning in Sydney and preparing for Europe I got carried away with myself and began thinking that life was a doddle, that professional golf was easy. I couldn't understand why some of the guys whinged all the time about how tough life on the tour was. There was nothing wrong with it so far as I was concerned.

"Maybe that was a natural reaction to what had happened. It was only a few months since I had been playing against mates for microwaves and toasters and here I was, having won a pro tournament on the Australasian circuit and come close in others. I'd won $100,000. What was so hard about this game?"

Greg Turner, with whom he was going to stay in Bagshot, Surrey, could have told him that what goes up must come down. Turning professional in 1984, Turner won the New Zealand PGA championship the same year, won the Fiji Open the following year and in 1986 won the Singapore Open and had his first success on the

European circuit by winning the Scandinavian Open.

Then came a drought which was only broken when he won the 1989 AMP New Zealand Open at Paraparaumu Beach, a success which helped clear debts he had incurred during his barren spell and restored badly dented confidence.

In many ways, Turner and Campbell are alike. Both enjoy themselves, are fun to be with and have had their ups and downs. It was appropriate Campbell had Turner to turn to during his European experience.

Turner laughs when he thinks back to the days when Michael Campbell, rookie, arrived on his doorstep in London.

"The thing about Cambo, to those who don't know him well, is that he comes across as cocky and arrogant, but he isn't as cocky as some people perceive him to be. I think he is quite insecure. It is important to him to have people around that he is comfortable with.

"When he first came over it was all fairly new to him. He didn't have people he knew or felt comfortable with around him, as he had been used to in New Zealand and Australia. Those he did know, Frank Nobilo and myself, he didn't know that well, and anyway we were playing every week and he wasn't.

"Cambo was stuck in London on his own, twiddling his thumbs, and had to be self-sufficient. It was all a bit of a shock to him.

"In all honesty, he had just come out of amateur golf where there were team managers and the New Zealand Golf Association looking after him. It is a different story when you get out there in the big bad world and there isn't anyone looking after you.

"We all go through that, and it is one of the things which makes difficult the transition from amateur to professional golf. All of a sudden you have to look after yourself.

"The American college system helped me. At that time I couldn't have done it any other way. It is different now. The amount of international experience today's players get by staying in New Zealand is vastly different to when I attacked the game at that level.

"I don't think the American college system is any different to the New Zealand Golf Association programme in preparing you to look after yourself. You have a golf coach cum manager at university who looks after everything for you, just as Michael had Roger Brennand as his manager while playing for New Zealand.

"The big difference with going to an American college is that you are living away from home. You become more self-sufficient by virtue of that. It is like going to university in Dunedin when you live in Wellington.

"I know during his early days in London, Cambo was a bit down about the fact that he wasn't getting as many starts as he thought he would, and remember having a long chat with him about it.

"I agreed it wasn't an ideal situation but I said, 'Look Cambo, you have to turn that disadvantage into an advantage as much as you can.'

"I told him that the advantage he had was that Frank, myself and the other guys get back from a tournament on Sunday night having played all week. We have Monday to turn around, do the laundry and so on, and then get out on the road again on Tuesday morning.

"I suggested that when he was getting a start he should go to the next venue on Sunday night. He would have the course to himself for the first day and a half; all those practice facilities. He could have played four or five practice rounds by the time the tournament arrived and still be fresh from a competition point of view.

"While Michael appreciated that was a good idea, he had been sitting around in London without any of his friends and he was glad to see us come back on a Sunday night.

"Monday was our day off and we would probably be going to the pub that night. Michael wanted to be part of it. The reality was that while he could be part of what we were doing he was forfeiting a head start he could have got on us for the next tournament.

"Instead of having that head start he was actually worse off. Not only had he missed out on a couple of days' familiarisation on a course which we knew but he didn't, but he hadn't had the week's golf we'd just had so he was underdone. He was getting all the disadvantages but I'm sure he learned plenty from going through those things."

While those back in New Zealand might have been wondering why Campbell wasn't playing well when he did get starts in European tournaments, Turner didn't think there was anything strange in him taking time to come to terms with a new environment.

"I don't think people appreciate what a difficult transition it is. It isn't just the physical side of the game. Most of these kids can go out in the New Zealand Open, compete and look physically as good a player as most of the professionals. That doesn't mean they can move into the big league and compete on a week-in, week-out basis.

"You have to adjust to all the things that go hand in hand with playing in such an environment. All those variables which go with managing yourself, going to different places, dealing with different courses, having to tee it up against guys who have been your idols. These are all things you have to adjust to.

"Looking back I believe I was lucky not getting straight on to the European or United States tours first up. I played for two or three years around the place so I had learned about life as a professional golfer before I got into a really serious playing arena. I think that is a good thing.

"When Marcus Wheelhouse and Mark Brown didn't get their cards in Europe in 1995 it didn't bother me. In some ways it would have been nice had they done so, but I think it is probably a damn sight better idea for them in the long run if they have to go and grind away for a year or two in the minor leagues so to speak – Australia, Asia, perhaps the Nike and Challenge tours.

"In those arenas they are playing with and against guys who aren't going to intimidate them too much. It is different teeing it up alongside guys you know you are as good as, rather than the Greg Normans of this world. It is important to get used to what it is like to travel and play professional golf every week.

"There are so many parts of doing that. None on their own seem significant, but when you put them all together it makes a heck of a difference.

"The difference between doing well and losing your card on the European or United States tours is probably only a shot a round during the year, so you are only looking for a shot a day, but all the outside influences can add up to at least that.

"When you start out you are fresh and enthusiastic. When things go well for a month or two, which it did for Michael in Australia, you begin to think it is easy and, when you are on top of the bubble it is easy.

"The difficult part comes when you fall off the top. How far do you fall? How quickly can you stop yourself? And how quickly can you get back on top?

"That is the test and ultimately it tends to be a lot more difficult than most people perceive, and certainly a bit more difficult than a young guy would perceive if he has immediate success when he first goes out there."

In retrospect, Michael Campbell would agree with Turner about all those things but he had to find out for himself, the hard way.

"When I got to England I was completely lost and didn't know what to do with myself. All the headlines I had got while winning and doing well in Australia now meant nothing, and I was nothing to the guys playing the European tour. Maybe some of them had heard of me but it didn't seem like it.

"I think I expected to carry on where I had left off on the other side of the world but that was never going to happen in the circumstances I found myself in. I didn't have a schedule, and inevitably when I did get a start in a tournament it would be a rush to get to the course after getting a telephone call saying I was in on the Monday.

"I'm not trying to blame anyone for me going a bit crazy at that point in my life but not knowing where I would be playing from one day to the next was part of the equation. So was not having any goals whatsoever.

"All my life I had set myself targets and goals, but here I was with the chance to play in Europe and I had no direction whatsoever. When I did get in tournaments I didn't take advantage of the opportunities which were presented to me. I was overawed when I arrived at some of those courses.

"My first European tournament was the Dunhill British Masters at Woburn. I was hitting balls on the practice ground when I looked round and saw Nick Faldo and Bernhard Langer doing the same thing a few yards away.

"It was a bit of a shock to me and I didn't handle it too well. I thought 'I'm here with the best in the world'. I became overawed. I started thinking 'I can't compete with these guys' which just isn't me, but my state of mind over there wasn't very good.

"Basically I was just having a good time in England. I had money in my pocket and the pubs were inviting. My pin ball machine technique and pool skills were being honed on a more regular basis than my golf swing.

"I couldn't see what was happening around me. I had blinkers on. When Turns was away playing I would get up in the morning and watch his Sky television. It wasn't unusual for me to stay there all day doing nothing. I became a channel surfer. I knew everything that was on television during the day.

"Practice was the furthest thing from my mind and yet that is what I had been doing for years. The only reason I was in Europe to play golf was because I had been prepared to spend hour after hour hitting balls on the practice fairway.

"Literally three minutes down the road was a golf course and driving range. Greg and Frank had arranged for me to be able to use the facilities at the course for practice, but I hardly went there.

"I thought, 'What's the point? I like things the way they are right now.' I had what at the time was a lot of money in my pocket so thought I would cruise along and have a holiday for six months. It would be easy to get back on to the treadmill when I wanted to.

"I feel sick now when I think back and realise how easily my attitude could have cost me my career. Instead of doing this book right now I could have been off in a pub somewhere drinking and probably not even playing golf at weekends.

"As it was I cost myself five or six months and a lot of money. I played in ten tournaments and missed the cut in every one of them. I was letting everyone down. Mum and Dad, who had done so much to get me here, all my family and friends, Mal, and my management team who were getting me starts in tournaments when I didn't have a European tour card.

"There were so many young players who would have given anything for the chances I was getting and I was just throwing them away. I was in a routine, a bad routine, and after a while it had got into my system. Thank goodness Mal arrived when he did."

It is hard to keep things quiet in any sport, and golf is no exception. I had heard that Campbell was really struggling in England and was enjoying himself rather than practising. I mentioned to Mal Tongue, who was joining Campbell in England in July prior to him playing in pre-qualifying for the British Open, that Campbell had apparently put on weight and that his swing didn't look the best.

Tongue probably got the first inkling that those comments weren't exaggerated when Campbell picked him up from the airport and took him to the Fighting Cocks bed and breakfast establishment in London. Campbell told Tongue he was going out and that was the last he saw of him for two days.

Going into pre-qualifying at the Royal Cinque Ports course, just down the road from Royal St George's in Sandwich where the Open was to be staged five days later, Campbell had played only four tournaments in nine weeks and was recovering from a rib injury sustained just before the British Masters at Woburn a month earlier.

By the time Campbell and Tongue reached Kent there was no time for practice before the first round of qualifying but Tongue did get a taste of how his protege's habits had changed.

"We went out with Peter O'Malley and his wife Gill and I watched Michael sink four or five pints. I couldn't believe it. He was playing golf the next day. This wasn't the Michael I knew.

"I said something to him about it but he said it didn't bother him, and he did it again the next night, probably to annoy me. It didn't bother me either. He was paying for it. Not only in money but on the golf course because he was missing a lot of cuts."

Michael Campbell remembers the incident well and how Tongue's arrival made him stop and think.

"Mal was on to me right away about what was happening and he was right. It had got to the point where it was quite frightening. I had become immune to the beer and, not playing tournaments regularly, I drank more and more.

"When I downed four or five pints comfortably, Mal, who I hadn't seen for months, looked at me dumbfounded. It hurt when he talked to me about it. I resented what he was saying, but it made me think about what I was doing to myself.

"A few months earlier that amount of beer would have put me on the ground, and it probably would now. At that time it was making no impression.

"Mal didn't hide how disappointed he was. I was fifteen stone and didn't care. Mal was as blunt as always. 'Michael, tidy yourself up or you will go nowhere in golf. Don't throw away that special talent you are lucky enough to have.' That was the turning point, and while I didn't make cuts after the Open I knew that I was on the road back to finding the Michael Campbell who had arrived in England."

Royal Cinque Ports was to bring only disappointment. Only 13 places in the Open were available to those playing that course and

The downs . . .

Michael hits out of deep rough at Paraparaumu Beach during the 1993 AMP New Zealand Open. It was a tournament he would like to forget.

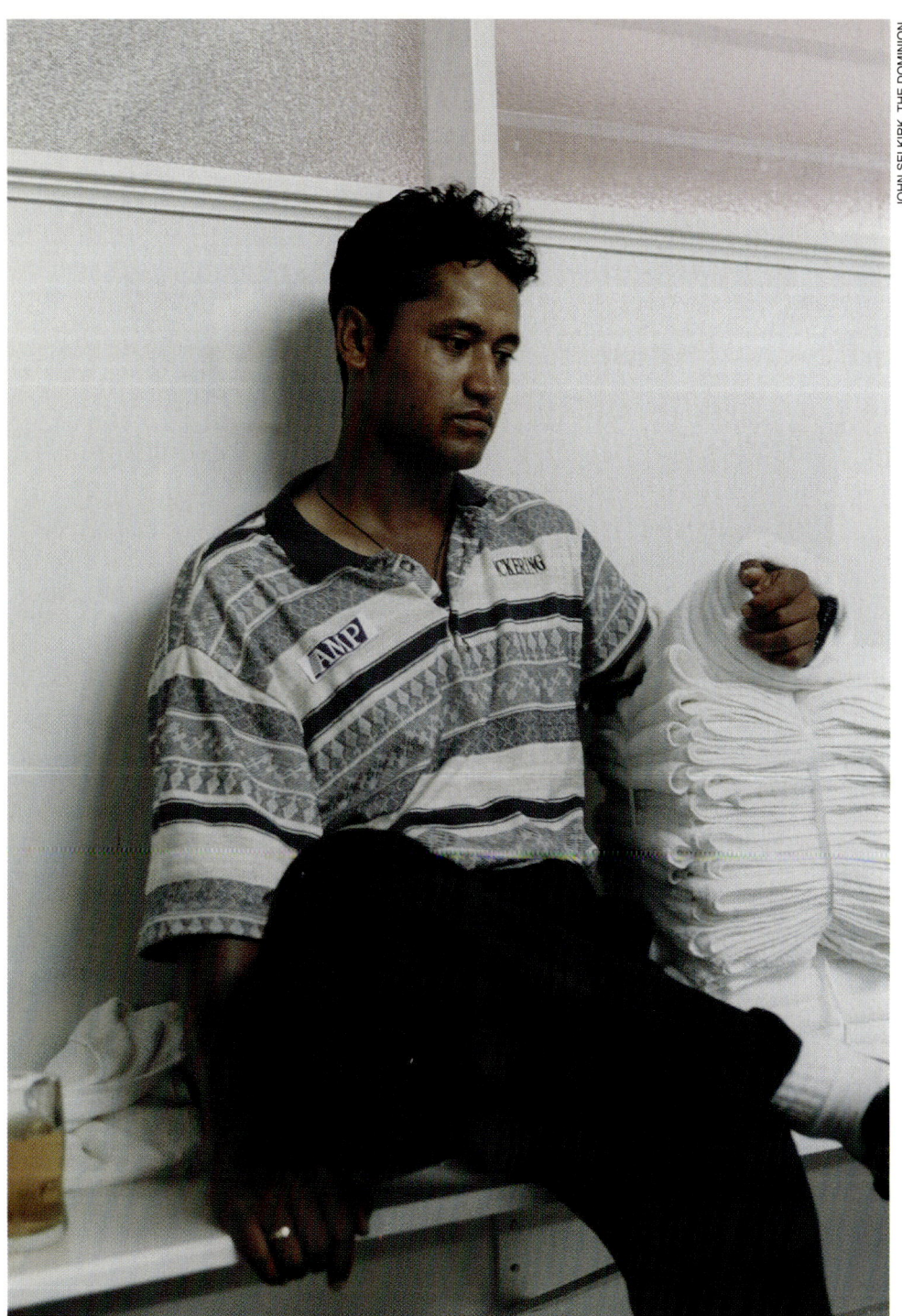

A downcast Michael Campbell in the locker room after being forced to withdraw from the 1995 AMP New Zealand Open at the Grange with a wrist injury.

Campbell was back in the field after an opening round one over par 73.

Mal Tongue hadn't had a chance to work with Campbell before that first round but the pair were out on the practice ground straight afterward and there was a marked difference the following day when, with Tongue caddying, Campbell shot 71, including four birdies over the last five holes.

"I felt unlucky with the weather during qualifying. On the first day I played in the morning when it blew a gale which later receded. In the second round it was calm in the morning and blew when I played in the afternoon.

"I was making all the excuses possible because at the time I hated Europe and what it was doing to me. Looking back it didn't do me any harm. It made me realise that it wasn't as easy as I thought it was. I had been pretty cocky about my good start in professional golf."

The day after Campbell missed qualifying for the Open Mal Tongue made him walk round the Royal St George's course with Greg Turner, Frank Nobilo, Martin Gates and Peter Fowler who were having a practice round.

It was obvious Campbell would have preferred to be anywhere other than where he was. The usual bright and breezy Michael Campbell was nowhere to be seen as he wandered around morosely watching when he knew he could easily have been part of it all had he applied himself.

"That was a great move by Mal because it made me all the more determined to play in the British Open the following year. It gave me something tangible to aim for at a time when I was feeling really miserable.

"Mal wanted me to see at first hand what I was missing. I saw all right, and it hurt that I was so close and couldn't be a part of it.

"As the other guys were finishing their round and we walked up the 18th I looked up at the grandstands on either side of the fairway and behind the green and thought what a wonderful sensation it would be to walk up there on a Sunday afternoon with the stands packed.

"Two years later I was to savour that experience. It was just as wonderful as I imagined but that day at Sandwich I just wanted to get my career back on an even keel."

Mal Tongue was with Campbell for six weeks during which they practised together and travelled to tournaments, but eventually it was time for Campbell to return to Wellington before going back on the Australia-New Zealand circuit and returning to Europe and the qualifying school.

"It had taken time for what Mal was telling me to sink in, but if the message needed hammering home it was when I got back to Wellington and saw Mum and Dad's reaction.

"They wondered what I had been doing in Europe and I couldn't blame them for thinking that way. I spent a month and a half at home charging the batteries and rethinking my goals.

"I had to put some direction back in my life and give myself something to aim for again. I did that, and while I failed to get my card when I went back to France at least I qualified to play in the Challenge Tour in 1994. I didn't realise at the time how important that was going to turn out to be.

"Finishing second in the Air New Zealand Shell at The Grange was also a timely confidence booster. What had started out as a fantastic year finished on a reasonable note. It was the middle of 1993 I could have done without."

8
Coach

The relationship between a golfer and his coach is like a marriage. There must be chemistry, compatibility and, above all, trust.

The golfer-coach partnership which has received the most attention in recent years is that between Nick Faldo and David Leadbetter. Faldo needed the utmost trust in Leadbetter to allow the coach to dismantle and rebuild the swing upon which his livelihood depended. That the reconstruction worked is history with the record books showing Faldo has won six Major championships since the change. Whether it will continue in that vein only time will tell. Sometimes you can tinker too much.

The partnership between Michael Campbell and Mal Tongue is certainly built on the ingredients of chemistry, compatibility and trust, and those who have seen them together over the last seven years will testify that there is unlikely to be a practice fairway divorce in the foreseeable future.

There have been separations; three of them during the seven years, but on each occasion they have realised how much one needs the other. They are like Morecambe and Wise, Torvill and Dean or Fred Astaire and Ginger Rogers. One without the other just doesn't seem right.

Whenever Campbell and Tongue come together they joke and take the mickey out of each other, till they get on the practice ground. The practice fairway is their office, though it is at times a fun-filled office with the other workers, Tongue's pupils, trading jibes with the star pupil.

Undoubtedly Campbell and Tongue are as stubborn as each other. That is probably what has made them so good together. Michael Campbell will tell you he wouldn't be where he is today without Mal Tongue. The coach, in his mellower moments, will admit that he loves Michael Campbell like a son, though as with all parents there have been times when he has despaired of his adopted offspring.

When their paths first crossed both were making their way in golf. Michael Campbell was a 19-year-old with tremendous potential and a terrible dress sense. Mal Tongue was a golf coach with a theory looking for someone to turn it into reality.

The first time Mal Tongue set eyes on Michael Campbell was on December 4, 1988. The date and what Tongue saw that day is etched in his mind.

It was on what might be termed the unfashionable Martinborough course and Tongue, an Englishman born in Nottingham, was still coming to terms with the more relaxed dress standards on New Zealand courses after arriving in Wellington five months earlier to work for the Golf Foundation.

While performing his duties for the foundation, Tongue had watched a couple of junior tournaments but hadn't had the chance to see much senior golf. He was at Martinborough, in the Wairarapa where Tongue was based, because one of Wellington's leading amateurs, Stu Thompson, whom he had recently started coaching, was playing.

Despite an atmosphere far more relaxed and easy going than he was used to, Mal Tongue was completely unprepared for Michael Campbell who, he had heard, was "a good little player".

"He had a Lakers cap on back to front, was wearing a Hawaiian type fluorescent teeshirt, with no collar, which was hanging out of his shorts, and the sole on his left shoe was hanging off.

"While the rest of the group he was playing in were dressed more appropriately, they didn't seem to care much about course etiquette. It was all so slipshod it was a joke. I was amazed that no one wanted to put the flag back in after they had finished putting.

"They were an undisciplined rabble really. We were sitting behind a green and one of them whacked the ball off the putting surface and it hit my wife, Gill, on the leg. They would have been thrown off courses in England.

"I remember watching Michael bogey the last hole to lose the tournament to Rodney Barltrop by a shot. And he smiled! I couldn't believe it. I couldn't understand how anyone could hit bad shots and find it amusing.

"Michael hit some fine shots that day but even after the bad ones, and there were a few of them, he would still keep smiling. He could hit five balls out of bounds and still have a big grin on his face."

Michael Campbell didn't know Mal Tongue had been watching him that day but when Tongue got home he couldn't stop thinking about the young Maori lad who could play superb golf shots seemingly without effort.

The coach got another glimpse, and that is all it was, of his future star pupil at the New Zealand championships at Taupo. With his tee shot on the first hole Campbell hit his caddy, who had stepped forward at the wrong moment, in the chest, poleaxing him. The poor caddy was taken to hospital while Campbell continued his round. Unfortunately he forgot to penalise himself on his card for hitting the caddy and was consequently disqualified.

"Michael stayed at the tournament for the rest of the week, but it was just a social occasion for him after the disqualification and I couldn't help feeling it was such a waste. He seemed to be enjoying himself though."

It was in April 1989 that Michael Campbell and Mal Tongue first spoke, at the Wairarapa 72-hole strokeplay championship in which 36 holes were played on both Saturday and Sunday.

"Michael had shot reasonable scores on the first day and was leading by one from Stu Thompson. At the end of the second round he came to me and said, 'You're Thommo's coach aren't you? Can you watch me hit some balls?' I watched him, made a couple of suggestions, and the next day he went out and shot 68, 67 to win by something like nine shots."

Campbell laughs when he thinks back to that day. "I remember asking him to have a look at me and to give me a quick lesson. I also know I didn't say please, but he gave me a quick band-aid lesson anyway. The way I played to win the tournament the following day . . . well, I thought he was marvellous. In fact, I thought he was a genius.

"I used to have a very arched reverse C action, very wristy and army. It was all feeling and not mechanical at all. Under pressure I was hopeless and the swing would break down."

Tongue was astonished that Campbell could pick up what he had told him so easily and put it into practice. After the prizegiving he was delighted when Campbell approached him for a chat.

"We talked that night and I said I thought it would be good if we could work together. I told him I believed he had something pretty special and we arranged to meet for our first real session the following Sunday at Te Marua."

The Te Marua Golf Club's course, which lies at the foot of the Rimutaka hills, was carved out of the wilderness and still boasts beautiful native bush. It has an opening par four hole, "Waterloo", which attracts golfers from far and wide. The direct shot from tee to green is across a deep bend in the Hutt River, which almost bisects the course. Even the cautious dog-leg approach on the hole must still fly considerable water. It is a daunting prospect for the weekend golfer, but it was the practice fairway that Tongue and Campbell were more interested in that first day, and again Campbell surprised Tongue.

"I couldn't believe how quiet he was. When he was with all the other lads he was this bright, ebullient person, but that day at Te Marua he was quite timid. I thought he was very shy.

"We went out to hit some balls and I wondered how he had been playing as well as he had. Michael had no pre-shot routine and no practice methods. I asked him how often he practised and he replied 'only half an hour at a time because it hurts my back'

"That day we spent almost three hours working on his game and it all went from there. The following week we met at the Hutt Golf Club which is when I took my first photographs of him. He was pretty big at that time and he got bigger as the year went on."

Tongue had been playing golf for four years when, as a 16-year-old, he landed a job as an assistant professional at the Wollaton Park club. During the time he was playing Tongue didn't have the benefit of coaching. He had ability, he says, but didn't know what he was doing so had no chance of succeeding.

It is something he regrets, which is probably one of the reasons he was willing to give so much of his time to promising young players in the Wellington region. It was as if he was trying to make up for what he had missed.

He might not have received any coaching while he was playing, but Tongue was coached as a coach and in 1979 got his first professional job at Ormansfield in Derbyshire. From there he moved on to the 1140-member North Shore club in Skegness and became more and more involved in coaching.

Chances to work with top players in England, where there are hundreds of coaches, are extremely limited, a scenario which led Tongue to try his luck abroad. Before heading for greener pastures, however, he met Helen Dobson and their achievements proved a forerunner of what was to come 12,000 miles away.

When Helen Dobson first went to Tongue she was a nine handicapper. By the time Tongue left for New Zealand she was on plus three and had won most of the major European women's amateur golf titles. Even after Tongue moved to New Zealand Dobson kept in touch, and on a number of occasions has travelled to New Zealand for tuition when she has felt her game needed it.

Now a professional, Dobson has won on the USLPGA tour, and perhaps it was no coincidence that her first success on that side of the Atlantic should come after she had asked Tongue to join her in America to tidy up her game.

In New Zealand, Mal Tongue didn't last too long with the Golf Foundation. There were those in that organisation who felt he was spending too much time with players such as Michael Campbell. Their attitude was that coaching potential top players should have been left to the national coach.

Tongue didn't agree. He had left England because he wanted the opportunity to be involved with top players. In Michael Campbell and Stu Thompson he saw the potential to do that. Soon he would add others to his stable but at the time getting to know and work with Campbell and Thompson was enough.

"Now that I was coaching both Stu and Michael it became really interesting. A huge rivalry developed between them. Each wanted to outdo the other, wanting to show me he was the best. It was quite intriguing for someone who had never had two really good players at the same time.

"The thing I liked was that they had a kind of innocence about them. This was something you wouldn't find in England. To have a golf coach seemed to be so special to Michael and Stu, whereas in England no one really bothered. It was expected that you would go to a coach if you were any good.

"I always got the feeling that these lads were going out there on the course to do well so they would get a pat on the head from me. As much as they were doing it for themselves they wanted to satisfy what we were doing as a team."

Young players are able to relate to Mal Tongue because, at times, he is like a big kid himself. When the youngsters began to make their mark in the Wellington team, Tongue looked forward to the evenings when he would sit with the players in their motel rooms to swap stories and listen to their dreams for the future.

The fact that he could relate to his kids didn't mean that Tongue was soft on them. Just the opposite. He is a hard taskmaster. If he was giving up his time, and that is what he was doing, and still is with his next crop of players, then he expected those he was working with to commit themselves totally.

Michael Campbell and Mal Tongue weren't long into their relationship when the first separation came following the Tower inter-provincial championships in November 1989.

"We fell out because of a few things which were happening off course and I didn't think he was putting enough into what we were trying to do. The only problems I have ever had with Michael are off-course or because of comments he has made.

"Three months after we had fallen out, and we had only spoken a couple of times during that period, I saw him play at the Wellington matchplay championships where he shot 88 and 82. I watched him at the South Island champs as well where he shot 342 or something for four rounds. It wasn't flash and he had been picked in the last nine to trial for the 1990 Eisenhower team.

"During the period we weren't working together it was as if someone had chopped his arm off. He had no one to respond to and I think we were both relieved when we sat down, settled our differences and began working together again. I know I wanted to keep going because he was special."

What made Michael Campbell seem so special?

"You never knew what was going to happen. When he teed off you wouldn't know if he was going to make eagle or a nine. Whichever one he made he would still have a big grin on his face.

"His talent is natural from the point of view of saying someone has fantastic hand-eye co-ordination, but no matter what, right through you never knew what he was going to do from one hole to the next.

"It was obvious he had that something special which none of the others had really got, but you didn't know whether Michael was going to use it or waste it.

"There was always a battle of wills between us. I suppose that is why I was probably so ruthless with him. Michael wasn't a troublemaker, but he was so difficult to control because he is incredibly stubborn.

"If he gets it into his mind to fight against you he will go all the way. At those times if you told Michael not to do something he would do it. Tell him to do it and he wouldn't. Anyone who gives in to him will never get his respect. That is the type of person he is.

"There are times, however, when stubbornness can be a good thing and that was true about Michael's golf. Where golf is concerned he knows within himself what is right or wrong.

"I began to realise towards the end of 1995, seven years after we got together, that some of the things I had tried to teach him he would never do only because it didn't feel right to him.

"He would never say no to me. He would play a game with me, but he wouldn't do it. It is technical things I'm talking about. Now seven or eight years down the track I'm doing things with people that I have learnt from Michael, simply because he knew deep down that what I had been asking wasn't right.

"Practising hard wasn't an easy thing for Michael to do because he was so gifted. I could honestly make adjustments to his swing in one day that would take other people months to adapt to.

"I could say I wanted the club in a particular position. He would watch me and I would put him into the position I was looking for. By the end of the day he would be doing what I wanted. I've never known anyone else take it in so quickly. He is freakish.

"The other lads called him The Adaptable Man. We were experimenting. I didn't know what I was teaching. I just believed in what I was trying to do. I had this shape pictured in my mind which I wanted to see but I didn't know what it was.

"I could have him swinging the club so flat on his backswing and he would hit the ball perfectly. Two days later I would say that it was too flat and we need to get it more upright. I would have him swinging like a windmill that same day and he would flush it again.

"The work ethic is something he learnt from me and the other lads working with me, guys like Stephen Scahill. Stephen had a huge influence on Michael's life because he was totally opposite. He didn't want to be told how good he was, he wanted to be pulled down. I've never once had to say to Stephen that he wasn't practising hard enough. Those things rubbed off on Michael."

Michael Campbell is the first to admit that there have been times when he has found standing on the range hitting balls hour after hour, day after day, week after week too much to handle. Had his coach been someone he could manipulate it might have meant more time off but it would probably also have meant a less illustrious career.

When Campbell resigned from Telecom to become a full-time golfer he was at the Manor Park club by nine in the morning and worked solidly on his game till five in the afternoon. All the time he was under the watchful eye of Tongue, who didn't at any time charge him one cent for his time, an investment which is now being well rewarded as part of Campbell's management team.

"I was so keen in those first few months after giving my job up. This is what I wanted to be doing – playing golf, not fixing telephone faults.

"The novelty began to wear off a bit when the weather got cold and after a while I started to sleep in and not get out to Manor Park till one o'clock. Mal told me straight. If I wasn't going to be there at a certain time then he wasn't going to coach me. There were a few times over the two years I was working there every day when I started slipping and became a bit lazy.

"Mal was always there to give me a kick up the backside and get me going again. I trusted him like I trusted Mum and Dad. When I felt like telling him where to go I bit my tongue because I knew that he was only trying to do his best for me.

"I trusted him with my swing as well. I put myself in his hands. There were times when I despaired. After six months working with Mal I could hardly hit the ball. There were times when I was shanking it, topping them, skying it . . . everything. But I had total faith in the guy. I trusted what he was teaching even when it got to the point where I said, "I can't do it.' Mal said, 'Michael please, just trust me.' I did."

In New Zealand, Mal Tongue has become almost as well known as Michael Campbell. These days there must be times when he gets fed up with being introduced as "Michael Campbell's coach", but that is the price he has to pay. While Tongue has been associated with a number of top amateurs who have gone on to become good professionals it is Campbell who has given him and his methods the most publicity.

In his early coaching days in New Zealand, cynics called Mal Tongue a washing machine salesman. Those coached by him were dubbed washing machines by their peers because of the action they used in the golf swing. Simply put, the body action advocated by Tongue moved backwards and forwards around the spine, similar to the agitator in a washing machine. No one is laughing any more.

New Zealand, where the golf scene is more relaxed, suits Tongue and he readily admits he has fallen on his feet on this side of the world. That he has been able to handle young players of different temperament, putting up with the idiosyncrasies of some, the tantrums of others, is because he knows what they are going through. He has his idiosyncrasies and tantrums as well.

Tongue has learnt as much from his boys as they have from him, but it is the relationship with Michael Campbell that has taught him the most.

Throughout his time in New Zealand, Tongue has defended his players through thick and thin. He has gone in to battle for them against officialdom if he believed they weren't getting a fair deal when teams were selected. In return he demanded their loyalty and no one has been more loyal than Michael Campbell, even though at times he has stretched Tongue's patience.

The pair's second separation came in 1992 when, as Tongue puts it, he fell out with Campbell and Stephen Scahill over a matter of principle, something he saw as a lack of loyalty to a teammate.

For five weeks he didn't speak to either player, totally ignoring them even though he was within feet of them every day. "They would look at me as if they were dying to say something but I would walk straight past them. In those circumstances five weeks is a long time. The Eisenhower Trophy was coming up and the New Zealand Golf Association was getting quite panicky that two of their players had fallen out with their coach.

"I told them I wasn't going to work with them. They were upset. I was upset. Eventually we got back together again but they knew how I felt."

Circumstances had changed by the time Tongue went to England to join a struggling Michael Campbell in 1993. No longer was Tongue giving his time for free. Campbell was a professional and he was the one paying for the trip, though that didn't stop Tongue speaking his mind.

He was quick to tell Campbell that he was drinking too much, and when he insisted Campbell walk the Royal St George's course with Greg Turner and Frank Nobilo after failing to qualify it was because he felt the need to impress on him what he could have if he worked hard enough.

Tongue had to put his foot down again the following week when they went to the Dutch Open at Leiden.

"I was carrying his bag in a practice round with Frank, Greg and Russell Claydon. We hadn't got there till that day, Tuesday, and he wasn't going to be able to play on Wednesday because it was pro-am day and he hadn't got a start in that.

"The others had played the Noordwijkse course before but Michael hadn't. After the first hole it poured with rain and gale force winds got up. The others walked in. Michael asked should we go with them. I said we would carry on. If I hadn't been there I think he would have gone in as well, but then he wouldn't have seen the course."

That trip to England and Europe in 1993 was a learning experience for Tongue. He had never been on the tour as a golf coach with a professional touring player, and when he talks about what was for both him and Campbell an adventure it is obvious he enjoyed it, despite Campbell's lack of success.

"Michael might have been having a rough time but we were doing things in style. Travelling business class and staying at superb hotels where the beer was something like $30 a pop. The only time we stayed anywhere rough was when we went back to near where I used to live in Skegness. There we stayed in a bed and breakfast where if you put your arm out you were in the other bed.

"Michael used to be out all the time. He was learning about life. I never went out with him. I would stay in the hotel room and he would come back at all hours waking me up so consequently I couldn't get him out of bed in the morning.

"But we had a lot of fun and never fell out. He was going through such a bad patch with his scores but he didn't seem to let it get to him whereas other players would have been distraught.

"Michael still behaved like he was a superstar. Not in a big headed way, but he would talk to anyone who walked past be it Vijay Singh or Colin Montgomerie. They probably had no idea who this Maori boy was, but even though he was struggling he never looked upon himself as being anything other than eligible to be in that company."

The third and, hopefully, last separation between player and coach came at the end of that year during the Air New Zealand Shell Open where Campbell finished second.

"Michael rang me to say he would meet me at 8.30 but didn't turn up till 10. The next day he was late again so that afternoon I went up to him on the putting green and asked could he make sure he was on time the following day as I also had Scahill and Thompson, plus some amateurs, to look after.

"He turned to me and said, 'I call the shots.' I didn't say anything. Next morning he was late again so I told his caddy Bryce Mawhinney to tell him I had gone home. I went back to where I was staying, got a cab to the airport and went back to Wellington.

"When Michael got back to Wellington after the tournament and saw me he was all cheerful as if nothing had happened. I was offhand with him. He asked me why I had gone home and I told him it was because he was late again. His reply was 'I would have won if you'd stayed'.

"I told him I had had enough. That I would work with him till February and that he could then go and see Denis Pugh, David Leadbetter or whoever he wanted but I wasn't working with him any more after that.

"I hated saying it but I told him that he would never be bigger than the game, no matter how many tournaments he won. Michael said he didn't want a new coach. He wanted to continue working with me and that if I would carry on he would change his ways and work harder.

"I said we would go till February and see how it worked out. We have worked great together ever since. When two people are working so closely there are bound to be times when things go wrong. We've had our ups and downs but have come through them."

It probably needed that disagreement to clear the air between them, though Campbell feels he was a victim of circumstances at the time.

"I was 15 minutes late that first day at The Grange and the second day I was half an hour late. The first time was my fault, but I didn't think the second was. I had left the car lights on overnight and got up to a flat battery.

"I was shocked when Mal went home and upset when we couldn't work things out straight away when I got back to Wellington.

"We didn't talk to each other and when you consider how close we had been for so long that really hurt. Practising by myself while he was working with other people just up the fairway made me realise that Mal was an integral part of not only my game, but my life.

"In the end I was the one who gave in and rang him up. I told him that I wanted to work things out because he was good for me.

"It was the end of a difficult period in my life. I had needed Mal and Mum and Dad to get me back on the tracks. I had been enjoying myself too much and was totally blind to the whole situation. Everyone was out of step but me.

"I was so stubborn but so was Mal. That's probably why we are such a good team."

At one time Campbell and Tongue used to spend a lot of time together off the course during tournaments, but as Campbell's commercial commitments have increased the coach has seen less of his pupil when travelling. That is something he has come to terms with.

"When I was at the 1995 Greg Norman Classic with him, Michael's Dad said it must be hard for me now that Michael had so many other things to do and couldn't spend the same amount of time with me.

"It doesn't bother me. That week he picked me up from the hotel every day. That was important to me. The 15-minute drive to the course gave us the chance to talk. He would go and put his shoes on while I had a chat to Max his caddy. We'd all go down to the practice ground and do our stuff. Michael would go out and play and when he finished I'd be there to talk about the round.

"That is where he is now. It isn't like when he used to play for Wellington and we would go to tournaments, have dinner and sit in the rooms telling yarns and having a laugh.

"Those were great days, but he has moved on from there. We have to move on with him."

9

Laying the Foundation

There was nothing spectacular about 1994 for Michael Campbell, though fate and a friend combined to make it a year in which Campbell laid the foundation for what was going to be one of New Zealand's sporting success stories 12 months later.

Back home in Wellington, for that is where home still is despite being based in Sydney and London for most of the year, for Christmas, Campbell was more relaxed than he had been the previous year.

The second placing at The Grange had been a timely confidence booster and Campbell prepared for the AMP New Zealand Open at Remuera in a better frame of mind than he had been in for a few months.

Despite what had happened in Paraparaumu a year earlier, Campbell loves playing on New Zealand courses. Home-grown players draw the biggest galleries and crowds are what bring out the best in Campbell.

It was no different at Remuera. Huge galleries turned out in the hot, dry conditions over the first three days and even when it became steamy for the final round they still arrived in droves.

Michael Campbell, Frank Nobilo, Greg Turner and Philip Tataurangi were the ones they wanted to see, and hopes were high that one of the quartet could hold off the overseas challenge. Greg Turner had won the Open in 1989 and Grant Waite, who wasn't in the field at Remuera, took the title in 1992, so New Zealanders were starting to lay claim to their own Open championship after it had been plundered for years by outsiders.

It wasn't to be. Frank Nobilo got closest, one stroke behind Australian Craig Jones, after a tournament during which the gently undulating Remuera course didn't play as easy as many were predicting. Turner tied for seventh, Campbell was equal 12th and Tataurangi tied 23rd.

With rounds of 73, 69, 71, 71 on the par-71 course it wasn't one of Campbell's most memorable tournaments but it was a solid start to the year. The next three tournaments were in Australia. Campbell had disappointing first and last rounds in finishing 38th in the Players Championship at Kingston Heath, but played much more solidly at the Heineken Classic, where he finished equal ninth, and the Australian Masters, tied for 24th, against top class fields.

There were two unproductive European tournaments and a trip to Indonesia, cut short by illness, before Campbell began to set his sights on qualifying for the United States Open.

Playing in a Major championship remained his number one priority, especially after the disappointment of failing to make the field at Royal St George's in 1993.

There was further disappointment for Campbell in America when he didn't qualify for the US Open. But it was while he was in the United States that fate, and friend Lucas Parsons, a former New Zealand amateur champion he had first met at the New Zealand Boys' championship when he was 15 and Parsons 14, combined to set him on the path to the big time in Europe.

Parsons persuaded Campbell to enter the St Louis Open, a tournament on the Tommy Armour satellite circuit which was being played at the same time as the US Open. Not keen at first, Campbell eventually thought he might as well give the tournament a go as he had nothing else planned for that week. It cost him a $US850 entry fee but it was an investment and a decision he will remember with satisfaction for the rest of his life. He will also look back and wonder what would have happened had he qualified for the US Open. Would he have gone on to win it, or finished in the body of the field?

There have been fairytale endings in Major championships, the most famous involving John Daly emerging from obscurity to win the 1991 USPGA. Daly drove all night to take his place on the tee at Crooked Stick after getting into the field as an alternate. The chances of that sort of thing happening again at the US Open were thousands to one but, as Mal Tongue has always said, with Michael Campbell you never know what is going to happen.

It was much more likely that at that stage of his career Campbell would have played solidly and finished creditably.

Forgetting all the conjecture, the St Louis tournament was to prove invaluable so far as Campbell's immediate future was concerned. It was in St Louis that Campbell learned how to win again; though compared with the majority of players on various tours around the world, his previous win, in Sydney 15 months earlier, had been relatively recent.

The major tours in the United States and Europe are the ones on which attention is focused throughout the year. But each of those tours has its own satellite events. Players use the Nike and Tommy Armour tours as stepping stones to the full United States circuit, while in Europe the top ten on the second tier Challenge Tour qualify to play on the Volvo European Tour the following year. Finishing in the top ten on the Challenge Tour is a better route than qualifying school, with more regular starts guaranteed and no mid-season re-ranking as is the case with school graduates.

How tough it is for a fledgling professional to earn a place on the European Tour, never mind get starts in tournaments, can be gauged from the number of players who vie for prize money on the circuit.

In the 1994 season 550 players earned prize money on either the Volvo order of merit or its two supplementary lists, while 235 players were listed on the Challenge Tour in which Campbell finished third with earnings of £29,707. Northern Ireland's Raymond Burns topped the order of merit on the Challenge Tour with £43,583, while at the other end of the scale was Denmark's Dan Stage who picked up just £77.

Throw in another 168 hopefuls who made it through to the final stages of the qualifying school looking for one of the 40 places available and how tough it is becomes obvious.

In 1993, when Michael Campbell went through the school, 183 players were fighting for the 40 places, many of them seasoned professionals who hadn't earned enough money on the tour and were seeking to regain their treasured card.

Michael Campbell was looking to qualify through the Challenge Tour in 1994, starting with the Memorial Olivier Barras tournament on the Crans sur Sierre course in Switzerland. His managers, IMG, had got him a start in that event. If he could perform well there he would automatically be in the field for future tournaments.

Europe was where Campbell's attention was channelled. The St Louis Open was really just an extra chance to get more competitive golf under his belt.

"Unlike the previous year, I had a plan of attack for Europe in 1994. The top ten on the Challenge Tour get their card for the Volvo Tour. I thought I was capable of winning two or three tournaments and getting into that top ten if I knuckled down, worked and played as well as I knew I could.

"During the first three months of the year I had just been ticking over. I was doing all right but wasn't quite on my game. I was probably still feeling my way back after the problems of the year before, still trying to regain my confidence. What happened in St Louis provided what I was searching for."

Off the course changes had been taking place in Michael Campbell's life. While in Sydney he had met Julie Wendel, the woman he was to marry in January 1996.

When Julie Wendel first set eyes on Michael Campbell the last thing on her mind was embarking on a life of travel. Definitely not with a golfer.

She had worked for a United States company which had a cruise ship operating in the Caribbean. Promotional work, staff recruitment and setting up offices were part of her portfolio. It meant constant travel. Julie also worked for a Japanese company which meant living in Japan for a while. She began to feel like a nomad and decided it was time to put down some roots.

Settled in Sydney, Julie Wendel was enjoying home comforts when Michael Campbell arrived on the scene, and the night the pair met she couldn't have known she would soon be on the road again . . . more than before.

"At that time I didn't know anything about golf. I had no interest in it at all. I thought it was slow and for old people. My dad played but my three brothers, like me, had no interest in it.

"One of my girlfriends from high school had begun working for the Australian Professional Golfers Association while I was away travelling and had obviously become interested in the game.

"She lived in the country and was staying with me in Sydney while going to watch one of the tournaments. I was talked into going along with her and I hated it straight away. I didn't know where to stand and didn't understand what was going on. I headed for the bar.

"My friend was quite interested in a golfer and he asked us both out to dinner as we were together. I was saying to her 'no dinner, no dinner'. I couldn't imagine anything worse than being stuck with a golfer all evening.

"They convinced me to go for a drink at the golfer's hotel which was alongside the course.

"We were chatting when Michael turned up. He made out that the guy we were with was his best friend, which of course he wasn't.

"Michael asked if he could join us and we chatted for a while. He said a friend of his was singing upstairs and would I like to go and listen. I'm a sucker for music so off we went.

"The singer was Lucas Parsons' girlfriend Gabriel. She is now his wife and one of my best friends. It was a pleasant night and Michael asked if I wanted to watch him play next day. I said yes but didn't really want to, so I turned up when he had finished.

"Our getting together wasn't a whirlwind thing even though he met my family quickly. When he was in Sydney he would ring up and we would go out. I didn't really take it seriously. He was a bit younger than me and I thought he was busy with his career."

When she first met him, Julie felt Michael was a little insecure.

"Michael has a lovely personality but at that time he wasn't as confident off the golf course as he was on it. He thought people were interested in him only for his golfing ability. That wasn't the case with me. I told him I would have preferred it if he hadn't been a golfer.

"The fact that he played golf didn't attract me, and neither did his earning potential.

"While we were getting to know each other I took him out for his birthday and thought I had better pay for it because he might not be able to afford it. I knew he travelled a lot and thought that would be really expensive.

"I knew he had been an amateur and my idea of an amateur was that if you show some potential then people will pay for you to go places, but there would be no money coming in.

"Now he was a professional he would have to pay for everything himself. Little did I realise that two years later when we were about to get married he would have won over a million dollars. It was a bit overwhelming really."

Given her feelings about the game at the time it wasn't surprising that Julie hardly watched him play golf as their relationship slowly developed in the early stages.

She did make an effort to watch him at an Indonesian tournament but found the weather oppressively hot. That, combined with the fact that she had no idea where to stand on course and no knowledge of the game itself, didn't make Julie too enthusiastic about the St Louis Open. When she agreed to meet Michael there she was probably thinking more of catching up with relatives she had in the American city rather than the golf tournament. Why else would she take a book to the course?

Julie had the use of a golf cart at the tournament and while Michael went about his business on the course she was quite happy to read her book and get a sun tan. Till the final day of the tournament that is. That was the last time Julie Wendel read a book on the golf course.

Going into the final round Campbell trailed the leader by five strokes. He had begun well with a 68, but slipped back with a two-over second round 74. A third round 70 had got him back among the leaders but there appeared to be far too much leeway to make up if he was to win.

While Campbell was making par on the first five holes Julie was happily reading her book. She quickly put it down when the course started buzzing as word of Campbell's charge spread like wildfire.

"All these people were rushing round talking about Michael. One of them came to me and said he just had five birdies in a row. I just said 'oh yes'. But then I began to think he was going to win it and I got excited.

"He did win it of course, and I got so caught up in my emotions. I was so proud. Was this really me feeling excited at a golf tournament? At home when golf came on the television I would switch channels."

Unlike herself, Julie said Michael seemed to take the day in his stride, but he was also feeling the elation of a special moment.

"It was the best I had played for a long time. In fact it was one of the best rounds I've ever had. Every part of my game came together.

Everything I touched that day turned to gold. I'm pretty hard on myself on the golf course, but even I was impressed with the way I played.

"I was so full of confidence once I got on the birdie roll at the sixth hole. Six birdies in succession was unbelievable and then I lipped out going for birdie on the 12th before getting another on the 13th.

"The only lapse I had was putting my tee shot in the hazard off the 14th tee. I made double bogey there, but had two birdies and two pars on the last four holes for a 65 to win by two."

Finishing first at the St Louis Open was worth $US40,000 to Campbell but winning was even more important, and he boarded the aircraft for Europe feeling that his career was about to take off again.

Julie also went to Switzerland and was to continue travelling with him from then on. That her presence on the circuit should coincide with an upsurge in Campbell's performances didn't surprise Mal Tongue.

"I noticed a big change in Michael once Julie came on the scene. He became a lot more balanced, a lot more rounded. He began to learn things he never would have just going around with the guys. Little things like going to restaurants, choosing a nice bottle of wine, eating proper food.

"He became more considerate to those around him whatever the surroundings. I noticed it straight away when I joined him in England before the British Open in July.

"Julie knew nothing about golf and during those early months on the tour with Michael she made a lot of sacrifices. It can be terribly boring waiting around in all kinds of weather for someone who is playing golf. Living in hotels, even if they are flash, for 10 months of the year isn't that great either."

The hotels Julie and Michael stayed in on the Challenge Tour weren't the five-star luxury ones they would get used to the following year, and Julie's first job when they checked in was to clear out the mini bar and restock it with crackers and cheese from the local supermarket.

The luxury coaches and courtesy cars which are part of the main circuit are nowhere to be seen on the Challenge Tour. It is all trains, planes and automobiles and it sometimes seems to take forever to get to a tournament.

While Michael had golf to concentrate on, Julie had concerns of her own. When a young golfer is battling to make his way two definitely can't live as cheaply as one and Julie found herself in a position to which she wasn't accustomed.

"We were expecting that I would be a financial burden just being there which was a weight on my shoulders when we went to Europe.

"I had been in relationships before where I had always had a job and paid my own way. I was very stubborn over that. Now all of a sudden I had to throw all those ideals away and I was travelling with and relying on this young guy.

"I didn't know how much money he had because I had never really asked, but I knew it would be difficult financially for me to travel with him. It meant asking him for things. 'Can I buy some shampoo please.' I felt humiliated at times.

"Europe is so expensive compared to other places. In St Louis it cost us seven American dollars to do one and a half loads of laundry in a laundromat. For that everything came back on hangars or nicely folded. The following week in Switzerland the same amount of laundry cost us $A155, and that wasn't in the hotel but at a laundromat.

"The Challenge Tour is so expensive and you can't really make money. You lose money even if you make the cut. To make money you have to be in the top three.

"That Michael won at his first event in Switzerland and won the next one as well took some of the pressure off. It was still tough but we were better off than most on the tour. Steven Bottomley, who tied for third with Michael at the British Open, spent five years on the Challenge Tour.

"Luckily we didn't have to go through that. I know Michael had had hiccups and problems in Europe the previous year, and even earlier in 1994, but it was lucky for me that by the time I came along as excess baggage I wasn't excess baggage at all.

"The Challenge Tour also helped me to learn about golf. It was a great educational experience and enabled me to find out what a golf tournament was all about. They don't get big galleries so you can walk in places that wouldn't be possible on the main tour. Michael would clear it with his playing partners and I would walk down the fairway with him and ask questions when the time was right.

"I began to work out the scoring and came in useful by helping them look for balls. It was great fun. Much more enjoyable than I had ever imagined golf to be."

Campbell won the Memorial Olivier Barras with a 10-under 206 for 54 holes, three better than Raymond Burns who was to become a friend as well as an adversary as the circuit progressed.

Campbell was popular in Crans sur Sierre. It was a small tournament but the locals make it a big event and the organisers adopted Campbell as one of their favourites. Michael and Julie left Switzerland with fond memories and headed for the next tournament, the Bank Austria Open on the Neusiedlersee-Donnerskirchen course.

After winning in Switzerland, Campbell was more relaxed than he had been for some time and it showed in his golf. He was enjoying the game again and some of the pressure had been lifted. As a winner he could now play in any other Challenge Tour event for the rest of the year. They might not have been as big as the main tour events but at least he was playing and enjoying himself.

The town where the Austrian tournament was staged looked nothing like the popular perception of that country. The course was in the wetlands, very flat and with very long grass. It was just as well it wasn't hilly or Julie would never have managed to finish the round as Michael's caddy.

"After that day I will always admire caddies who carry the bags day after day, week after week. I had a trolley but I was still huffing and puffing trying to catch up.

"I was just bag pulling. I didn't go near the greens or anything, but at the end of the day I was buggered. I also noticed that when I was pulling the bag I wasn't the girlfriend any more. I was the caddy. It was subtle, but obvious.

"I quickly decided the job wasn't for me but it took me till midnight to pluck up the courage to say that I hadn't liked it. Michael started laughing. He said he had been waiting all night for me to tell him that because he hadn't enjoyed having me doing it either.

"We were both relieved we had the same views on the subject."

Campbell won the Austrian event by two shots from England's Stuart Cage, later to finish eighth on the order of merit, with a 12 under par total of 276. In two weeks Campbell had played seven rounds of golf in 22 under par. Never had his confidence been higher.

Despite his superb run of form there was no chance of Campbell getting above himself. Not with Greg Turner around.

Turner, like Campbell, had to qualify for the British Open at Turnberry despite being a seasoned European touring professional. Both were drawn to play at Western Gailes and Turner recalls a practice round on that course before qualifying began.

"Michael was brimming with confidence after three wins in succession when we went for a practice round with Martin Gates and Lucas Parsons.

"It was the first time I'd seen him since he'd won those events, the last of which was the previous week. As usual there was a bit of banter going on and when Michael got on to the tee we carried on yarning to each other.

"He jokingly turned round and told us to be quiet. I said, 'Great, you win a couple of monthly medals and you think you are the king pin.' That cracked him up.

"That night he said, 'You bastard Turns, you were saying something to me out there weren't you? But you're right, they are just monthly medals aren't they?'

"I said, 'No, they are more than monthly medals Cambo, but you are here for the British Open this week.' "

Turner, with his sense of humour and quick turn of phrase, might have been good at making sure Campbell kept his feet on the ground and his head out of the clouds, but he was just as forthcoming with encouragement. He let Campbell know what he really thought of his winning streak.

"I told him it doesn't matter where you win, there is nothing like it in golf. The pressure you come up against coming down the stretch in a tournament, whatever tournament it is, is something you have to handle. Obviously the bigger the tournament the greater the pressure.

"I've never led the British Open down the stretch and I would imagine that is as intense as it ever gets, but it is only a more intense version of the same thing. I'm sure it is almost the same in a Challenge Tour event. There probably aren't as many players chasing you, and it isn't as intimidating with Joe Masamimo from Italy alongside you as it would be if it was Greg Norman. But it is still pressure you have to withstand."

Campbell remembers those words from Greg Turner clearly.

"After talking to Greg about it I finally realised that winning money wasn't the real issue. Holding a trophy in both hands was the most important thing. Winning those tournaments, and another which was to come later in Germany, was great even though they weren't big money events."

Twelve months earlier, after failing to qualify for the British Open, Campbell had left the Royal St George's course after being forced to watch Turner and his mates play a practice round with a defiant "I'll be back". He was true to his word.

Two rounds of 69 at Western Gailes, where Turner finished second with 65, 67, saw Campbell through qualifying and in. Michael Campbell from Titahi Bay was going to play in the British Open.

Most rookies, and that is what Campbell was and would still be the following year in Europe, having qualified to play in the Open would have been happy to organise their first practice round with a couple of mates they knew well. Not Campbell. He had his first practice round with world No 1 and defending champion Greg Norman.

"The last time the Open was held at Turnberry Greg Norman had won it. What better person to play with. I had got to know Greg quite well by that time and it seemed natural to ask him for a round.

"He said he would fix up a couple of guys to play with and see me on the tee next day. When I turned up he was with Brad Faxon and Davis Love. Greg said I was his partner and that it was Australasia against America.

"It was when they began talking about what they would play for that I realised I had stepped into a different world. They were playing for $US1000 a hole! I couldn't afford that so I played for a hundred pounds. Perhaps I should have risked the thousand because Greg played brilliantly, shot nine birdies in a 62 and we won easily. Davis Love paid me with two fifty pound notes. I got him to sign one of them and I still have it.

"I had four birdies myself but it seemed like one. I felt like a spectator.

"As we walked from a green to the next tee Greg would pull out his marker pen and sign caps, books or whatever they put in front of him. It is on practice days like that when he goes out of his way to be accessible to the fans. I felt like asking for his autograph myself.

"The whole day was something I will never forget. It might only have been a practice day but the atmosphere was unreal. There I was, playing with the world's best golfer at the biggest tournament in the world. It took a bit of getting used to.

"The whole thing was fantastic. People had told me what it was like to be at a Major. How different the atmosphere was to other tournaments with the huge stands and massive crowds, but to experience it first hand as a player . . . it is hard to describe how I felt."

Greg Norman probably wishes he had kept Campbell as his partner for Wednesday's final practice round.

On the Tuesday night, soon after Norman and Campbell had taken the money from Faxon and Love, Tom Watson was on the telephone to Jack Nicklaus telling him that he had "a couple of pigeons" lined up for a four-ball match in their final practice.

"Who are they?" asked Nicklaus.

"Norman and Price," Watson answered, and they both laughed. The following day, to their intense satisfaction, Watson and Nicklaus shot a better-ball score of 60 to wipe out Norman and Price.

It was Nick Price who had the last laugh in the 1994 championship, however, winning the Open title 12 years after he had handed it to Watson at Royal Troon by butchering the last six holes, while Watson sat in the clubhouse thinking he had finished second.

The moment Michael Campbell had been waiting for arrived at 2.45 on July 14, 1994, when he heard the magical words, "On the tee, Michael Campbell, New Zealand."

The previous day, on finding out his tee time, I had jokingly told Campbell that rain was forecast for Thursday, starting at 2.44. I couldn't believe it, and Mal Tongue has never let me forget, when it started to rain just as Campbell was taking his one iron from the bag to step on to the tee.

Standing by the first tee on the opening day of the British Open is an education. Players who have been on the tour for years suddenly turn to jelly. It is hard to believe but in the first round of the Open you see shots which would embarrass even an average player. Not Campbell. He bisected the first fairway with as sweet a one-iron into the wind as you would wish to see.

That he carded a two-over 72 and followed it with a 73 in the second round to miss the cut by two didn't make the occasion any less special for Campbell. At his second attempt he had got to play in the British Open. He repeated his vow of 12 months earlier: "I'll be back."

Michael might have been having a good time but Julie definitely wasn't. After the relaxed atmosphere of the Challenge Tour where she had been able to wander where she liked, when she liked on the course, the Open was a bit too much for her with its restrictions.

"When we hit Turnberry I thought 'yuk'. I didn't like the atmosphere, there were too many people . . . the whole thing turned me off. With all the shops and – I couldn't believe – a grandstand where people would sit just to watch the players hit balls on the practice ground. It was too much like a circus and the golfers were on show.

"It was freezing cold and I had towels round my head because it was raining. I was in a bad mood the whole week. I tried to be supportive to Michael but I kept thinking 'What is this, what am I doing here?'

"My attitude to it worried Michael a bit because this is where he wanted to be and it was obvious I wasn't enjoying it.

"Then we went back to Switzerland for a Volvo Tour event on the course where Michael had won at his first start on the Challenge Tour. This time the grandstands were up. I began to get quite excited. It was somewhere I had been before but I could feel the vibes and the totally different atmosphere in the town and among the people.

"It was exciting, too, because he was leading at one point during the first day. I think the significance of him leading on a main tour event spun him out because he didn't fire on the second day and missed the cut.

"The trip had changed my outlook, though. By the time we got to Australia I was in the groove and knew what my role was."

In his first tournament back on the Australia-New Zealand tour, the Queensland Open at Windaroo, Campbell showed he was still in good touch by finishing second, two strokes behind Lucas Parsons. Campbell was disappointed not to win for the fifth time in 1994, but if he couldn't then he wouldn't have wanted anyone other than Parsons to lift the trophy.

Besides the winner's cheque and trophy there was another bonus for Parsons when he returned to the room he had been sharing with Campbell all week – two bottles of Moet champagne. Campbell and

Parsons have a standing bet on their performances when they play the same tournament and Campbell couldn't resist reminding his roommate that he was still six bottles up on the New Zealand v Australia bet.

The hot and humid atmosphere of the Tanah Merah Country Club was the venue for the tour's next tournament, the Singapore Open, and Campbell was reasonably satisfied after finishing tied for 14th.

At the Alfred Dunhill Masters in Bali the following week, Campbell finished seventh, four shots from Canadian Jack Kay. Campbell was interested to note that just one shot in front of him was European order of merit winner Colin Montgomerie, with Vijay Singh another stroke better off in third place. It was a yardstick which told Campbell he was holding his own in good company.

After such a performance Campbell was disappointed to finish 39th at the Victorian Open and then went into a mini form slump which saw him miss three cuts in succession before he finished the year with a 48th placing at the Air New Zealand Open.

10
Caddy

It was almost inevitable, given the chain of coincidences connecting them, that Michael Campbell and Max Cunningham would end up working together.

Cunningham was Michael's mother's maiden name, both Michael and Max played their teenage golf at the Manor Park Golf Club, albeit a decade apart, each has a wife called Julie, and both began playing golf left-handed before switching to the more orthodox way.

They joke that they were always meant to become a team, for that is what a player and caddy must be; it was just a matter of when it would happen.

It happened towards the end of 1994 when Max was left with time to fill when his employer, genial Scotsman Sandy Lyle, had completed his relatively sparse programme of 24 tournaments for the year and gone into hibernation for the northern hemisphere winter.

There was no need for Lyle to chase from one end of the world to the other as has become the golfing fashion in recent years. If he didn't win another dollar on the golf course it wouldn't really matter. He was set up for life after a golden patch during which he could seemingly do no wrong in the 1980s.

When he edged out Payne Stewart to win the British Open at Royal St George's in 1985, Sandy Lyle became the first home winner of the championship since Tony Jacklin in 1969, a feat which guaranteed lucrative sponsorships galore. Three years later Lyle became the first Briton to win the United States Masters title. His win at Augusta opened the floodgates with Nick Faldo winning for the next two years and Welshman Ian Woosnam carrying on where Faldo left off. But Lyle was the first, guaranteeing entry to the world's biggest tournaments and meaning even more sponsors were queuing up clamouring to be associated with him.

Working for Sandy Lyle was, according to Max Cunningham, the easiest job in golf. In finding since leaving Lyle "the next easiest job in golf" with Campbell he counts himself extremely fortunate.

Ironically it was because Lyle had been there, done it all and was more than comfortably off financially that Cunningham felt the time had come for him to find another employer. He loved working for the Scotsman, who was generous, courteous and talented, but it was becoming frustrating.

"Being with Sandy meant I got to all the big tournaments such as the US Masters, which was great. The problem was he wasn't doing anything at those tournaments. The talent hadn't left him but he wasn't using it. I began to find it hard being around someone, even though he was such a delightful person, who minimised his talent.

"It was also starting to cost me money because there were no percentage cheques coming in. I was starting to go into debt to caddy for him. I would look at my credit card and realise I was getting further into debt. Being married by then I wondered how long the situation could continue."

While at the British Open in Turnberry Cunningham had spoken to Michael Campbell about the possibility of carrying his bag during the Australia-New Zealand tour later in the year while Lyle was on holiday.

"At that time I didn't really know Michael at all. He knew me and I knew him because of us both coming from Manor Park but that was about all. While I hadn't had much to do with him, I had heard a lot about him. Trevor Thompson, the secretary at Manor Park, is a good friend of mine and he had told me about this Maori kid with loads of talent.

"It was a very casual approach at Turnberry. I asked Michael who was working for him down under. He said he had been using Bryce Mawhinney who he knew from Wellington and asked why I was inquiring.

"I told him I would be interested in working for him as I had the summer off. Michael's biggest worry was that he couldn't afford to pay me what I was getting with Sandy but he said he would think about it.

"When he came back and said he would like me to join him in Australia he was still concerned about not being able to pay what I was used to. I decided to take a chance and told him to pay me if he played well.

"Actually, he played poorly at the Australian Open, but despite all that, he looked like he was very close to playing well and it wasn't long before I was glad I had taken the gamble with the terms we were working under."

Max Cunningham was born in Wellington, went to school in Silverstream and completed his education at St Pat's College Silverstream. He was 11 years old when a friend of his brother, who was 13, asked if he would like to join him for a round of golf at Manor Park where he had just started playing.

"I shot 132 using my mate's father's clubs and was hooked, absolutely hooked. His dad was left-handed, as I was at the time, so it was handy. I played at every opportunity from that moment."

Cunningham played left-handed till he was 16 and on a nine handicap. One day while watching Terry Kendall, who was the assistant professional to Bob McDonald at Manor Park, hit balls on the practice ground, Cunningham took a couple of swings with one of Kendall's clubs. The professional said that he could swing pretty well right-handed. As right-handed clubs were easier to come by in those days, Kendall suggested Cunningham play right-handed. He did and, amazingly, was back on a nine handicap within 12 months.

University didn't appeal to Max Cunningham. Travel and golf occupied his thoughts more than anything and for a while after leaving college he would work during the winter and play as an amateur on the reasonable professional circuit New Zealand golf at the time enjoyed. There were good tournaments in Dunedin, Christchurch, Hamilton, Mount Maunganui and Miramar as well as wherever the New Zealand Open happened to be played in a particular year.

Cunningham made the odd cut, missed a lot; shot a lot of 78s and 80s, but posted the occasional good score. He didn't, as he puts it, really know what he was doing but he did know he was thoroughly enjoying it.

There was one tournament, the Caltex at Paraparaumu Beach, which Cunningham still remembers vividly after being drawn to play with big names Graham Marsh and Stan Peach for the first two days.

Last off in the first round in front of a big, expectant gallery, Cunningham could hardly keep his hands steady enough to put his ball on the tee at the first. A skied tee shot made it over the hill and after a two iron to the green Cunningham sank the putt for birdie. After 11 holes he was even par and one ahead of Graham Marsh. Cunningham ended up shooting 76 and Marsh 71, but what happened that day shows Cunningham is a more than useful guy to have as your caddy.

A dislike of Wellington's winters sent Max Cunningham in search of the sun. Since he began reading golf magazines he had wanted to play the courses he read about, such as America's Pebble Beach and Spyglass Hill. For six months in 1978 he drove himself round the United States in a van doing just that. His girlfriend of the time joined him at the last minute and while she didn't play golf happily followed him around to see America. The pair drove 16,000 miles through 38 states and by the time they ended up in London at the end of 1978 they needed to settle down for a while to catch their breath.

Cunningham hated London at that stage. He had arrived from San Diego in September, just as the weather was getting colder. Having flat hunting and job seeking on the agenda didn't make the place appear any more attractive. When he landed a job with Shell Oil as an internal auditor the fact that he ended up working for an alcoholic Scotsman didn't exactly endear him either.

Cunningham was told by his boss that it was important he was in the office by nine each morning. That was no problem, but the reason he had to be punctual – "we go to the pub at 12.30 and that's it; we don't come back" – fazed him somewhat.

Living in Holland Park wasn't conducive to getting on to the golf course and Cunningham's life became a pattern of going to work, drinking afterwards, drinking on Friday night, drinking on Saturday night and going to a pub somewhere on Sunday. It was a lifestyle he came to detest and after two years of such a humdrum existence it was back to Sydney where he ran a golf discount store and worked for Daiwa before deciding that nine-to-five jobs weren't what he wanted.

Caddies, coaches, managers & mentors . . .

That's how it has to be Michael. Mal Tongue and Michael Campbell still spend time at Manor Park fine-tuning his swing.

Michael and Maori Golf Foundation Director Vic Pirihi who has been a supporter of Michael's from early in his career. Pirihi was always there to help but he didn't lie down and roll over when Michael beat him in the final of the 1991 Maori Golf Championships.

A night off in London for fellow professional Greg Turner, Michael's caddy Max Cunningham, Frank Nobilo's caddy Anthony Knight and Turner's caddy Charlie.

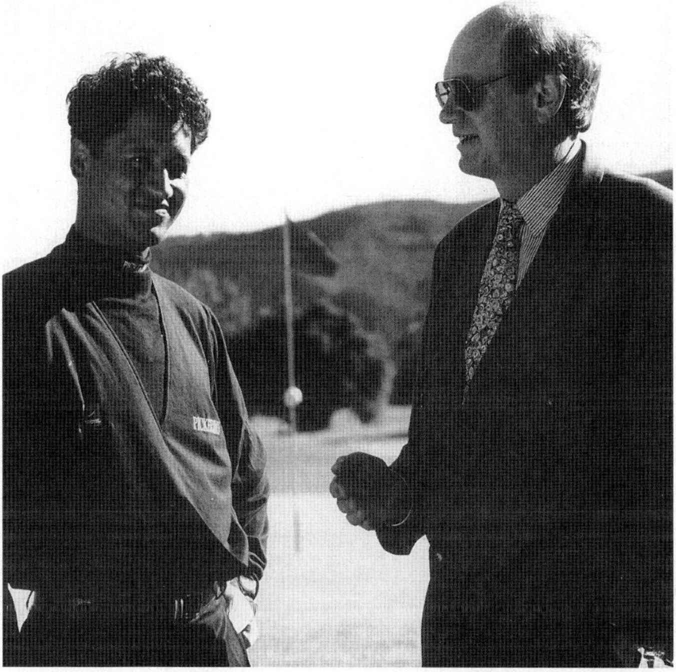

ANDREW COLLINS COLLECTION

Michael and his lawyer Andrew Collins get together at Manor Park instead of in the office.

MARK ROUND

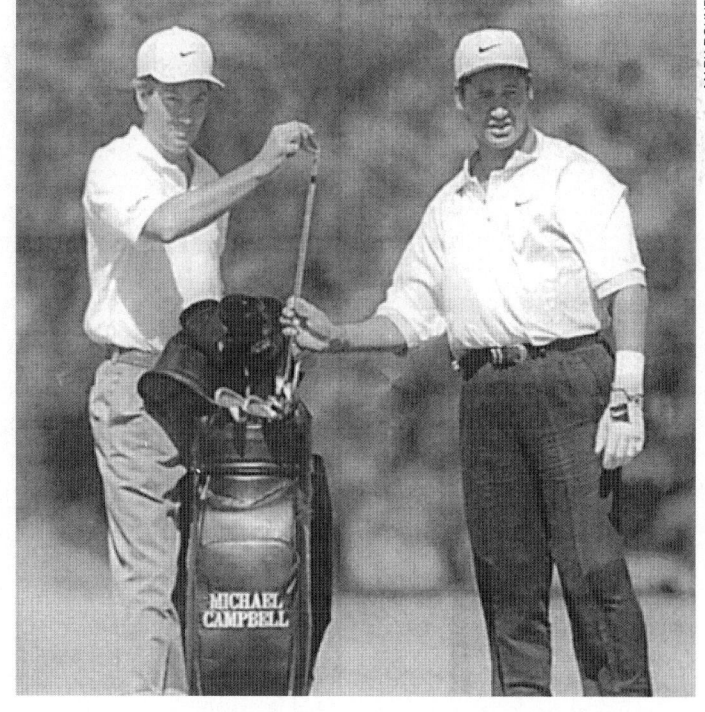

That's the club Michael, believe me. Max Cunningham and Michael Campbell work as a team on golf courses throughout the world.

Greg Norman at the 1995 Johnnie Walker Classic in Manila.

After losing his job with Daiwa because of his boss's insensitivity over his father having cancer and him wanting to go back to New Zealand to see him one Easter, Cunningham accepted an offer from Stuart Reese, a good mate, to go to Europe and caddy for him on the tour for six months. It was the start of a lifestyle he has come to love.

"Stuart paid me £120 a week and ten per cent of what he won. It doesn't sound much now but in 1985 it wasn't a bad deal. I had quite a bit of money saved up so I was never struggling, and I quickly began to enjoy the life.

"Stuart never became the player he could have been. He had a tremendous amount of talent but didn't get the results he should have.

"At the end of the year I went back to Australia thinking I would have to get another nine-to-five job but fortunately Ossie Moore asked me to work for him. Ossie had won the Australian order of merit that year. He seemed to finish second every week I carried his bag. I thought this is a nice way to earn good money.

"I went back to Europe with Ossie but he was another of those guys who didn't make use of the talent he had. He played a bit like Michael Campbell. Hit it long, left to right and had all the shots. Greg Norman described him as a wonderful player but he had an incredibly negative outlook and that eventually cost him.

"Ossie was a good guy. I had a great time with him but he just couldn't do anything in Europe and that was where the money was. He would play well every year in Australia then go to Europe and miss cuts.

"I was still undecided about making caddying a full-time job. I had a spell with Terry Gale in 1987 and he took me to Japan, which was a great experience, before Rodger Davis stepped in and offered me a job.

"That's really when I thought to hell with a nine-to-five job. I realised I could make a good living out of carrying a bag. Rodger was a real pro and it was stepping up a little for me. As good as Ossie Moore was I don't think he ever became a pro. He always had an amateur side about him, whereas Rodger Davis was the ultimate pro. Nothing was left to chance.

"Rodger had a routine for practice before he played, another for after the round. He was always on time for practice.

"While I had a bit of bad luck with him being out for a few

months with a neck injury, I made a great living with him. He won five or six tournaments including beating Fred Couples in a playoff at the Bicentennial tournament which was worth $500,000 to him and $50,000 to me.

"The last time I carried Rodger's bag, at Palm Meadows in January 1990, he beat Curtis Strange in a playoff to win again but I had problems off the course at that time."

The problem for Max Cunningham was ME, chronic fatigue syndrome, the onset of which – though he didn't know what it was – he had noticed in 1989. The condition got progressively worse till Cunningham couldn't stay awake for six hours a day. When Rodger Davis went to the practice ground after a round to hit balls Cunningham would go to sleep with his head resting on the golf bag. "Rodger wouldn't be able to wake me up. He would kick the bag and I would carry on sleeping as if in a coma. I couldn't continue in the job like that.

"I went back to New Zealand and started seeing doctors in Auckland. You name one, I probably went to him. One guy did every test possible and I came out a hundred per cent. Everything was fine. There was nothing wrong with me, except I was sleeping twenty hours a day!

"In the end they diagnosed it as ME and after almost two years it disappeared almost as quickly as it had arrived."

Max Cunningham was soon back on the golf course with American John Morse who asked Max to join him soon after winning the 1990 Australian Open. He accompanied Morse to Asia and Europe but the American didn't enjoy either the travel or food in Europe. He headed home and Cunningham teamed up with Sweden's Per-Ulrik Johansson.

"I really enjoyed working for Per who was good to be with. I thought he was going to be an incredibly good player. I think he got into the technical side a bit much but the year I was with him he made over £250,000.

"While I was with Per, Sandy Lyle made me an offer I couldn't refuse. Before deciding anything for the following year I went with Sandy to Jamaica for the Johnnie Walker World Championship which was guaranteed money.

"I spent $3300 on a return ticket and when I got there Sandy immediately wrote me a cheque for the ticket, paid me five per cent of $62,000 and gave me £500 for the week. It was all above what I imagined he would do for that week.

"It was a difficult time for me. I had worked for Per Johansson for one year, done well and he had paid me a tremendous bonus. I rang Per up and told him that Sandy had offered me a job. His reaction was typical of the man.

"He said, 'This is a business. You're not in it for fun or the travel. If it is an offer you don't feel you can refuse, then don't. It is no different than me changing my golf clubs when someone offers me a better deal. No hard feelings.'"

Max Cunningham seems to always end up with nice guys, which isn't the case with a lot of his peers on the tour. Many players are difficult to work for, demanding everything from the caddy they employ while making life difficult and uncomfortable for him at the same time. Seve Ballesteros's adventures with caddies, and how difficult and demanding he can be, have been well documented. I interviewed Billy Foster, a down-to-earth and likeable Yorkshireman, while he was working for Ballesteros. He had to ask permission from "the boss" before he agreed to talk to me. While Foster had only nice things to say about Seve there was always the impression he wasn't letting his true feelings out.

It seems my impressions that day we talked in Southport weren't far out. The pair have since parted with Foster telling Ballesteros in no uncertain terms what he thought of him and the way he had been treated.

Seve Ballesteros has always been the darling of the galleries whether he was playing in Europe, England, where he was idolised after winning the British Open for the first time at Royal Lytham and St Anne's, or the United States where he produced arguably the greatest array of shots Augusta has seen to win the Masters.

The public can get the wrong impression of players from their demeanour on the course. Some who look angelic can be more like the Devil away from the course, while the opposite can apply.

Colin Montgomerie has come in for stick from media and public alike for his on-course tantrums. Away from the golf course he is a charming person. While covering the 1991 Open at Royal Birkdale I stayed in the same private hotel, the Warwick, as Montgomerie. He was with his family and many convivial evenings were spent in the lounge.

Cunningham has got to know Colin Montgomerie well and isn't surprised that was how I found him.

"Alistair McLean, Colin's caddy, is another with a sweet job. When they see Colin huffing and puffing and carrying on on the course people think he must be a right sod and that he gives his caddy a hard time. They couldn't be more wrong. Colin has never directed abuse at a caddy in his life. He knows the guy is doing his best and if things do happen to go wrong he didn't hand him the wrong club on purpose. On top of that Colin is incredibly generous."

When a golfer and caddy get together nothing is put on paper. There are no contracts binding one to the other. It is appropriate given the nature of the game that agreements are sealed through an old-fashioned handshake.

That was how Michael Campbell and Max Cunningham sealed their partnership and Cunningham must have wondered whether he had done the right thing when the pair got off to such a shaky start at the end of 1994.

Cunningham, however, felt that Campbell wasn't far off playing well, even though he was missing cuts. What he saw at the AMP New Zealand Open at Heretaunga in January 1995 convinced him he would be on a winner if he continued working for his fellow Kiwi.

"To finish third at the New Zealand Open after one of the worst putting displays I had seen was incredible. He played absolutely brilliantly apart from on the greens. I thought, 'This is it. If he can play like that in Europe he will make a fortune. I want to work for this guy.'

"We didn't get a chance to discuss the future after the Open because he had to dash off to Dubai and I had had no plans or ticket to go there. He finished third in Dubai with an Australian, who had seen him at Dubai airport and realised I wasn't with him, carrying his bag, and fourth in Manila the following week using Mark James's caddy.

"He made fifty grand, which I was really thrilled about having worked two months for him and having made nothing! When I met him in Perth the following week he said he was sorry I hadn't been there, especially as I had made no money before Christmas.

"All of a sudden there was no shortage of guys wanting to work for him. Twenty-five guys rang or faxed him asking could they have the job and when I saw him in Perth I said, dreading the answer, 'I suppose you've got another caddy now?' He said, 'Of course not. You've got first choice if you want it.'

"Of course I wanted it. I had an obligation to caddy for Sandy Lyle at the Masters but Michael was good about that and said I should go.

"It was while we were sorting things out between us in Perth that I asked him what he thought he could make during his first year in Europe. He said £200,000 to £250,000.

"I thought, 'God, if he actually thinks he can do that it is pretty impressive for a first year player.' The average player in his position would probably admit to being happy if he could make £100,000, and have his fingers crossed saying that.

"By the time we left St Andrews after the British Open he was up to £250,000."

Campbell and Cunningham have slipped easily into a tournament routine which works for them.

Arriving at the tournament venue on a Tuesday, the first thing Max will do is buy a yardage book from Graham Heinrich, who makes a nice living from what is a lonely job. With 144 players in a field, and as many as 20 players preferring to carry a book themselves on top of the one used by the caddy, it is, at £9 a book, a good little earner.

Out on his own the week before everyone else arrives, Heinrich, who has caddied for Peter Fowler and Mark McNulty and has a talent for drawing, measures the course with a laser and checks on changes from the previous year.

It now saves Cunningham walking the course himself before Michael plays it for the first time, though in 1995 he would often be there Monday night to do that anyway.

"Michael will go out and play a practice round which gives us the chance to double check Graham's yardage book, though if there is a typographical error someone will soon notice it and tell everyone.

"A lot of players want their caddy to pace the course before they play to double check everything. I don't see the point of that. Many of the courses we play on now often have six or seven holes over water which the caddy can't pace anyway.

"It was a bit different in 1995. I was back working for a rookie so

I would often be out on Monday before Mike saw the course for the first time on Tuesday.

"Michael had never seen the courses and wouldn't be able to play on the Wednesday because he wasn't in the pro-ams. It is totally different now. Michael has seen the courses and is in the pro-ams every week.

"He isn't keen on playing more than one practice round, which makes sense. It is important to see the course but why waste all your energies on practice rounds?"

Once the tournament gets under way, Campbell will hit a few balls and have some putting practice before heading out on the course and may return to the practice ground for a while to wind down after the round. The post-round session, including putting, lasts no longer than an hour before he and Max might go for a quiet beer and relax.

"The intensity level is quite low when compared with a guy like Bernhard Langer, who seems to be grinding, grinding, grinding from the moment the sun comes up. That's just his way of doing it. He has a different outlook to someone like Michael."

The life of a caddy looks attractive when his man is winning and the cheques are coming in. On the other side of the coin expenses have to be taken care of, and they also have to be paid when a player is missing cuts and there is no money at the end of the week apart from the retainer.

Those who aren't making money will go to the discount shops and buy their own cheap air tickets. The problem with that is the tickets aren't changeable so if your man misses the cut you can't go home on Friday night.

When your player isn't playing well the caddy has no control. If a player is performing really badly the caddy will be making no money and has no control over his life or his income.

"That is a bad feeling. I got it with Sandy. I was working for a guy I enjoyed being with but going into debt at the same time. I thought, 'God, here I am 40 years old, I'm doing a good job and getting no result.' It gets to be more than the money.

"I love the game and love being around it, but as hard as you try you can't fix Sandy's putting or what is going on in his head."

The majority of caddies go through the golf travel companies who will have airfare and hotel deals going for the week. Whether they stay at the same hotels as their player is up to them.

"A player's hotel might be £90 a night for a double and the travel company will mention a nice hotel round the corner which is only £40 a double.

"Depending on how I feel or what town it is I will probably go to the cheaper place. Sometimes you have no choice and have to stay at the same hotel as the players.

"While at a tournament I see a bit of Mike. I eat with him here and there, perhaps have a beer but we certainly don't live in each other's pockets. We are together six days a week as it is. He does his thing, I do mine.

"There is no player-caddy thing about Michael. That isn't the case with a lot of players on the tour. The vast majority would never think about going for a beer with the caddies but people such as Mike, Sandy Lyle and, believe it or not, Colin Montgomerie don't think twice. They love to relax and chat with the caddies."

There isn't much that happens on tour that escapes the notice of the caddies. They are the eyes and ears of the circuit. They are the ones who know which players tread the thin line between manipulating the rules and being called for cheating.

Golf is a gentleman's game and, considering the number who play, relatively few players cheat, but they do exist. One caddy on the US tour walked off the course and left his player with his bag and a red face after the player declared an air shot while under a tree had been a practice swing. "I can't work for you," the caddy said and left him to it.

From the outset of their relationship the Campbells and Cunninghams have got on well together. There was a concern when the partnership was evolving as to how it would work, but Julie Campbell says it has worked out well.

"Obviously you think about what would happen if we didn't all get along when we were stuck together. We needn't have worried. It has been great.

"It would have been impossible had we not got on, though we would have had to make an effort. Michael and Max have a good working relationship and that has to take priority. We may not have been friends in different circumstances, but because we both knew how important it was we grew close pretty quickly.

"We maintain our space. They spend time with their friends and we go out with ours."

Teaming up with Michael Campbell was the best thing that could have happened to Max Cunningham when it did. With Sandy Lyle not playing many tournaments Cunningham was losing his enthusiasm.

Once with Campbell, however, the enthusiasm returned as Campbell's ebullient nature rubbed off on Cunningham. When the results started to come it was a bonus. The credit card bills which Cunningham had been running up while carrying the bag for Lyle were able to be paid off, and the caddy couldn't wait to jump out of bed and get to work whereas a few months earlier he had had to drag himself from beneath the sheets each morning.

Campbell, too, was delighted to have him on board and after some initial teething problems everything fell into place.

"It took Max and myself about four months to really get to know each other on and off the course. We are obviously different types and we go our different ways. In the early stages we went through a few problems but it all settled down.

"Every player has his own routine. I like to get to the course an hour and a half before my tee off time. I like everything planned between then and tee off. When we first started working together he did things differently to what I was used to.

"There was sometimes bad timing. When I wanted him he was gone. That doesn't happen any more. Luckily both of us are organised people. Sometimes you can have an organised golfer and a disorganised caddy, or vice versa. In our case we both dot the I's and cross the T's which means we are in the right frame of mind when we hit the first tee.

"There is a stability about our relationship which isn't always apparent in other partnerships.

"Max is very professional. He has worked for some top players and the experience he has picked up while with those guys is a big help to me."

Much is made during television commentaries at golf tournaments about club selection and the discussion which inevitably takes place between player and caddy before one is removed from the bag.

Max says Michael is incredibly easy to club for because he hits the ball so consistently. Ninety-nine times out of a hundred Michael and Max agree on which is the right club.

Michael Campbell says he is always willing to listen to a suggestion from his caddy but admits that, like himself and Mal Tongue, he and Max are both very stubborn when they are sure they are right.

"While we are usually on the same wavelength there have been a few club selections we have disagreed on.

"A perfect example was on the last hole at the 1995 Irish Open, a par four with water on the left-hand side. It is either driver and six iron, or three wood and four iron to the green. I was sixth or seventh with one hole to play. I had had the chance to win when I was one behind with four to play but I'd gone bogey, bogey, bogey so had slipped back.

"The sensible shot was to play three wood for safety, four iron to the middle of the green, make par and finish sixth or seventh.

"Because I'd had a chance to win and wasted it I didn't care if I finished sixth, seventh, tenth or twentieth. On the last tee Max said, 'Cambo, I think it's a three wood.' I said, 'No way. Give me a driver.' 'Cambo, it's a three wood.' 'Give me the driver.' I ended up in the water, made bogey, finished 12th. I should have listened."

It is a caddy's job to get the best out of his player on every shot. Sometimes it isn't easy. If a player has decided it isn't his day and is going through the motions it is difficult to change his frame of mind. Campbell normally isn't that sort of player but once he is out of contention in a tournament can tend to go into cruise mode if allowed. That was something Julie noticed in Scotland during his last Challenge Tour event.

"Michael knew he already had his card for the following year's main tour but he had to play the last tournament as he had to have competed in seven events on the Challenge Tour to qualify for the order of merit.

"It was a horrendous week with terrible weather capped off by 36 holes being played on the last day. Michael was in contention going into the last day but it soon started slipping away from him.

"On the second 18 holes it looked like he needed a miracle to win, but second place was still within his reach. I was walking on fairways then because the Challenge is much more relaxed than the main tour. As we walked along I said he could still come second, but he seemed to have lost interest. He just wanted to get out of there.

"The leader then lost four shots, and the lead, in one hole. I said to Michael, 'Well there you go, you never know do you?' He ended up third but could easily have won it. It was a learning curve for me. If Michael can't see the win he doesn't play with the same aggression.

"Max is good when the pressure goes on, helping to break it down hole by hole, shot by shot. People think Michael is calm and unruffled when he doesn't throw tantrums like some players. That is because he is good mannered. He is feeling just as much inside as other players but doesn't let it bubble over and get out."

There was much discussion about Campbell's club selection when he lost the Greg Norman Classic by one shot to Craig Parry with a bogey on the last hole, a par three, at The Lakes, after going through the back of the green. Cunningham is adamant Campbell would take the same club again today.

"I went to the front of the tee to see if the wind was hurting or helping us. Without even giving him the yardage I walked back to him and said, 'What's your gut feeling here?' He said five iron. That was all I wanted to know. Mike asked how far it was. I told him 194. He said, 'Five iron.'

"As soon as Mike hit it he said, 'I killed it.' It pitched pin high and went over the back.

"In the locker room Mike Clayton said, in his usual sarcastic way, 'Nice club.' 'It landed pin high Clayts,' I replied. Grant Waite was sitting alongside and he said, 'You would never have given him a six iron there. He never would have hit it, and you never would have picked it so don't feel bad about it.'

"We get some wrong, but we get most right otherwise we wouldn't have won £400,000 in the year would we?"

At the end of their first year together Michael Campbell asked his caddy what he thought the strength of his game was. Max Cunningham didn't hesitate. "Temperament," he said.

"Michael doesn't realise how good his temperament is, because that is just the way he is.

"He is laid back. At the end of the day if it is 78 or 68, what the hell, it's not life or death.

"Unlike a lot of players when they finish a poor round Michael doesn't dwell on it. It is rare that he even mentions what has happened. Occasionally out on the course he might say something. At The Lakes he started the second round with double bogey on the first and a bogey on the third. Walking to the fourth tee he said, almost with a smile, 'That's not the kind of start we wanted is it? I don't know what went wrong there.' I replied that he would just have to make a few more birdies than he had originally thought. He ended up shooting 68, five under par!

"I have never left the course with Mike in a courtesy car or gone to the locker room and listened to him analysing what has happened. He believes that some days it works, some days it doesn't.

"That is how I think as a caddy. I certainly don't hang my head because he is having a bad day. They are going to be few and far between. He is trying his hardest. It would be a different story if he was hitting it on the run and heaving clubs in the bag as some players do, but that isn't his style. He always tries. Some days you just can't tune in."

During his time on the European tour with Campbell, Cunningham watched other people's reactions to Campbell with interest.

"The guys over there on the tour began to realise just what a good player he is. When people like Colin Montgomerie start commenting about how good his game is you know he has that something extra.

"A lot of the younger guys on tour were in awe of his game. Mike shoots the easiest 67s I've ever seen. He has fabulous hand-eye co-ordination. He has a rare talent.

"The last great player was Tom Watson. I think I might be working for the next."

11
Media

Observing Michael Campbell work the world's golfing media in the St Andrews press centre after his magical third round 65 at the British Open was akin to watching an actor manipulate an audience with a powerful performance.

Developing the talent to evoke a wide range of emotions from his audience can take an actor years. Here was a young New Zealand Maori golfer in his rookie year on the European tour doing just that, seemingly without effort.

Every grin, grimace, wipe of the brow, touch of the hat or roll of the eyes by Michael Campbell was seized upon by a gathering of hard-bitten journalists who can, if it takes their fancy, make life hard for the touring pro.

Get on the wrong side of them and it takes a while to turn things around. Nick Faldo will tell you that, as will a number of his peers who have had form slumps magnified out of all proportion as reporters seek a fresh angle or attempt to upstage their colleagues with an "exclusive".

Press conferences at an event such as the British Open are made up of a mixed bag. There are the tabloid writers seeking sensationalism and taking quotes out of context to satisfy the boss back in the office who is looking for a back page lead story.

In 1990 American Scott Hoch was asked to a press conference after being drawn to play the first two rounds in the same group as Nick Faldo, who had won the US Masters in a playoff when Hoch missed a tiddler of a putt.

Hoch related how he and Faldo had met some time after for the first time since the Masters. Faldo enquired how he was and Hoch joked that he hadn't had much sleep since the fateful day. Faldo unthinkingly rubbed salt in the wound by saying he hadn't had much rest either, with all the commitments which came from winning the Masters.

"I could have punched him," Hoch said with a laugh. It was meant as light relief and was taken that way by most who were there. The next morning, however, one paper carried the headline "I Could Have Punched Faldo's Lights Out Says Hoch".

Hoch was horrified. On meeting Faldo at the first tee he attempted to explain but Faldo told him not to worry. He didn't read the newspapers during Open week and, anyway, he knew how they twisted things.

The other side of the story is when a player bursts into the press centre in a self-righteous rage to confront a journalist he alleges has misquoted him. The aggrieved player soon backs off when the accused reporter plays a tape with the alleged misquote on it.

Despite the reputation the tabloid reporters have, most of them are personable people who don't believe they are half as bad as they are painted. To be fair they aren't, most of the time.

Then there are those from the "quality" papers. They aren't averse to a bit of scandal, but their primary purpose is to write about the golf, not what one player thinks of another's sex life.

The magazine writers are different again. While they sit in on the press conferences, once it is over they will attempt to grab a few minutes, or more, with the subject to expand on what he has just said. By the time their work appears the Open will have long gone and they are looking for something a little different for their readers.

Television and radio personnel do their interviews separately from the written media. As is the case in all sports world-wide these days, television calls the tune and the various television stations get first crack at a player once his round is finished. Television interviews are of necessity, through time constraints, superficial. It is when the golfer faces the written media that his background and the ins and outs of his round are delved into in detail.

At the Open the written media are next in line after the television stations, before the player leaves the press centre via the temporary radio studios where post-round interviews are conducted.

The Open press centre is run by a charming Scot by the name of David Begg. David is a warm and courteous man, but should any reporter or photographer break the rules woe betide him or her. While he leaves everyone in no doubt as to who is in charge, the players are quickly put at ease with an opening quip where necessary. When David Begg knows a potentially controversial or embarrassing issue will be raised he endeavours to move into that particular area with sensitivity.

If an interview is going to be productive you would hardly start by saying to a player who had been in contention and just had a triple bogey on the penultimate hole, "Well you made a right mess of the 17th didn't you. Why was that?" That question has to be asked but if it is the first one posed there is likely to be little else come out of the discussion.

When a golfer enters a tournament one of the conditions under which he does so is that he makes himself available for interviews. It is rare that a player will refuse to talk to the media after a round. Should any do so it is a fair bet that, given a few minutes to regain their composure after what may have been a bad round or traumatic finish, they will return to talk about their exploits.

Golfers at the top level tend to be extremely articulate. What could be expected to be a five or ten minute interview can extend far beyond that time as the player gets a taste for the job at hand and starts discussing not only his own game, but that of others in the field, or something completely unrelated to where the interview started out.

You can put money on a press conference involving Jack Nicklaus running over time. Nicklaus loves to be the centre of attention. He runs the interview rather than those trying to ask the questions. He can be irascible, charming, dogmatic and personable all in a matter of minutes. The odds are that something will come out of a Nicklaus press conference.

Seve Ballesteros is wonderful to watch in action. His accented English is excellent but the way he uses his hands, shoulders and brown eyes to make his point add colour to his interviews.

When Nick Faldo enters a press conference it is possible to feel the tension, especially if he hasn't had the best of days. Inevitably in the last few years Faldo has been among the favourites to win the Open. He has won twice since 1990, but even when he has an off day there are a number who request that he attend to find out what happened. I suppose those who ask for him to come in feel there is safety in numbers rather than approaching him one-on-one to ask what went wrong.

On the Australia-New Zealand tour there are always a number of young players fresh to the game. It is particularly noticeable at the New Zealand Open, which is the first tournament for many after gaining their tour cards at the PGA qualifying school.

They are delighted to be interviewed but the mere sight of one or two reporters arriving, notebooks in hand, to watch them play their final holes can, it seems, affect them adversely. If there is a photographer or television cameraperson in the group it can be even worse for the novice professional.

Those asked to attend the press conferences, which at the British Open can attract around 200 reporters, have usually just done something exceptional during their round. Others are approached individually by those interested in their rounds for other reasons, for example they may be from a newspaper's circulation area.

In the case of New Zealand players there are usually few journalists wanting to talk to them, unless they have done something special. In that case they will probably be asked to a conference anyway.

When I first began covering The Open seven years ago I would talk to Frank Nobilo, Greg Turner or Bob Charles along with no more than three or four other journalists, including radio stations.

As New Zealand's golfing stocks have soared, more people are interested in them and, because of the way they are playing, the Kiwis are getting asked into the press centre more often. During the 1994 Open at Turnberry, Greg Turner and Frank Nobilo were both to the fore in the early stages and David Begg teased me that after not having had a New Zealander at a press conference for years I had had the pleasure of two within an hour of each other.

It was into such an arena that Michael Campbell had to step after his superb third round which included that shot at the 17th, which everyone present knew was going to dominate the back pages of every newspaper the following day, not only in England but throughout the world.

Covering golf for a newspaper is different to any other sport. Whereas a soccer, rugby or tennis match is played in front of a reporter, what is happening in a golf tournament is spread over a wide area.

Those charged with describing events in the following day's

newspapers can't be everywhere, which makes post-round interviews so necessary. They need to find out how a birdie was picked up on a particular hole, or what disasters befell the player when he had a quadruple bogey on the 14th.

It is possible to cover the tournament from within the press centre, where television sets showing the telecast are scattered throughout the working area. Radio reporters with bulletin commitments have no choice but to watch the action on television and follow the tournament's progress through the excellent scoring system. They will dash out to grab a few words from a particular player but basically they are chained to their desks the moment the tournament begins.

Some writers choose to do their reporting from the television screen and the interview room, but what is the point of being at such a wonderful and exciting event if you don't get out and sample the atmosphere.

It was amusing to watch a number of reporters arrive out on the course as Michael Campbell made his way through the last few holes of the third round. They wanted to steal a march on their rivals by finding out a bit about the young man before he faced their colleagues. Maybe they would hear of something which wouldn't come up at the conference later.

A reporter out on the course doesn't miss out on what is happening back at the press centre with a transcript of every press conference available to those who can't make it back from the outer reaches of the course.

Michael Campbell's first dealings with the New Zealand media usually took place at the back of the 18th green during amateur tournaments. Often there would be just one reporter, sometimes a couple or, on a good day, three.

As he progressed through the amateur ranks into Wellington's Tower inter-provincial team and began performing well at national tournaments, Campbell would be confronted by up to half a dozen journalists, and was inevitably bright and breezy, even after an indifferent round.

Reporters quickly learn which players to avoid after a bad round, those they should allow to have a cooling-off period before approaching. At no time did Michael Campbell come into that category.

The strokes . . .

Michael chips to the green during the 1995 British Masters at Northampton where he finished second to Scotland's Sam Torrance.

Michael tees off in the Dubai Desert Classic where he fired the first shots of his 1995 European campaign by finishing third to Fred Couples.

Putting during the 1995 Greg Norman Classic. Michael chased winner Craig Perry all day but finished one stroke behind after hitting his final tee shot too well!

Michael lets rip off the tee during one of the finest rounds of his life at St Andrews. Michael shot 65 during the third round of the British Open to lead the field by two going into the final round.

Always willing to talk after a good round, Campbell was never reticent after a disappointing performance. There were times when things hadn't gone as he hoped that Campbell would see a journalist in the vicinity of the 18th green or locker room and say, "Come on, let's get it over with."

Amateur golf in New Zealand and Australia gets more publicity than in most other parts of the world. Overseas competitors at Eisenhower Trophy and Espirito Santo tournaments in this part of the world were amazed at the coverage in the local papers and on television and radio.

Being in such a spotlight during the early stages of their careers has helped Michael Campbell and his New Zealand and Australian contemporaries to cope with media demands which increase dramatically on turning professional and starting to win tournaments.

When he faced the world's press at St Andrews, Campbell could have been excused had he stumbled his way through a conference which was standing room only, a situation which normally exists only for a Faldo, Nicklaus or Ballesteros. The composed way he handled the moment earned him many new admirers.

"I was having fun. It was a fantastic feeling. In my favour was the fact that I was different.

"I was the new kid on the block. Even though I had been doing well on the European tour no one knew a lot about me and most of the Americans there knew nothing at all. They were intrigued about where I came from, my background, culture, heritage and so on."

Inevitably in such a setting the first questions Campbell had to answer – apart from telling the gathering how he had played that shot – were about his name and what connections he had with Scotland.

He explained how his great-great-great-grandfather, Logan Campbell, travelled from Edinburgh to New Zealand, married a Maori lady, became Mayor of Auckland and had a place called One Tree Hill dedicated to him. That was enough to immediately endear him to the Scots in the room.

Next on the agenda for the media boys, who were now in a feeding frenzy, was the haka. While the Europeans knew all about the haka through the All Blacks it was new to the Americans. Campbell explained to them as best he could what it meant, and that St Andrews wasn't an appropriate place for it to be performed.

"Things threatened to get out of hand with the haka. I had joked about doing the haka on Tuesday. I said if I was leading Greg Norman by three I'll do the haka on the first tee. Now they wanted me to do it!"

The Americans still seemed perplexed about the haka, but they were already going off on another tack. Racism. Had Campbell had problems with racism? Was he able to play on any course he wished in New Zealand?

Campbell handled the questions they were throwing at him with the same adroitness he had shown out on the course an hour earlier. No, he told them, he hadn't had any racial problems, and yes, he could play anywhere he liked in New Zealand where Maori and Europeans are treated equally.

"I wasn't surprised by the questions about racism. Some journalists want something different. Not just about golf. To them bad news is good news. Faldo breaking up with his wife is juicier to them than if he holes in one or wins the tournament.

"Of course I have come up against racism and when they asked about it I could have gone either of two different ways. I could have spoken out about it and it would have raised more questions. Where and when, with whom?

"Instead I told a little white lie and said I hadn't had any experience of racism. This was a day about golf. I was feeling proud to be a New Zealander. Why should I start talking about racial problems in my country. It would have made their day had I said I had suffered discrimination."

It is worth recording how respected British columnist Ian Wooldridge put the questioners and their motives in perspective when he wrote in the *Daily Mail* the following day:

> Naturally they would never have addressed the same question to Dame Kiri Te Kanawa, but a 26-year-old Maori golfer who had just stamped his mark on the Open Championship was obviously fair game for the patronising treatment.
>
> Had Michael Campbell ever been hit by racism? Had he ever suffered from discrimination? The charming young man with a name half Marks and Spencer and half Scottish, who hails from Wellington, the most English of New Zealand cities, who now lives in Tooting Bec in South London and is about the same colour as any white person who's just come back from a fortnight on the Riviera, did not take umbrage.

"No," he said, "I've never had any difficulty with any class system back home. I carry the flag for New Zealand, not Maoris or Europeans. And no, he added, he had no more intention than his compatriot Bob Charles of performing the haka on the first tee. Maori war dances, he felt, were hardly appropriate at St Andrews.

The questioners were American who, for some reason, appear obsessed by race. This was the second time this year we've heard them grill a young golfer about his mixed ancestry, as though probing for an outburst of exasperation.

The first was in April at the US Masters where the intended victim was the brilliant American teenage amateur, Tiger Woods. Happily Woods, who is as black as Jesse Owens or Muhammad Ali, saw them coming.

"Tiger, what's it like to play at the Masters?" "Good," said Tiger, "it's a wonderful tournament."

"But this is the Masters Tiger. How about that?"

Tiger certainly knew all about that. The Masters is played at the Augusta National where, for most of its history, the only blacks on the premises were caddies or waiters. It still has only two black members. Tiger also knew what they were driving at and he wasn't going to say "Massa, I'se so grateful to be admitted to your wunnerful world."

Utterly polite, expressionless so that not even a glance could be misconstrued, he replied, "I've just said, it's a wonderful event."

"Yeah, and you're a smart-ass," breathed one of America's most venerable golf writers. Race has never been a big issue in golf in Britain. Yes, there's been discrimination against women, Jews, Catholics, Masons and, at certain clubs, distinguished public figures just because a closed-shop membership didn't like the cut of them.

It is not the most liberal of sports but this gratuitous questioning of a Maori golfer revealed not only a stupendous ignorance of New Zealand but struck the only jarring note I heard throughout the 124th Open Championship.

Incidentally Dame Kiri is also an accomplished New Zealand golfer. Maori, naturally.

During the conference Campbell mentioned in an off-hand way that he had suffered some bad press in New Zealand. He was referring to those disputing his Campbell ancestry but the journalists had no way of knowing that.

Earlier in the interview Campbell had said he was in much better condition than when he missed the cut 12 months earlier at

Turnberry. He told them he had lost two kilograms in weight.

Within minutes of the conference ending the tabloid journalists descended on the two New Zealand media representatives wanting to know what that remark was all about. They sniffed a John Daly type story. Had Campbell been drinking excessively? Had stopping helped him to lose weight? They took some convincing that wasn't the case and that Campbell hadn't expressed himself well when he talked about bad press.

"You don't think about those things when you are up there facing a couple of hundred journos. You have to think quickly. You are thinking of lots of different things. When someone asks a question you react naturally with the first thing that comes into your mind. Sometimes it is the wrong thing to say.

"It was so different in New Zealand when I would talk to two or three reporters almost informally. Now I was facing a couple of hundred people with a microphone stuck in front of me.

"Doing well on the European Tour leading up to the Open had helped. After some of those tournaments I had been in front of thirty or forty journalists. As I said, it was fun that day – even if one or two did try to trip me up. They were the minority. Everyone else seemed to be pleased for me.

"In that sort of situation you can tell when people are rooting for you rather than trying to put you down. Ninety-nine per cent of the journalists in that room were happy for me. That meant a lot. The others? They aren't worth worrying about."

Michael Campbell earned the media's respect again the following day when he had to front up within minutes of seeing his dream snatched away. The way he handled himself as he told them that he would be back, that he was proud of the way he played in finishing third in only his second Open, that he was naturally disappointed that he couldn't cap it off, led one English colleague to say as we walked out together, "You guys have got a hell of a player there and he's got a mind to match his swing."

12
European Rookie

When Michael Campbell began his 1995 campaign he had the added incentive of needing the money playing well would bring.

While Campbell has always insisted he enters golf tournaments to win for the satisfaction, rather than for the money on offer, he has the same problem as the rest of us. He has to earn money to live, and the life he leads, with all the travelling involved, doesn't come cheaply.

Towards the end of 1994 Michael and Julie, his wife to be, had bought an apartment in the exclusive Bellvue Hill suburb of Sydney. Within weeks of completing the purchase, and taking on the mortgage commitments, Campbell began missing cuts in Australia.

Back in New Zealand those following Campbell's progress wouldn't have dreamt that the brilliant young player had the same money worries many of those reading and hearing about him had to cope with. He had, after all, earned over $100,000 in prize money during his Australia-New Zealand rookie year and gone on to win four tournaments in 1994.

The four tournament wins in 1994 were, however, worth more for the future rather than money in the bank. The $US40,000 Campbell won in St Louis was more than useful, but that was quickly eaten into when he moved on to Europe and the Challenge Tour he had identified as his best route to the big-time Volvo Tour.

Campbell's first Challenge win in Switzerland brought a cheque for £8200 and success the following week in Austria £8330. Not bad for a week's work most would think, but getting to and from those tournaments, along with the accommodation costs for him and Julie, took a fair slice of the rewards.

When Campbell returned to Australia at the end of 1994 he had earned the right to compete on the Volvo Tour, but there wasn't a lot of money left in the kitty. Worse still, over the next few weeks the bank account wasn't getting topped up as cuts were missed.

Even the laid back, easy going Campbell was beginning to get concerned. Everyone in golf might have been predicting a great future for him, but bank managers don't take such things into account when they have loaned money. As Julie says, it wasn't an easy time.

"We had so much expense at that time and nothing coming in. There were legal fees and we had to start from scratch in buying furniture.

"There was hardly any money left in the bank and we had big repayments to make. The pressure of that probably had something to do with Michael missing cuts late in 1994 and we began to think we had made a big mistake in buying the apartment.

"The problems we had were no different to those other people go through. There was a difference in the way we were perceived though. People read about the money a golfer wins and think it goes straight into the bank.

"There are all sorts of things to be deducted before we see any of the money and then we have our own expenses to pay. It isn't only the mortgage. It costs a fortune to travel and live in Europe. I'm not saying we are hard done by. Far from it. But it isn't quite as easy as it seems."

It was against such a backdrop that Michael Campbell stepped out for his first tournament of 1995, the AMP New Zealand Open in Wellington. The Open was being staged at the Wellington Golf Club's Heretaunga course for the first time since 1987, when Ireland's Ronan Rafferty beat American Larry Nelson in a playoff.

It might be known as Windy Wellington, but for the New Zealand Open the capital city turned on four fabulous days and the sun began to shine on Michael Campbell once more.

The Wellington Golf Club was celebrating its centenary. How fitting it would have been had a New Zealander – a Wellingtonian even more so – won the Open that year. Australian Lucas Parsons spoilt that scenario and Campbell had to settle for third even though for four days he had hit the ball as well as at any time during his career.

Having coach Mal Tongue around during his preparations was an advantage Campbell hadn't enjoyed in Australia over the previous two months. Tongue was delighted with Campbell's form going into the tournament and had he been able to get the putter going it would have been a different story, according to Tongue.

"His ball striking that week was second to none. Had his putting been on he could have won easily. Andre Stoltz, who played with Michael during the first two rounds, said if Michael had been putting well he could have given everyone a 10-shot start and won.

"I could tell from that tournament that it was going to be a good year. He had just bought the apartment and told me he needed to win some money. Getting off to a good start at the New Zealand Open gave him the boost he needed.

"After his next two tournaments, in Dubai and Manila, he had secured his European Tour card for the following year and he was able to go and play without worrying about that.

"Michael had things sorted out for Europe this time, he had a plan. He was going to a good base in England and his close friend Lucas Parsons was going over as well. But most importantly, Julie was travelling with him most of the time and that gave him more stability. He was able to get away from golf with Julie whenever he needed to."

Stephen Scahill, who travels on his own, agrees having Julie along would have made a difference to the way Campbell felt compared to his previous trip to Europe.

"I doubt whether he would have dwelt too much on the negatives if things had gone wrong again, but it is a release to have someone there. It is different having someone to talk to who cares about what is happening to you. You can also do other things, such as have a nice dinner or go to the movies. It means you aren't thinking about golf all the time whether your game happens to be going well or poorly."

Michael Campbell found Dubai an intriguing place and the field for the Dubai Desert Classic presented a challenge he was now beginning to feel he was ready for.

"Dubai was a bit of a culture shock. The first thing which hit me was the women walking round completely covered, apart from their eyes. You don't see that down Lambton Quay!

"I think I enjoyed myself so much that week because the place was so different. The golf course was fantastic and the field the tournament had drawn was outstanding. It was like playing in a Major. Seven of the world's top ten were there and I didn't feel intimidated.

"It is hard to put my finger on what it was, but I was really looking forward to playing with these guys. In the past I would put on a brave front, but inside was a bit overawed at teeing it up against such names as Fred Couples, Colin Montgomerie, Ernie Els, Greg Norman and Nick Price.

"In Dubai I treated it as just another tournament, which it was despite all the big names. I was feeling pretty good after the New Zealand Open and playing in the company of top players brings the best out in you.

"When you are playing with someone who is struggling you can tend to struggle yourself. If you are playing alongside such as Fred Couples, Nick Price or Greg Norman then you get dragged along.

"I was reasonably satisfied after the first two rounds had brought me a 69 and 71. I had been hitting the ball as solidly as in Wellington. This time the odd putt was dropping and that makes a hell of a difference.

"In the third round I really got the putter going and made nine birdies in a 65. It was a great feeling and by the end of the day I was two shots behind Fred Couples and Colin Montgomerie who were the joint leaders.

"On the final day a 67 left me equal third with Nick Price and Wayne Riley. We were four shots behind Couples who beat Montgomerie by one.

"I was really pleased to get third because a good finish was needed to do so. There was no point during the final round when I thought I could win the tournament. I was always three or four behind and after nine holes was actually eight off the lead.

"A birdie at the 12th got things going and it snowballed from there with birdies at the next two holes. The highlight of the round for me – probably for the whole tournament – was the eagle I made on the last hole. It was the only eagle there on the day and it earned me a £3000 bonus.

"I was looking at just a top-ten finish till the eagle. It enabled me to pass a few players. I had decided to go for broke and my playing partners looked at me as though I was mad when the driver came out on 18, a par five. The tee shot cut the corner over trees and luckily the ball ended up on the fairway.

"From where it finished there was 210 yards over water to the pin. That was when I hit the best three iron of my life to 14 feet and sank the eagle putt. It was perfect, but sometimes you can hit what you think is the perfect shot and it doesn't turn out as you hoped. A wind gust comes up and you finish up going too far left or right and end up in a bunker or out of bounds. This was one of those shots where I hoped for the best and it turned out to be everything I hoped it would be."

Before he left Dubai there was another thrill for Campbell when Fred Couples made special mention of him during his acceptance speech at the prize-giving. It was, Couples said, good to see talented young players arriving on the scene. Couples went on to welcome Michael Campbell to the tour and said he was impressed with the way the young New Zealander had played.

Michael Campbell and myself had an arrangement whereby he would ring if anything worth writing about happened to him during his travels. The calls, as were those to coach Mal Tongue, were usually collect. The morning of his third placing in Dubai, however, the telephone on my desk at *The Dominion* rang and there was Campbell on the line, not an operator asking would I accept the call. Times had changed.

As can be imagined, Campbell was excited, and wanted to share the moment with friends while waiting for a connecting flight to Manila, where the Johnnie Walker Classic was to be played, in Singapore's Changi Airport. He had already spoken to his family and Mal Tongue.

Campbell was able to make the calls because he was travelling business class and enjoying the facilities of the first-class lounge at Changi. He knew how fortunate he was to be able to indulge himself in such a manner.

"Because it was a long flight I had decided to go business class. I wasn't going to arrive in Manila till Tuesday so thought it would be more relaxing to travel in comfort.

"I knew how lucky I was to be able to do that. You think about the guys who are just struggling to find enough money to get to tournaments and feel for them. Had things not panned out the way they did for me I would have been doing the same thing.

"It doesn't help to have you in the right frame of mind for the next tournament if you are scrimping just to get to the course. Travelling the way I did doesn't guarantee you will play well, but at least it gives you the opportunity to perform to the best of your ability.

"I wasn't looking forward to playing in Manila. The last time I had been there was as an amateur with the New Zealand team and had been sick as a dog, so was hoping for better luck this time.

"It was important to put the thoughts of what had happened during that previous trip out of my mind. I tried to be totally positive and Dubai had given me something to build on in that regard.

"The field in Manila was even stronger than Dubai with Bernhard Langer and David Frost coming in. It was the strongest field I had been up against, apart from at the Open at Turnberry.

"A 74 wasn't the best of starts, but after a 66 and 68 I went into the final round two shots behind Fred Couples. That day I had a great chance to win a European Tour event but blew it with a poor piece of course management.

"As on my previous visit to Manila I was making regular trips to the toilet on the morning of the final round. This time though it was more a case of nerves than food poisoning, but you still try to tell yourself it is something other than being tense."

Campbell was playing with Fred Couples and showed the American he had been spot on when he had praised him the previous week in Dubai. A birdie at the first hole and an eagle at the second told Couples that he wasn't going to have things all this own way over the final round. By the seventh hole Michael Campbell had sole possession of the lead at 11 under par only for disaster to strike at the par-four eighth.

"I can still see that damn hole. After a good drive there was only 125 yards to the front of the green, 136 to the pin. Nothing more than an easy nine iron, I thought. I had 120 yards to carry the water guarding the green but just as I hit the ball a big gust of wind came up and I thought 'Oh no.'

"The ball finished up in the water and I made triple bogey. While I fought back well for fourth that one shot had cost me the chance to win because I was only three behind Fred at the end.

"It was pretty hard at the time but I had to keep telling myself that these things happen and that life has to go on. Looking back on it now I'm sure it wouldn't have happened if I'd had Max as my caddy rather than a stand-in. That shot on the eighth was bad course management. All the trouble was at the front of the hole. The only thing at the back was a bunker.

"Even though I had to settle for fourth it was a big day for me. Playing with Fred Couples was a thrill. We might have been basically going head to head but Fred still found the time to encourage me.

"After my disaster at the eighth hole Fred Couples came alongside and said, 'Come on Michael, you can come back from that.' That is something I really love about golf. Playing any other sport there is no way an opponent would be so pleasant. Actually trying to help you through a difficult period even though you are trying to beat them.

"Colin Montgomerie was also in our group. It was a bit daunting at first playing alongside the European tour's top player and one of the leading guys from the American circuit.

"There was a great atmosphere at the Orchard course that day. There must have been around 30,000 people on the course and at times it seemed they were all following our group. They must have seen me as the underdog, which of course I was, because they were encouraging me more than the others. 'Come on, come on Michael' they were shouting at me as I walked to each tee. It was fun and I think Fred and Colin could see that I was enjoying it.

"This was what I had dreamt playing professional golf was all about. Competing against guys like Fred Couples and Colin Montgomerie. It was happening sooner than most people imagined, including myself I suppose if I'm totally honest, but it was happening.

"Two good finishes in fields which contained the world's top players was fantastic. It made the disappointments of Europe eighteen months earlier seem even further in the past. That period had taught me plenty though. It had come hard on the heels of success in my first few weeks as a pro. Now I had to make sure the same thing didn't happen again.

"I'd finished third in Wellington, third in Dubai and fourth in Manila. That really was something to build on and this time I wasn't going to let it slip."

The third and fourth finishes in Dubai and Manila, both part of the Volvo Tour, were the making of Michael Campbell's year. The media who travel with the circuit were now in no doubt as to who

Michael Campbell was, and he headed back to the Australia-New Zealand tour for the Heineken Classic at The Vines in Perth feeling on top of the world. Another fourth placing kept the adrenaline flowing – and the mortgage payments up to date.

With two third and two fourth placings to his credit from four weeks of golf, Michael Campbell was flying high not only on the golf course but off it as well. The media wanted to know all about him, sponsors were keen to attach his name to their products and the praise of peers was ringing in his ears. It would have been easy for Campbell to get carried away, to let it all go to his head. Unlike 1993, however, he was in a more stable situation.

Julie hadn't been with Michael in Dubai or Manila. When he returned home she immediately noticed a difference in his attitude.

"The self-confidence and self-belief which had perhaps been missing before was very apparent. Had I been with him every day for those two weeks I may not have noticed the change but I couldn't miss it when he got back to Australia.

"I think people back in New Zealand also began to believe that Michael Campbell really can play golf and compete with the best. That meant a lot to Michael as well. While Michael has always looked confident and self-assured on the golf course, sometimes away from it he hadn't been. Now he was. After that trip he really believed in himself."

If Campbell needed confirmation that he was now in the big time, it came when he was chosen for the Australasian team to take on Southern Africa in the inaugural Alfred Dunhill Challenge at the Houghton Golf Club in Johannesburg.

Before that there was the Australian Masters on Melbourne's Huntingdale course, and while Campbell had made headlines in New Zealand through his fine performances over the first few weeks of the year he wasn't satisfied with the way he was playing. There had been, he said, a few bad shots creeping into his game even while he was posting good scores.

Mal Tongue arrived from New Zealand, diagnosed that the problem related to Campbell slipping into bad habits with his posture and alignment, and quickly rectified the problem as a six-under round in a pro-am at Royal Melbourne prior to the Masters showed.

Going into the Masters, Campbell felt more confident than in the year's earlier tournaments but his confidence didn't translate onto his card as rounds of 76, 72, 77 and 69 left him tied for 43rd spot in the strong field.

While he would have liked to finish higher, Campbell was satisfied his game was now almost back in the shape he wanted it and couldn't wait to get into a team situation at the South African tournament. He was representing Australasia rather than New Zealand, but it still filled him with pride that those selecting the team rated him among the region's top players.

The Alfred Dunhill Challenge is meant to be the southern hemisphere's answer to the Ryder Cup, which is played for between Europe and the United States every two years. While the Dunhill Challenge is unlikely for many years to mean as much as the Ryder Cup, which is steeped in history, Australasia and Southern Africa had to start somewhere.

It was a special moment for the Australasian players when they set off on their historic journey, with no one more excited than Michael Campbell.

Terry Gale, who had just resigned as chairman of the Australia-New Zealand PGA after a nine-year tenure, was the non-playing captain of the Australasian team and he paid Michael Campbell the ultimate compliment by describing him as "the best swinger in our team". There is nothing special about that comment on the surface till you realise that also in the Australasian team were Greg Norman, Frank Nobilo, Greg Turner, Vijay Singh, Robert Allenby, Wayne Grady, Lucas Parsons and Mike Clayton.

It was a big call by Gale but Campbell didn't let him down. In the morning fourball on the opening day of competition Campbell teamed up with Greg Norman. While the Australasian pair lost three and one to Retief Goosen and David Frost, who made an amazing ten birdies in a 15-hole stretch from the third tee to the 17th green, Michael Campbell did his share to keep them in the match with seven birdies.

Campbell lost twice during the tournament. He and Wayne Grady were beaten in the foursomes, the same pairing had a half, and Campbell had the satisfaction of winning his only singles match when he was one up on Wayne Westner. Southern Africa had the last laugh though as they won 14-11.

"It was the first time I had played with Greg in a competition round. In the past it had only been in practice rounds so this was my first chance to be close to him in a really competitive atmosphere.

"While we concentrated on our own games I studied him closely at every opportunity and learnt a lot. The way he holds himself round the golf course, his body language, his routine, how he maintains a level of concentration . . . everything.

"Being part of the team was a big thrill both on and off the course. I had met all the guys in the team before but it had been mainly small talk. The trip to South Africa broke the ice. It gave me the chance to get to know them socially because it was a fun week for the families as well as the players. All the wives, girlfriends and fiancees were invited and we had a ball.

"After the second round on the Friday the players and their partners, along with the media guys, were invited to a fabulous mansion for a barbecue.

"For an hour or so we were entertained by African dancers and all the time Turns and Frank were badgering me about showing them some New Zealand culture and doing the haka.

"I said it would be too embarrassing but they wouldn't let go and eventually all my teammates were saying 'Cambo, it's time for the haka.' In the end I gave in and did it.

"I'm glad I did. The scene was perfectly set. The atmosphere, the circumstances . . . everything was right. Two cultures were meeting. While I was performing the haka there were some kids behind trying to do it with me. They had seen the All Blacks do it on television.

"The whole trip was brilliant, not only the golf but what surrounded the tournament.

"For me the highlight was meeting Nelson Mandela the night before the event began. It was a dinner for the players and officials only, no partners.

"We were all in awe of Nelson Mandela. When you looked at him sat there so quietly you couldn't help but think about what he had been through over so many years. And now he was president of South Africa.

"Even people like Greg Norman and Nick Price were spellbound. It is usually them who people are in awe of. Now the tables were turned. I've been lucky enough to have some special moments to savour so far in my life. Vancouver with the other guys in the New Zealand team and what happened at St Andrews. That night ranks right up there along with those.

"While in Africa a few of us – Robert and Nadina Allenby, Lucas and Gabriel Parsons and Julie and myself – took the opportunity to go on safari for six days.

"It was great fun even though we were bounced around in a jeep for up to six hours some days. That was all made worthwhile when we saw a leopard which we were told was quite rare.

"On safari we stayed in nice places but they were all open air. Lying in bed under a mosquito net in open air huts we could hear lions roaring. I couldn't help thinking the mossie nets wouldn't be much use if a lion came in for a look and was pleased that they had guys posted round the perimeter making sure they stayed out.

"Whether they kept their eyes open all night I'm not sure. There was one night when we listened to a lion roar for about half an hour. Next morning there were lion tracks through the camp.

"The signs in the camp said that elephants, which would come in and drink out of the swimming pool, had right of way. We didn't argue, but it was an elephant which gave us our biggest shock on the trip. It was even worse than David Frost's ten birdies.

"We went round a blind corner in the jeep and there in front of us was a bull elephant. He stood there staring at us before giving us what the guide said was a mock charge. As the elephant came hurtling towards us the guide was telling us to keep cool and calm.

"Keep cool! With this elephant, weighing God knows how many tons, and its massive tusks racing at you. I nearly stopped breathing.

"Apparently it just wanted to stamp its authority but I wasn't too sure about that. It stopped six feet from the jeep, turned round, snorted, waved its trunk and went. I tell everyone that it was a fantastic experience but at the time I was scared to death.

"We hired our own plane for the six days which ensured we got about a lot. One night I started thinking about just how lucky I am to be able to play golf so well. The average age of the six people in that plane was 25 and here we were jetting about Africa. If it wasn't for golf none of us would have got such a chance. We have a lot to be grateful for."

13

Making an Impact

Michael Campbell arrived in Europe already in the top ten on the Volvo order of merit courtesy of his earnings in Dubai and Manila.

The European Tour's expansion into Asia was attracting more top players, with Fred Couples making the most of the opportunity to play in Dubai's Desert Classic and the Johnnie Walker Classic in Manila by winning both. In those same tournaments Michael Campbell had proved he could compete with the best.

Now Campbell wanted to continue that form in Europe itself, particularly in England where he was to base himself for the northern summer.

Home for the next few months was to be Tooting Bec in London, where Michael and Julie would share a house with Martin Boswell and Brenda Horsfall. The stylish house with a beautiful rose garden in a quiet street provided the perfect environment and atmosphere in which Campbell could prepare for a busy European season. It was also somewhere to relax when he wasn't playing golf, being well away from the Bagshot area – tagged Ramsay Street – where most New Zealand and Australian golfers live.

Between leaving South Africa and arriving in London, Campbell had spent ten days in Wellington working with Mal Tongue. He had also played the Malaysian Masters in Kuala Lumpur where he finished tenth, leaving him with an expectant feeling when he and Julie arrived at Heathrow Airport.

The Open . . .

A moment to savour for Dad. Thomas Campbell carries his son's bag down St Andrews' first fairway during a practice round for the British Open.

Father and son on one of St Andrews' most famous landmarks, the Bridge of Sighs.

"That shot" out of the bunker at St Andrews' infamous Road Hole from a different perspective showing the club house in the background. Michael signed the photograph as a souvenir for family and friends.

The frustration for a coach being outside the ropes. Mal Tongue, nervous as usual, watches Michael play the sixth hole during the final round of the British Open.

PHIL SHELDON

A wonderful memento of a great day. The player recording the lowest round in the British Open receives a solid silver replica of his scorecard. Michael Campbell won that trophy in 1995 at St Andrews.

This is better than riding a bike in Titahi Bay! Michael disembarks from his friend JP McManus' private jet in London after flying from Scotland the day after finishing third in the British Open.

At least we can still smile. Julie and Michael relax after the traumatic last day of the British Open.

The sun seemed brighter, the wind less chilly, than when he had arrived at the same airport two years earlier. In reality it was Michael Campbell who had changed. There was a bounce in his step familiar to New Zealanders and Australians but as yet not often seen by European golf followers.

Campbell made a promising start by finishing equal eighth at the Catalonia Open in Girona, and was in 39th position when rain caused the abandonment of the Cannes Open after two rounds the following week.

Then came two missed cuts within three weeks – his only misses of the year – at the Italian Open in Milan and the Spanish Open at Club de Campo. Sandwiched between was a creditable 15th placing at the Benson and Hedges International Open at the St Mellion course in Plymouth, England.

Such is now the depth of the European Tour no player is able to dominate. When the field lined up for the British PGA championship at Surrey's Wentworth Club, apart from Couples' two wins in Asia, every European tournament had been won by a different player. It was to be Bernhard Langer's turn at Wentworth, but Michael Campbell, with his red socks, would be the one grabbing the headlines in New Zealand with a stunning finish which took him to within a stroke of Langer and into a tie for second place with Per-Ulrik Johansson, caddy Max Cunningham's former employer.

"I played solidly during the first three rounds at Wentworth with 69, 73 and 71. In the fourth round, however, I was struggling a bit. For the first 14 holes it was a battle to stay level with the card, needing eight one putts in succession to do so. One of those putts was for bogey after I'd been in the water on the eighth, one was for birdie, and the other six for par.

"From tee to green my game was poor but my short game was brilliant. That day showed me that if you can hang in and keep somewhere near the lead anything can happen. It started to happen for me on the 15th hole where I holed a seven-iron for eagle when I was hanging around 20th position.

"For that second shot there was 194 yards to the pin, downhill, down breeze. The ball pitched probably ten feet short of the pin, spun left and into the hole. One shot like that can change your whole state of mind. The adrenalin started pumping and my confidence began to bubble. Perhaps it was the red socks which did the trick. New Zealand were involved in the America's Cup and I kept reading about Peter Blake's lucky red socks. I thought it couldn't do any harm to be patriotic and wear some myself. It worked.

"On the 16th and 17th holes putts from around ten feet gave me birdies, and I picked up another on the last from twenty feet.

"When I finished, Bernhard Langer still had five holes to play. Everyone was asking did I think he would slip up and give me the title. My answer that I expected him to carry on and win was honest.

"Langer is a world-class player and under pressure there is probably none better than him. He needed to make a mistake to give me the win or a playoff, but I didn't expect that to happen. It wasn't a surprise that he made his way safely home.

"Players do make mistakes in such situations. You lose focus on what you are doing and attempt a shot you wouldn't normally consider. Your concentration slips and you do stupid things. That had been my problem when I was leading in Manila and took a nine-iron for my second shot at the eighth when, with all the trouble at the front of the hole, the sensible club was an eight iron.

"I'm sure it has happened to Bernhard as well in the past, but somehow you don't think of Langer ever making such an error of judgement. He goes out on the course and just keeps grinding it out, making pars and pulling a birdie out of the hat when it is needed.

"Finishing so well was a big thrill for me though. I had picked up five shots on the last four holes for a 67. Just as importantly it was the first time I had really shown what I could do in England. It was nice to be recognised where I was going to be based."

Why Campbell had been struggling from tee to green came to light two days before his next tournament, the English Open at the Forest of Arden course in Warwickshire. Leading New Zealand amateurs Mark Brown and Marcus Wheelhouse, in England to play some amateur events, called in to see Campbell and immediately picked up a slight flaw in his swing.

"Mark and Marcus noticed a difference in my swing right away. They told me my posture was out of kilter and that my shoulders were too open. They helped me adjust it. The three of us work with Mal Tongue so they picked out the fault straight away. You could say they were Mal's eyes.

"It made a big difference because I was able to shoot a five-under 67 on the first day of the English Open. After such a start it was disappointing to finish only 24th."

Between the English Open and his next tournament, the Deutsche Bank Open-TPC of Europe in Hamburg where he finished seventh, Michael Campbell was invited to play in a pro-am in Ireland. He accepted, fell in love with the country, and made himself a new friend.

"I had heard so much about Ireland that I couldn't resist going for a couple of days. The country was every bit as lovely as they said. The people are golf mad and they introduced me to Guinness. I didn't like it at all the first time but it began to grow on me. Now I love it.

"The pro-am was organised by JP McManus. For some reason he and I just hit it off and were quickly getting on like a house on fire. I didn't realise when we first got together how wealthy he was. On the tour you meet a lot of wealthy guys who love showing off how much money they have. JP is nothing like that. He doesn't say a lot about himself. When I asked him what he did for a living he said he was a wheeler dealer.

"After the pro-am he flew myself and three other players from Shannon to Hamburg in his private jet. There we were in this brand new $25 million Falcon. It was a different world.

"I decided then and there that I want one myself. I hate airports with the queuing you have to do at the best of times. One day I intend to have a private jet; my own little toy. Some people might say it is pretentious to talk like that but it is important to have ambitions. That is one of mine."

The following month Campbell was drinking Guinness again at the Irish Open in Kilkenny. He tied for 12th there and picked up another nice cheque for finishing 18th at the Scottish Open on the difficult Carnoustie course the week before the British Open.

Twelve months earlier Michael Campbell had arrived in Turnberry for his first Open unheralded and virtually unknown after getting through pre-qualifying. It was a completely different story at St Andrews. With five top ten finishes and £186,220 in prize money on the European Tour in his rookie year, Campbell was getting rave reviews.

Experienced writers were picking Campbell in their ten best prospects for the Open, despite the bookmakers offering 100-1 against him winning. The *Daily Mail's* Michael McDonnell listed him as one of six potential winners, saying, "It may seem unusual to include the name of a man who has yet to win on the European Tour, but Campbell is no ordinary player."

Getting so close – only one shot away from forcing his way into the playoff – and missing out was obviously extremely disappointing for Campbell. He was, however, making sure he concentrated on the positives which came out of the Open rather than the one negative – that he failed to hold on to his lead in the last round. How many world-class players have been in his position going into the last day of a Major championship and ended up the same way. Plenty, including the biggest names in golf. Ask Greg Norman!

Campbell had shown he could compete with the world's best golfers on one of the world's toughest courses and beat all but two of them. And he was only one shot away.

It was important to Campbell that he played well two weeks later at the Swedish Open in Barseback. He said he didn't want to be known as a one-week wonder, though how anyone could think that after what he had achieved over the first seven months of the year is hard to imagine.

In Barseback, Campbell began strongly with 69 and 71. In the third round he consolidated with a 70 before dropping away slightly in the last round with 76, a number he was beginning to dislike intensely, to finish tied for tenth.

It had been difficult for Campbell to concentrate fully during his time in Sweden. He did his best to focus on the job in hand, constantly telling himself that every tournament was important. Subconsciously, however, Campbell had been thinking about the Open and the tournament he would be contesting the following week at Los Angeles' Riviera Golf Club – the USPGA.

When Campbell arrived in Los Angeles on the Monday night to prepare for a second Major within three weeks his nerves were already tingling. More experienced players had told him that playing in a Major was always something special, no matter how many times you did it.

Nerves were usually in evidence going into a regular event, they said, but a Major . . . that was different again. The atmosphere, the huge crowds, having the world's top players gathered in front of hundreds of media, and millions watching on television throughout the world. That is a Major.

"What they had told me was right. The four Major Championships are different. The hairs on the back of your neck stand up when you walk through the gates of the course.

"Going into another Major so soon after playing well at the Open was exciting. I was full of confidence and determined to show what had happened at St Andrews wasn't a fluke. There were moments, however, leading up to the USPGA, while we were settling into Los Angeles, that I felt some apprehension.

"It was probably fear at not living up to what I had achieved in Scotland. You can be confident and apprehensive at the same time. Even though you feel great it doesn't take much to ruin a round. One shot can do that.

"Everyone's expectations of me were so much higher because of what had happened two weeks earlier. The newspapers were saying 'Michael Campbell is here after a top performance at the British Open and should do well again'.

"My expectations were also higher, and so were those of people watching on television back home in New Zealand. When the tournament finished I rang Mal and he told me about a telephone call he had received from a man asking what was wrong with me that I could only finish 17th in the USPGA. What was wrong with me? You begin to wonder what people think you are.

"If you do well in your chosen sport in New Zealand, be it as an All Black, a Silver Fern, a shooter or a squash player and you make one mistake or have one bad day it is all magnified. Because I had done well at St Andrews some people expected me to go well all the time. It doesn't work that way.

"It is impossible to be on top of your game all the time, particularly in a game like golf. Things change week by week. Sometimes you can't quite see your putts. The next week the opposite happens and you can see every little break. If you feel good and are putting well it makes it so much easier.

"In a tournament 144 guys start off on a Thursday. All of them are quality golfers and which one wins becomes a combination of many things. There can only be one winner each week. Who it is can depend on a very fine line.

"Winning is nice. No, it's great. But it isn't everything. Learning about yourself and your game is nice too. Every time I go out to play, wherever it is in the world, I am learning. Learning from what happens to me and learning from those I am playing with, not only about their golf but about them as a person.

"That is why I want to play practice rounds with the top players. On the Tuesday of the USPGA I played with Greg Norman, Jack Nicklaus and Vijay Singh. If you can't learn from those guys there is something wrong with you.

"Norman is brilliant but when you consider how long Nicklaus has been playing and how many major titles he has won it is mind boggling. Just to share his thoughts is a privilege.

"These players are only too willing to share their knowledge with someone like myself who hasn't been on the tour long. You just have to ask them.

"During practice rounds you ask them where is the best place to go off the tee, left-hand side or right-hand side? Where do they think the pins will be for the tournament? Once you know that you can go and have a putt in that area of the green and a good look at it.

"If the wind blows from right to left or left to right, where is the best place to miss the green? Is it short right, short left or through the back. At St Andrews, for instance, it is better to be through the green rather than short of it.

"I take all these things in. The one thing I've done this year is to listen to other people's opinions. Obviously they often differ. I drag in and filter out the things I need to know. I'm always looking, watching and listening.

"Once you play with the best players you start to play like them. You are in their slip stream a little bit. When you talk to them it is always positive, whereas when you play with guys who are struggling on the Australasian or European tour it is the negative things you hear about, because that is how they are feeling.

"Right from the start I made sure I hung around the best players. I want to think like them. For some reason they have really accepted me. I think it is respect. They know I can play the game."

It is hardly surprising that Michael Campbell began to feel apprehensive in the days leading up to the USPGA. It seemed everyone at the Riviera Golf Club wanted to congratulate him on the way he had played at St Andrews.

Between the locker room and practice fairway or putting green it was the fans who wanted to shake his hand or pat him on the back. Once at the practice area it was players such as Larry Mize, Scott Hoch and Mark O'Meara who wanted to shake hands with the New Zealander.

"I couldn't believe the impact I had made in the United States. It shows the influence television can have, especially ESPN. People were whispering as I went past 'That's Michael Campbell, that guy from the British Open.'

"This time people knew I was Michael Campbell from New Zealand. That I was a Maori, not a native American or Mexican or Indian or Pakistani. That was important."

Everyone in golf knows Campbell as Cambo, though Sam Torrance tried to attach the nickname Soupie, after Campbell's soup which is popular in Britain. It didn't catch on, but the mischievous Torrance still uses it because he knows the Kiwi doesn't like it.

On the Tuesday at Riviera, Campbell was on the practice green, about 20 yards from the first tee, when he heard someone shout "Cambo".

"I turned round and it was Tom Watson. 'Do you want to join us and make up a four?' he asked me. I had to tell him I was going off in a few minutes with some other guys. But Tom Watson was another of my early heroes, someone I aspired to be like and he was asking me to play with him.

"That night back at the hotel I went through the day in my mind. It was hard to believe what had happened to me. Not only had Tom asked for a game but Lanny Wadkins and Mark O'Meara had wanted me to go with them."

Do some of the other rookies, for that is what he still was despite what had happened over the past seven months, show any jealousy because he hangs around with the big names?

"Perhaps some are jealous, but I never hear about it."

That may be because it is hard to dislike Michael Campbell with his easy-going, laid-back, sunny nature. Confident yes, but big-headed, no. That is something those at the top of their profession appreciate.

"Greg Turner told me that when I first went to Europe I was very cocky. I've lost that now because I don't need to be cocky. When you are young you want to be the best player in the world, so you tell everyone that is what is going to happen.

"When you reach the stage where you are as good as the next guy you don't have to say anything. They know it. They can feel your presence."

The tournament itself provided satisfaction for Campbell who tied for 17th with an eight under 276 for the four rounds.

A second round 65 was the highlight. To shoot 65 in successive majors was an achievement which didn't go unnoticed by players and media alike. During that round Campbell narrowly missed hitting Julie when he pushed his drive into trees after being distracted while swinging on the tee of Riviera's par-five 11th hole.

Julie ducked for cover, and looked up to see her fiancee's ball come to rest alongside a dirt access road. It was then Campbell showed his class by hitting a superb five-iron shot which found a gap through the towering gum trees which stood between him and the green. For his third shot Campbell hit a wedge shot to nine feet and calmly rammed the birdie putt into the hole. With that five-iron shot Campbell reaffirmed he belonged in Major championships.

The following week, Campbell took part in the Invitational tournament at Castle Rock. It is a stableford type competition with five points for an eagle, three for birdie, none for par and minus two for bogey. He made the first cut, but missed the second and tied for 26th.

Before arriving in Los Angeles, Campbell had decided the two weeks he was to spend in America would give him an idea how he felt about the country, with a view to playing the United States tour in the future. When he got back to London Campbell reflected on what he had found.

"The crowds are much bigger in America and the lifestyle is a lot different. In the United States you get a car every week, it is cheaper to live there than in Europe, the same language is spoken throughout the tour and you don't have to change money all the time.

"In Europe you go through passport control twice a week, change currency all the time and learn bits of the language. In restaurants you guess or use sign language. But you get by, and it can actually be a lot of fun."

Campbell's first European tournament on his return was the

European Masters in Switzerland and there were fond memories of the course on which it was being played, the Crans-sur-Sierre. It was there that Campbell had kicked off his Challenge Tour campaign the previous year with a win.

Campbell's liking for the course came through again as he tied for 11th with rounds of 71, 66, 69 and 70. One of the key components of Campbell's profitable 1995 campaign was consistency. It wasn't a case of second or third one week and missing the cut the next. When he left Switzerland Campbell had played 21 tournaments in just over eight months. In ten of those he had finished in the top ten, including being in the first four six times. At the Trophee Lancome in Paris the following week he tied for 14th.

The Dunhill British Masters at Northampton came next. It was to be another case of so near but yet so far for Michael Campbell as he finished one stroke behind that great Scottish competitor Sam Torrance.

The final round turned into a head-to-head battle between Torrance and Campbell, and if there was one thing the New Zealander could take solace from it was that, despite all the invaluable experience 42-year-old Torrance had picked up during his 25 years as a professional, he felt the pressure just as much as Campbell who was in his rookie year on the European circuit.

The intensity of the battle between Campbell and Torrance, particularly over the last six holes, was such that Torrance couldn't at the end control his emotions and broke down in tears. "You would think," Torrance said at the time, "that after 24 years on the tour that I would have learnt to control my emotions. I couldn't today."

A disappointed Campbell said after the round, "I'm always knocking on the door and, as the saying goes, if you knock enough the door will open one day.

"It was hard to take at the time. I was hurting pretty bad that night. I kept talking about a learning experience but it was getting me down.

"I had actually got the lead outright after a birdie at the 13th, but for some reason misread the green on 16 and three-putted. Going into the last, which was a par-five, I was level with Sam but put my tee shot in the lake.

"I don't know what happened on the 18th tee. I don't think I was trying to force the issue. It was just one of those breaks that happen in golf. The pleasing thing was that I had hung in with Sam who is a fierce competitor.

"For all that, I had really wanted to win that tournament. After being so close so many times during the year I needed to win again."

That loss appeared to knock Campbell's confidence. At the Irish Open he tied for 45th and was equal 57th at the German Masters as the European Tour drew to a close. In the final tournament, the Volvo Masters at Valderrama in Spain, Campbell had regained his touch to finish 28th in a strong field.

Michael Campbell had set his heart on winning a European Tour event in 1995. That he didn't was a disappointment but he had to be proud of a European campaign which brought him two seconds, two thirds – one in the British Open – and a fourth, along with five other top ten finishes.

To top it off, Campbell finished fifth on a star-studded order of merit with earnings of £400,977, by far the best performed rookie on the circuit.

There was further disappointment when it was ruled Campbell couldn't win the Rookie of the Year title because he wasn't European. It was a ridiculous decision but, typically, Campbell refused to condemn it.

"I know I was Rookie of the Year and that is what matters to me. Okay, they couldn't give it to me officially but everyone knows I won it. For the second time in three years I was Rookie of the Year on a professional golf circuit."

Despite all the money he had won, and the accolades he was being showered with, Michael Campbell couldn't settle till he had won a tournament. He was grateful for the plaudits from media and his peers, but winning a tournament was what was driving him on.

"It was very frustrating. Right from the start of the year I had been getting close without being able to make the breakthrough. The previous year I had won four tournaments. It didn't matter that they were secondary tour events. There is no feeling like winning. You don't think about the size of the cheque you will be getting when they hand you the trophy. The feeling of holding a trophy in your hands is special.

"The reason I'm playing golf is to win tournaments. The money is great but winning is everything. While we are all materialistic to an extent I can honestly say the golf means more to me than money.

"It is all intertwined. Beating the top players is important and generally they only play in the richer tournaments, so if you are finishing ahead of them you are going to be making money.

"Having Julie with me was invaluable when I was getting so close only to finish up disappointed again. I began to feel it would never happen."

Julie's heart went out to Michael when she saw how hurt he was each time he got close without being able to finish the job.

"Michael was so disappointed at those times. He would be quite hard on himself for the first couple of hours. Then it would come in waves. He would be fine for a while and then perhaps later in the night, or maybe the next day, he would start thinking about it again."

Campbell went straight from Valderrama to Jakarta for the Alfred Dunhill Masters, the first tournament on the second stage of the 1995 Australia-New Zealand circuit. Julie returned to Sydney to prepare for their wedding, which was to take place in January.

In the first two rounds at Jakarta's Emeralda Golf Club, Campbell shot 69 and 65 on the par-71 course to trail Craig Parry by three strokes. In the third round Campbell was three under the card on 68 while Parry had a one over 71 to leave the New Zealander one ahead going into the last 18 holes.

Campbell had a good feeling about the last round but was wary after what had happened to him over the previous ten months. He was also well aware that players the calibre of Parry, Mark Mouland, Vijay Singh and Wayne Grady were snapping at his heels, waiting for a chance to pounce. When he spoke to Julie by telephone on Saturday night she knew the emotional state Campbell was in.

"I was probably more nervous than him. I knew that this was one he had to win. Subtly it was hanging over his head . . . being the bridesmaid. When people keep saying it over and over it can get to you. I didn't want him to have to go back to Australia and New Zealand with people saying it was a shame he hadn't managed a win during the year.

"If this one slipped away the hurting would have continued, but I didn't want him knowing how I felt. I attempted to be blase about the whole situation, trying to make it sound like one of the Challenge Tour events he used to win easily.

" 'Oh, look. You are in such a great position, just go out and win it like you did on the Challenge Tour.'

"When I spoke to him after the fourth round and he had won he sounded absolutely dead. He put everything, his whole heart and soul, into those 18 holes."

I know what Julie was talking about. Michael Campbell spoke to me straight after his round from the media centre in Jakarta. He sounded so relieved, but shattered at the same time. Usually bubbly, Campbell was more subdued in success than when finishing second and trying to put on a brave face.

"The relief just poured out of me that night in Jakarta. It is impossible to describe how I felt. I could say elated, but that isn't quite right . . . it was different to how I had ever felt before. Someone told me during the press conference that the prizemoney for coming first took me over a million for the year, but at that moment money was the last thing on my mind.

"I had wanted to win so badly it was hurting going into the last 18 holes. When it was over I was just glad it was over. All year I had been playing so well that I knew a win had to come sometime. But I began to wonder when.

"The wait had been terrible. You hear people wondering if you knew how to win. That success in Jakarta took a huge weight off my shoulders. The last couple of hours of the round were a blur, though I believed I was going to win it after the 14th hole.

"I had a two-shot lead playing it, and while I birdied the hole Craig bogeyed it for a two-shot swing."

Campbell had a brilliant six-under 65 in that last round to finish 17-under on 267 and eventually had five shots to spare over Australian Craig Parry and Wales' Mark Mouland, who tied for second.

Unfortunately the celebrations had to be put on hold with a 5am rise the following morning for a flight to China where, along with Frank Nobilo, he was representing New Zealand at the World Cup.

New Zealand tied for fifth in China with Campbell quite satisfied with his performance in shooting 69, 71, 67 and 68. At least he finished each round with the same ball, which was more than Frank Nobilo could say after having his ball stolen by a spectator during the second round, something which also happened to Scotland's Sam Torrance in the last round.

When Campbell finished 37th at the Phoenix Open in Japan and 28th in the Australian Open at Melbourne's Kingston Heath he appeared to be tiring after a hectic schedule which had him playing in six countries over a six-week period.

That theory was laid to rest at The Lakes in Sydney when Craig Parry and Michael Campbell had the finish of the Greg Norman Holden Classic to themselves. This time Parry came out on top by one stroke with American Brad Faxon three shots further adrift in third place.

Parry led Campbell by two going into the final round and the pair had a titanic battle throughout the round with Campbell fighting back from a mid-round stumble to be level playing the par-three last hole.

With the adrenalin coursing through his veins, Michael Campbell hit a five-iron further than he would normally expect on the 194-yard hole. The ball went through the back of the green, Campbell chipped and two-putted for bogey and the title went to Parry who made his par.

"Again that was just one of the things which happen in golf, but thank God I had won in Jakarta. Had I been still looking for my first win of the year and that had happened I would have been devastated."

As he prepared to cross the Tasman for the AMP Air New Zealand Open, Michael Campbell reflected on a marvellous, if at times frustrating, 11 months.

"It was a combination of a lot of things. My personal life was very settled with Julie. We had gone through a few problems the previous year, but that is going to happen in any relationship. The important thing was we had ironed them out and were to be married.

"While ball striking has always been the strong part of my game, I've often been below average with chipping and putting. During 1995 it improved and I was third on the putting stats in Europe. I used to be a flashy putter but now I'm more consistent.

"One of the reasons for the improvement in my short game is

that I've asked the best players for advice on it. Larry Mize, Ben Crenshaw, Colin Montgomerie, Bernhard Langer, Greg Norman – you name them, I've asked them.

"I went to Seve Ballesteros and Greg Turner about chipping and Peter Fowler and Frank Nobilo about short chips and bunker play.

"I was also a lot fitter during 1995 than during the previous 12 months because I started eating the right foods. I cut out meat and potatoes. Instead I ate fish, vegetables and greens. I felt fitter and played better because of it."

The amalgamation of the New Zealand Open and Air New Zealand Shell tournaments into one $500,000 event was a logical move and while American Scott Hoch was invited to play as one of the star attractions Michael Campbell was the player everyone wanted to watch.

Huge galleries followed Campbell over the first two days. A first round one under 69 left Campbell in a comfortable position only for disaster to strike on the sixth hole during the second round.

Campbell had been experiencing a few problems with his left wrist for the previous two or three weeks but put it down to wear and tear from the punishing schedule he had just completed. He wasn't overly concerned. Once the New Zealand Open was concluded he would be able to have a well-earned rest.

Nothing could have prepared Michael Campbell for the pain which shot up his left arm after playing his second shot on the sixth hole. While his playing partners moved on Campbell sat in the middle of the fairway, willing the pain to go away. It didn't and while the rest of the field continued Campbell withdrew and made his way back to the clubhouse.

The withdrawal shook everyone, on course and watching on television. Campbell sat disconsolately in the locker room not wanting to talk to anyone, preferring to wait an hour or two for a press conference.

It was there that Campbell and the tour physiotherapist explained what had been diagnosed as a tendon injury. It shouldn't, the physiotherapist said, cause too many problems. A rest would put things right and Campbell should be able to continue as normal in the New Year.

It sounded good but on the Saturday when he was having the

injury treated while everyone else was out playing, Campbell started to think things might not be as simple as they first seemed.

Two weeks later Michael was beginning to wonder if he would play again.

14

A Touring Life

Aglamorous life, or a hell of a way to make a living? How someone feels about playing golf for a living will very likely depend on what his form is like when asked that question.

As in all walks of life, there is no black and white answer. Besides the opposite ends of the scale – at the top where such as Nick Faldo, Greg Norman and Nick Price look down on the mere mortals, to the bottom where young rookies risk eating from street vendors in Bangkok because it saves them a few dollars – there are numerous grey areas

The world of professional golf is no different to any other workplace. Those at the top of the pile get the perks, those at the bottom battle along picking up the crumbs, hoping to one day enjoy the spoils of their endeavours.

The Air New Zealand Shell Open was always one of the last events on the Australia-New Zealand circuit. Consequently it attracted any number of young pros desperate to earn enough money at the tournament to get them into the top 100 on the order of merit. Being in the top 100 would enable them to avoid the trauma of attending qualifying school in an attempt to regain their card. If they could get into the top 60 and avoid pre-qualifying for tournaments the following year, all the better.

Inevitably one of the real battlers of the tour would throw up a good round at the beginning of the Air New Zealand tournament. To see the hope and excitement in their eyes when that happened made

Tooting Bec . . .

Martin Boswell and Brenda Horsfall (left) were always waiting at their home in Tooting Bec with dinner and a smile on Sunday nights when Michael and Julie returned from European tournaments.

Off to do the washing. Michael trades clubs for a bike on Monday morning to go to the laundrette.

I cooked this! Brenda Horsfall and Michael show off his culinary efforts.

Caddy Max Cunningham and his wife Julie join Michael at a barbecue in the garden of their Tooting Bec base.

Michael and Australian professional Lucas Parsons, who first met as amateurs at a junior championship in New Zealand, in a lighthearted mood.

Dressed up for a night out. Michael, Julie, Nadina and Robert Allenby.

Grant Duncan, Michael's friend and accountant, Nick Price and Michael at a Masters International get-together in Florida.

"That's My Man!" Unassuming Irish millionaire JP McManus with his horse "That's My Man" after it won a race in Ireland. McManus now wants to call one of his horses "Michael Campbell"!

up for having to watch the despair of others as they lost any prospect they had of picking up a decent cheque with a poor opening round.

If those who started well were still in contention going into the final day, and virtually assured of enough money to allay their fears of going back to school, an almost carefree attitude would replace the intense approach they had arrived with.

Many of the young, and not so young, professionals on the Australasian tour spend the whole year just trying to make enough to survive. Comparing that with the lifestyles of the rich and famous who compete for the big money at Major championships and other prestigious tournaments is like looking at night and day.

The Turnberry Hotel, which stands in regal majesty looking down on a championship golf course which has a modern but tasteful clubhouse, is a symbol of success. When a golfer can afford to stay in luxury at the Turnberry Hotel he has made it. The same applies to The Old Course Hotel at St Andrews.

Michael Campbell stayed at The Old Course Hotel while playing for New Zealand at the Dunhill Cup during 1995, and was new enough to such surroundings that he couldn't resist taking photographs from his bedroom window.

Places like Turnberry and St Andrews aren't part of the normal golfing world, however. They are for the big names competing in Major championships or Dunhill Cups. On the European Tour the rest of the year is spent waiting in airport lounges, passing through passport control twice a week, travelling to and from hotels and airports, changing currency . . .

If a golfer is playing well he will be able to stay wherever he wishes without worrying about the cost. There is also a chance that those running the tournament will have paid the golfer's airfare to get him there. Those who are going through a barren patch will want to watch their pennies without looking as if they are scrimping; putting on a front for their peers.

Michael Campbell's performances during 1995 had made him one of the players tournament organisers wanted. It was nice to be wanted, even better to be looked after. The travelling and hotels could still be a drag, but at least he had Julie with him, and it was a much different story to when the pair were making their way round Europe on the Challenge Tour.

A typical week for the Campbells during their time in Europe now is:

Tuesday:

Out of bed when it is still dark, around 5am. The night before Michael and Julie will have packed their respective bags. Many people would do it differently, but that is the way which works for them, according to Michael.

"Our regular taxi driver, Tony Tucker, picks us up from the house. We have agreed on a set price for each trip to and from the airport, but most importantly Tony is reliable. That is important when your job relies on being somewhere at a certain time.

"The trip from Tooting Bec to the airport isn't like the twenty minutes most of the Kiwis and Aussies have from where they live in Bagshot. With a smooth run it takes us about forty minutes. If there is a lot of traffic it can be up to an hour, but the time passes easily the way we chat with Tony.

"Once at the airport we take off to wherever that week's tournament is. Our arrangements are made through one of the three travel companies which take care of travel for the golf professionals. You book your flight and accommodation with them and they check you into 'golf' hotels, which understand a player's needs.

"Another advantage is that they have a bus waiting to drive you to the hotels, which can be an hour or more from the airport. Often the caddies are on the same plane. They don't usually stay at the same hotels as the players. They do, however, jump on the bus to save money.

"Hotels never seem to be close to the airport. I travel in my golf clothes so I can go straight to the course by about lunch time while Julie goes to the hotel."

Julie has her priorities sorted out in advance.

"I check in all our stuff and empty the mini bar. Then it is off to the local supermarket, where everyone probably speaks a language I don't understand, to buy stuff to fill up the mini bar. I don't care how much money Michael earns, I think it is a total waste to spend five dollars on a bottle of water.

"After unpacking it is often impossible to get an iron, but I do the domestic stuff while Michael is at the course registering and getting his bearings.

"Tuesday night we usually chill out and do nothing. We have been up since the crack of dawn so probably have an early night."

Wednesday:

Pro-am day. In the early part of the year Campbell wasn't playing in the pro-ams so their schedule was a little easier. Now he is in them all, though they are different to what he was used to in New Zealand and Australia.

"The pro-ams before big tournaments in New Zealand and Australia are taken seriously, with the dinner which follows usually being formal. In Europe they are much more casual. Sometimes there is an informal dinner, other times nothing at all.

"Each night is really our own. Often we have dinner with other players. We never go sightseeing. Sometimes Julie will go with a girlfriend on Wednesday while I'm playing the pro-am but not often. We want to do that sort of thing together when we get chance. One day we'll do a European tour without golf tournaments getting in the way.

"We try to make dinner a bit interesting if we are close to the centre of a city. Mostly though we don't do much apart from concentrating on the golf tournament. That isn't the way everyone approaches it but that is what we are there for. I believe if you start doing a lot of other things it deters you from your main purpose.

Thursday:

Golf, dinner, bed.

Friday:

Golf, dinner, bed.

Saturday:

Golf, dinner, bed. "Boring, isn't it?"

Sunday:

Julie takes over while Michael concentrates on his golf.

"Hopefully he is teeing off late because that means he is in contention to win. We pack our suitcases and take them with us to the golf course. If we have to stay for the prize-giving, great, though it means a few dramas for me as I change the travel plans.

"If there is a change I also have to make sure I get hold of Tony Tucker because he will be planning to meet our original flight. It is just nice to know he will be at the airport waiting for us. We normally arrive back around 10.30 at night and it is one less thing to worry about.

"Martin Boswell and Brenda Horsfall, the people we stay with, usually have dinner waiting for us at the house, which is really nice. Having a home-cooked meal to us is like other people going out for a meal.

"Often there are calls from the New Zealand media when we get home and Michael always takes them, even if it interferes with dinner.

"Martin and Brenda have been an integral part of our last two years and Sunday night is when we catch up with what they have been doing during the week. They have been great. Martin is a social golfer and loves the game. When we have a week off we spend it with them and their friends.

"The house has a beautiful garden and we love being home, so don't go out doing London-type things. We are far more likely to have a barbecue in the rose garden.

Monday:

Michael gets the push bike out to do the washing at the local laundrette. "It might sound crazy that here I am having earned around £400,000 in Europe and I'm riding a borrowed push bike. Actually it makes sense and is enjoyable. Insurance problems in England and Europe mean you can't borrow cars. Brenda and Martin would happily loan us their car but it just isn't worth it.

"Julie separates the whites and darks, I put the bags on the back of the bike and pedal off to leave them at the laundrette to be picked up later.

"There isn't a lot of talk about golf even though Martin and Brenda are interested in how I am going. They ask how it went when we get back on Sunday night and we might talk about it for half an hour, then it is forgotten.

"When I go back to New Zealand now I've had to get used to being stared at or asked for an autograph wherever I go. In Tooting Bec no one would have a clue about who I am or what I do for a living.

"Every week at the dry cleaners I leave my name and address and it doesn't have any effect whatsoever. Even the week after the British Open they didn't bat an eyelid. It is great. For the guys living in Bagshot or Wentworth it is a different story. There are so many golf people living in those areas that everyone wants to talk golf even when they are in the supermarket. Tooting Bec is great."

If Michael and Julie are grateful for the anonymity they enjoy living in Tooting Bec, then Tooting Bec should be grateful to them for putting it on the map, says Martin Boswell.

"It has become quite a joke. We are always thanking Michael for all the mentions Tooting Bec now gets in the newspapers and on television. When the commentator has no golf to talk about for a moment he will say, in a surprised tone, 'and Michael Campbell lives in Tooting Bec'.

"The only other person to give the place so much publicity was Citizen Smith in the television programme about anarchists. His motto was 'Freedom for Tooting'. That shows the type of place it is.

"It is a typical south-west London suburb, full of terraced houses, very Victorian. There are tiny roads which are full of traffic. Many people in Michael's position, when asked where they live, would hesitate to say Tooting Bec.

"Not Michael. He is so unpretentious. Golf does get talked about but not that much. We talk about everything. You could say we have a lot of social evenings.

"Michael and Julie have been great fun to have around. In the early days Michael was quite subdued because he wasn't getting out on the golf course enough. He was frustrated and would pace up and down the house. It was a different story in 1995 when he was playing virtually every week, and doing well."

There is more camaraderie on the European Tour than on the United States circuit, where everything is set up for families and people tend to stick to their own. One of the big differences between the two tours is that in America a player will have around 12 hotels to choose from at a tournament venue. A golfer travelling with his wife and children will tend to go to one particular hotel, single guys to another and couples will be split up around the place.

In Europe most of the players are staying within a short distance of each other, if not in the same hotel. At the end of a hard day on the golf course it is time for a shower back at the hotel before meeting up with friends in the bar for a drink and a discussion on where to go for dinner.

Those who have been in the particular city before lead the way in choosing restaurants. Eating together helps everyone feel at home and means grappling with the local language is done collectively. Having no language difficulties, Campbell admits, is one of the advantages of playing in the United States which is where he will eventually end up for the biggest part of the year.

When that happens, Michael and Julie will miss the closeness of the European Tour which, they say, is one big happy family. It doesn't matter where Michael is on the order of merit in relation to other players, everyone gets on no matter what prize money they have won.

They point to Steven Bottomley, who finished equal third with Campbell in the British Open, as a prime example. For five years Bottomley struggled to get on the main tour through the Challenge circuit and qualifying schools. Now he has made it he is just one of the boys. While Bottomley and Colin Montgomerie might be at opposite ends of the scale in earnings over the past few years they can often be seen having a beer together.

The hotel bar is used more as a meeting place than a watering hole. There will always be the exception to the rule, but most players will have one beer while they are deciding where to eat and then settle for a glass of wine with their meal.

It was in the hotel bar in Manila that Campbell met Sam Torrance for the first time.

"Sam was chatting to Mark Mouland, myself and a few other guys when he asked what my nickname was. I told him everyone called me Cambo. 'What about Soupie?' said Sam. I told him I didn't like that which was the worst thing I could have said. Sam still calls me Soupie when I see him but, thankfully, I squashed it with the other guys."

There are groups of players who spend a lot of time together while on tour. Inevitably Australians and New Zealanders tend to be attracted to each other in a foreign environment.

In Campbell's case a lot of time is spent with Michael Clayton, who can be ebullient and laconic at almost the same time, Peter "POM" O'Malley, Peter "Chuck" Fowler, Wayne "Radar" Riley, Robert Allenby and Lucas Parsons. The odd one out is Scotland's Andrew Coltart who has become a special friend of the Campbells.

"Andrew has the voice of Sean Connery, which is why I think Julie likes him. We call him Moneypenny and he is great fun to be with. A lot of the Europeans are more staid than Kiwis or Aussies, especially the English with their conservative backgrounds. Not Moneypenny. He is a real joker who knows how to enjoy himself.

"He played on the Australian tour in 1994 and won the PGA championship. That was a story in itself. He thought he was already qualified to play in the Australian Open but then found he wasn't. They told him he had to win the PGA to get in. So he did. Andrew formed an allegiance with the Aussie guys and when he goes out to dinner it is usually with the boys from down under.

"The other lads we pal around with are down-to-earth Australians and if Greg Turner is around he will be there too. Greg is a fantastic guy to be with. He has a fund of stories to tell and the way he puts them over is brilliant."

With his serious on-course demeanour Robert Allenby doesn't appear to fit in with Campbell's other friends. He gives the impression of being a very serious young man, but that, according to Campbell, isn't so.

"Rob has a heart of gold. His biggest problem is that he is very hard to get to know because he is a shy person. We really got to know him and Nadina on safari in South Africa. Julie at first thought Rob didn't like her but it was only his shyness holding him back.

"He comes from a close-knit family and hasn't experienced a lot of life. In the past he has lost his temper on the course but he is controlling that now. Rob does get uptight when he plays golf. He has been under tremendous pressure from early on through the expectations of the Melbourne media who worship him and call him the Greg Norman of Melbourne.

"Away from the course he is a completely different person. His family, his friends and the media have for years been telling Rob how great he is. There is nothing wrong with that, because he is a very talented player. But it does no harm to have your bubble burst a few times. That is what Lucas and myself do to him, which is why I think he is so comfortable in our company. We have a good laugh at each other.

"It isn't that Lucas and myself are ganging up on him either. Lucas spends most of his time bursting my bubble!"

There is often friction between players on tour which isn't surprising given the sheer competitiveness of at times highly-strung sportsmen travelling the world together. For months they are virtually living out of each other's pockets, a situation which leads to clashes.

Occasionally there are accusations of cheating, though such incidents are few and far between. More often it is merely a clash of personalities which causes the problem.

"You can get offside with someone and at the next tournament find yourself playing in the same group for the first two days. If there is tension between playing partners it isn't conducive to either playing to their potential.

"It is worse though if you are drawn with someone who throws tantrums. No one really wants to play with those who spit the dummy. When that happens it can distract those playing alongside.

"It can be embarrassing when someone is performing in front of a gallery. Those playing with him feel it just as much as the spectators. In some ways you feel like apologising to them because of what a fellow professional is doing."

While Michael Campbell has been making money on the tour he has been losing a few pounds off course to Colin Montgomerie with a long-running series of bets from which Campbell is sure he will emerge the winner, even if not in monetary terms.

"We were flying back from a tournament just before the All Blacks played Scotland in the quarter-finals of the World Cup. Monty was sitting two rows down the plane and among the banter I shouted down, 'Monty, how about a bet on the quarter-finals?' I offered him 17 points start. He wanted 21. How much? Monty said a hundred pounds. We settled on two hundred because I was so confident the way the All Blacks were playing. They won the match but I lost the bet.

"I saw him the following week in Hamburg and asked for a chance to get my money back on the first two rounds of the tournament – £200 on which of us would have the lowest round each day. By the end of the week I was £600 down.

"Now whenever we play at the same tournament we have £100 on each round on who will shoot the lowest score. At the end of the year I had lost £600, which wasn't bad going. All the guys think I'm crazy picking on Monty to bet with. Two years in a row he has won the European order of merit.

"It is a challenge taking on Monty because he is the top player on the European tour. If you are going to take someone on, I say make it the best. You can only improve your own game. I look at it from the point of view that if I am taking money off Monty then I'm going to be in contention for the tournament."

Michael Campbell makes a habit of taking on the best, whether it be betting with Colin Montgomerie or practising with Greg Norman. Campbell has never been shy of asking questions of the world's leading players and these days he and Greg Norman practice together when their paths cross at tournaments. When Campbell thinks back to his first meeting with Greg Norman he laughs.

"It was at a dinner leading up to the 1993 Australian Masters and I told the mate I was with that I was going to talk to Greg Norman and ask him for a practice round. He thought I was joking.

"I wasn't. My plan was to speak to him before he started the entree, but I couldn't pluck up the courage. No problem; after the main meal would be okay. I was really nervous. When someone has been your idol for as long as Greg Norman had been mine it isn't easy to just walk up and say something. You are afraid you will make a mess of the moment and it will be gone forever.

"After the main meal I was still too chicken. He was my idol. I'd copied his swing, the sliding right foot and the arched back, things like that.

"We finished the dessert and I was still trying to pluck up the courage when I saw he was leaving. I said to myself, 'Mike, this is your last chance. Go and talk to him.' If he could have heard me talking to myself he would have thought I was a nutter.

"I went up to him and said, 'Mr Norman, I'm Michael Campbell.' He replied, 'Oh yeah, I've heard about you.' That gave me a real boost so I took the bull by the horns and asked if we could play a practice round together the next day. Sure, he said, and the following day I went out with him and Peter O'Malley.

"I remember on every hole I would ask whether he would use one iron, three wood or driver. He gave me advice on how to play the Huntingdale course. He was probably fed up with all the questions I was asking, but if he was it didn't show because since then we've got on like a house on fire. He has taken a liking to me for some reason.

"Julie and myself had dinner one night with Greg, his trainer and Craig Parry and it was a lovely night. Unfortunately, most of the guys are too intimidated by him; they don't think he has time for them. I tell them to just go up and say hello. Greg Norman was in the same position himself at one time which is why I am sure he is only too happy to put something back into young players.

"He gave me his numbers and said I should give him a call, that we could go out in the boat, do some fishing or scuba diving. I have always been honest with him and he has reciprocated. I told him that I appreciated his help but knew that he was a very busy man. He gave me the stare and said, 'Cambo, when I was your age I often felt lost. I would turn to players like Nicklaus, Palmer and Trevino to help me out.'

"What he is doing for me, and others like me, is a bit of a payback for the help he received when it was needed. But you have to ask. He doesn't know you are waiting to talk to him.

"I've heard people say bad things about Greg, but it is only because they have had brief dealings with him, probably when he was flat out. He has an amazing presence and is so confident it brings out the lack of confidence others have. It means they get intimidated by him."

Julie will testify to the presence Greg Norman has. A very confident person herself, Julie was scared when she first met the Great White Shark.

"He does have this way about him which makes you feel inferior. He has it down pat. I think he learnt it through competitiveness. I had mixed emotions when I first met him. I was in awe but because he was so wonderful with Michael, so really caring about him, I thought he must be a pretty good guy.

"When we had dinner with him during the Dunhill Cup in Scotland I was really impressed. He is a normal guy from a normal background who happens to have become a superstar. Greg Norman is someone who goes out to be the best every time, and is a very smart businessman.

"Both Greg and myself have a great passion for scuba diving and we talked about that for a long time. I asked would he take Michael with him when they happened to be in the same city which had water and a hot climate. He said he would love to. I hope it happens because if Michael began to like it we would have something to share as a pastime. I love water but Michael doesn't. He gets seasick."

Michael Campbell loves playing on the European Tour. How long that remains his priority remains to be seen. During 1996 he is splitting his time between Europe and the United States.

The first time British Open and USPGA winner Nick Price saw Campbell play, at the 1992 Air New Zealand Open in Auckland, he said that American courses would suit him. "The way Michael drives he is made for the United States," Price said. "I'm in the top third in the States for distance off the tee and he was up there with me, and past me a couple of times."

America may be where Campbell's destiny is, but in the meantime he has been having a ball with his mates in Europe.

15
Friends and Advisors

Fellow touring professional Greg Turner sums up Michael Campbell perfectly when he says, "The great thing about Cambo is what you see is what you get."

Turner is well qualified to make such a comment. He was able to observe Campbell at close quarters through the low point of his career, in Europe during 1993, when the younger New Zealander was struggling within himself to find direction. At that time Campbell was staying with Turner in Bagshot, England.

Since then Turner has watched with satisfaction the way Campbell put his career back on track to make a meteoric rise up the world rankings into the top thirty. It would be exaggerating to say that Campbell may not have made it to where he is today without Turner's help. But the advice, straight talking and, perhaps most importantly, the company Turner was able to provide in difficult times did play a part in getting Campbell on the right road.

"I like Cambo and hope I have been able to help him. When you are the new kid on the block it is nice to have someone around to try and ease you in. But I never tried to mollycoddle him. He knows I call a spade a spade, and we have never let him get away with too much.

"I get on well with Cambo and increasingly so. There are no pretensions about him. He is honest. If he doesn't understand something, he tells you. If he wants to know something, he asks you. If he doesn't want to do something, he doesn't do it. You know where you stand with him.

"Michael is good fun and has a good sense of humour but, most importantly, he has a bloody good heart. He has made mistakes. I've heard stories about him pre-pro days. I also witnessed him in England early on.

"He has developed a lot as a person. He had the potential to get on the wrong side of the tracks, but he hasn't because he has a bloody good heart."

Turner has always known how to enjoy himself. Campbell is from the same mould. The difference between the pair during their early professional days was that Turner generally knew when to say no.

"I've always liked to loosen up a bit. Now and then I've had more than I ought to have at the wrong time. But, in general, not very often. Sunday and Monday nights I like to have a few pints. When I have a week off Janie and myself like to have barbecues, get people round and have a few wines.

"I'll always share a bottle of wine with someone at a tournament during the evening, but there is a difference between doing that and waking up with a hangover.

"Nothing against Cambo, but from what I've seen once he gets past a certain point he is unlikely to say 'Enough, I'd better hold back.' He is more likely to carry on drinking for another three hours. Therefore it is important he doesn't fall into that trap. It is something he realises and has acted accordingly."

Turner says that his partner, Jane, and Michael's wife, Julie, get on as well as he and Michael do. That, he says, is important in a touring situation where you don't take your neighbours with you. It is important to have people around who you respect and enjoy the company of.

Jane got an early taste of Michael Campbell's openness the first time they met, as Turner recalled with relish.

"We had roomed together during the Dunhill Cup qualifying in China and I was speaking to Janie on the phone every night. When he came across to London a couple of months later I picked him up at the airport and we went to the house.

"We share the house with a New Zealand girl, Kate Walker, who is a lawyer. Martin Gates, an English professional, was also living with us at the time, and when we arrived Gatesy and Kate were in the living room chatting.

"Cambo knew Martin already so I introduced him to Kate. Then we went through to the kitchen where Janie was making dinner. I introduced him and he said, 'You live here as well do you?' Janie said, 'No, I'm just the cook and washer woman.' Cambo turns to me and says, 'Oh, so that's your bit of stuff in the other room is it Turns?'

"He got a clip across the ear from Janie, but that is Cambo."

New Zealand's other European-based golf professional, Frank Nobilo, isn't as close to Campbell as Turner, but he quickly realised what potential Campbell possessed.

During the 1994 British Open at Turnberry, Nobilo, in response to a question about the depth of golfing talent in New Zealand, told a press conference after a particularly good round of his own that "young Michael Campbell already strikes the ball as well as anyone in the world".

The comment was made on the same day that Campbell failed to make the halfway cut, but Nobilo sticks to his assessment. "Michael always had a little bit more than other kids of his age. I think a lot of it is to do with his attitude.

"I remember talking to Martin Crowe about understanding what a New Zealand sportsman is all about. Generally speaking, New Zealanders are a little bit naive and normally quite shy in their approach to sport.

"Michael wasn't like that, which was going to be an advantage in comparison with a lot of other players who have come out of New Zealand. He was prepared to take the bull by the horns and I think that is why he has done so well."

Nobilo is right. Not many young players fresh on the pro circuit would dive straight in and ask Greg Norman for a practice round. It might have taken Michael Campbell all night to pluck up the courage to pop the question to Norman, but he did it and has reaped the benefits, with Norman's influence gaining him starts in tournaments which may not have otherwise been open to him.

Michael Campbell and Greg Norman have developed a rapport. Through that relationship Campbell was quickly rubbing shoulders with the world's top players. While Campbell might be considered fortunate by some to have been befriended by Norman, it wouldn't have happened had he not been such a talented player and so open as a person.

While Campbell is mixing with the rich and famous these days – Tom Cruise and Nicole Kidman for instance at Nicole's sister's wedding – it doesn't mean his old mates have been forgotten.

That was never better illustrated than by the guest list for the glittering wedding when he married Julie in Sydney. More than 70 family and friends crossed the Tasman to be with Michael on his big day. Manor Park teammates such as Murray McDonald and Grant Duncan, along with Wellington players Martin Pettigrew and Lance Phelps mixed with Aussie stars Craig Parry, Peter O'Malley and Robert Allenby. They wanted to be there with their friend Michael Campbell, not Michael Campbell the star golfer.

Grant Duncan and Murray McDonald were in the Manor Park team when Campbell arrived at the club. Murray had been the team's number one from the late 1960s right up to the time Campbell appeared on the scene.

There was no resentment of the talented Campbell. He was welcomed and supported by everyone in the team, with Duncan and McDonald in particular treating him like a young brother and looking out for him. Whenever he returns to Wellington from his travels he makes sure he can spend a night with Murray and Vanessa McDonald, Grant and Henia Duncan or John and Helen Pihama.

Murray McDonald and Grant Duncan have fond memories of those early days with Campbell. They point to an old team picture with Campbell in his white pointed shoes, and recall how he was the Michael Jackson of Manor Park. "Put the white golf glove on him and he had all the gear."

"Michael really enjoyed himself. He didn't drink much when he came to the club. I suppose Grant and myself, along with some of the other guys in the team, were responsible for introducing him to the brown stuff," Murray McDonald says.

"Cambo wasn't a noisy guy, but once he got going you couldn't stop him as we found out on one of our annual trips to Blenheim with the Manor Park team. We went to a night club, but when the guys decided it was time to leave Michael didn't want to know. He was enjoying himself and was going to stay on.

"By the time he left the club Michael couldn't remember which motel we were staying at, so he just went to sleep where he was, in the street. The police brought him to the motel and asked did he belong to us! The good thing about Michael is that he never gets aggressive . . . unless you are trying to get him out of a nightclub!"

Julie Campbell will agree that her husband is a bit of a party boy. When she first met him, Julie, knowing nothing about golf, had no idea that he may have to be up at 6am for an early tee off.

"We would be out quite late and I would be oblivious to him having to be up a few hours later. Once I found out I made sure it didn't happen. When I began travelling with him I would encourage him to go to bed early when playing the next day."

While he might be a pussycat away from golf, Murray McDonald soon found out how aggressive Campbell played once out on the golf course. When new players arrived at Manor Park they were invariably paired with McDonald, the side's most experienced player, for foursomes matches.

"From the first match it was always 'Should I have a go at this Mac?' Cambo has always been the type of player who wants to have a go at things. He was never one to sit back and just be content to play a round of golf, waiting for something to happen.

"Players such as Michael and Stephen Scahill took New Zealand golf into a new dimension. When we broke par it was out of the ordinary. With those guys it was a case of how many under par they would be. I know they were playing full time as amateurs, but even so . . ."

The younger element in the Manor Park team loved to party which often led to Campbell, Scahill and Rohan Welsh turning up to matches at the last minute. Team manager John Marsden took them to task about their late arrivals, deciding that they should all stay at the same place the night before matches to ensure they turned up on time.

"Of course, it wasn't that simple," remembers Grant Duncan. "Before one match, at Otaki of all places, which is probably the furthest we travel, they got on the grog on the Friday night and woke up late. I was the first player off for Manor Park. It took me 35 minutes to play the hole. I paced it out three times as I played for time while we were waiting for them.

"Our second guy took twenty minutes to play the first. By this time they were on their way with Michael telling the other two that if he got a speeding ticket it was going to be split three ways. It must have been the quickest trip ever between Titahi Bay and Otaki.

A new partner . . .

Away from the golf course and on safari. Julie, Michael, Nadina and Robert Allenby, Gabriel and Lucas Parsons take time out from representing Australasia in South Africa.

A night out with the Zimbabwean team for Michael and Julie during the 1995 Dunhill Cup at St Andrews.

The newly-weds.

Tom and Maria Campbell with Julie and Michael during the wedding reception at
Sydney's Ritz Carlton Hotel in January 1996.

Michael and Julie with Michael's nephew Dylan.

A rare chance to do some sightseeing. Julie and Michael outside Edinburgh Castle.

Scarsie was terrified. He was as pale as a ghost when they arrived, while Rohan lay down in the back of the car the whole way because he couldn't bear to watch what was happening. Then they went out on the course and played as if nothing had happened."

Grant Duncan has become more than a friend. He has been part of Campbell's support network since he turned professional. When Campbell and Scahill left the amateur ranks Duncan said if they ever needed tax advice he was happy to provide it.

When Campbell won the Canon Challenge in only his fifth tournament there was no shortage of people telling him to invest in this venture or that scheme. Campbell turned to Grant Duncan for help, and his friend was only too happy to put off those wanting Campbell to invest by telling them he needed the cash flow at that stage of his career.

"There were so many things happening to him it was important that an independent person like myself should be there if he needed someone to talk to. I didn't get paid by him which meant I remained independent and objective. I didn't have a stake in him apart from our friendship."

Michael Campbell doesn't forget his friends. When he represented New Zealand in the 1995 Dunhill Cup at St Andrews Grant Duncan was his guest for the week, an experience worth more than money to Duncan.

Grant Duncan is fiercely loyal to Campbell. He still doesn't accept payment for the services he provides. He cares about what happens to Michael Campbell and if he can help it Campbell will have no problems.

The last thing a professional golfer needs is having to worry about extraneous stuff off the course. The successful players have managers. Michael Campbell is no exception. He started out with IMG and at the end of 1995 switched to Masters International, which also looks after the interests of Nick Price.

There are things which need the personal touch, however. When Campbell won the St Louis Open he found he needed an American social security number for tax purposes so he picked up the telephone and asked Grant Duncan, back in New Zealand, to help.

What sounded an easy problem to solve became difficult, and Grant Duncan found himself in hot water with United States bureaucrats because he had the nerve to make an addition to one of their forms.

"The Immigration Department faxed me a social security form which asked for the person's race. It had boxes for White, Hispanic, European, Negro or Red Indian. Michael didn't fit into any of those categories so I ticked the European box and wrote underneath that he was a New Zealand Maori.

"The immigration people rang and said no one was allowed to amend their forms. Then there were more problems because I signed it for him and they wanted Michael, who had gone back to Europe, to fly back to the United States to sign the form in front of them. That is the type of hassle he doesn't need when he is trying to concentrate on his golf."

Wellington lawyer Andrew Collins is also part of the Campbell network. Collins has helped Campbell immensely during his rookie professional years, though they may never have got together had it not rained heavily during a corporate golf day sponsored by AMP, the insurance company which is New Zealand golf's major sponsor.

"We were watching Michael and Stephen practice when it started to pour with rain," Collins remembers. They continued practising but I headed for the clubhouse along with my brother David, who is an AMP agent. Over a few drinks David said someone should help Michael and Stephen who, it was rumoured, were about to turn professional.

"David came up with a proposal he wanted to put to AMP and I rewrote it for him before he submitted it. AMP said they would sponsor Michael, Stephen and Mal Tongue. It meant that the two players had a bit of cash in their pocket when they turned professional.

"Michael appreciated my help and a little later I got a call from Murray Macklin at the New Zealand Golf Foundation. He said Michael was in his office, that IMG were keen to sign him and that Michael wanted someone to check the proposal over for him.

"Michael recognised his limitations in the area of contracts. I was happy to help him and our relationship grew from there."

The relationship between Michael Campbell and Andrew Collins became vital when management group Masters International appeared on the scene wanting to represent Campbell when his contract with IMG expired.

The initial approaches from Masters International were made before Campbell's sensational performance at the 1995 British Open. They believed he was going to develop into a world-class player and wanted their company, which is headed by South African millionaire John Bredenkamp, to be part of his future.

Campbell's success at St Andrews was also the catalyst for IMG to realise they had a hot property on their hands which it would be in their interest to keep. IMG were aware Campbell had been the subject of approaches from other management companies and began to make every effort to retain him as one of their clients.

Michael Campbell had some misgivings about what IMG had, or had not, done for him. IMG, for their part, conceded that Campbell was justified in some of the concerns he expressed about their relationship. Things would improve if he stayed with them, IMG promised.

Despite feeling he hadn't been handled as well as he could have been by IMG, Michael Campbell didn't find it easy to walk away from a company which had supported him when he was starting out. There were also some strong personal relationships he had formed with IMG personnel – Angus Hawley in particular – to consider.

While Campbell was in Los Angeles for the USPGA, after his third placing at St Andrews, IMG made a last attempt to keep the New Zealander in their stable.

"I got a call from Tom Campbell asking if I would like to go to the USPGA because Michael was meeting IMG representatives while he was there," Collins said.

"The meeting was scheduled for the Wednesday evening before Thursday's first round. Because I was making the trip at the last minute the meeting was postponed till Thursday evening. That was a concern to me because Michael was playing in a Major golf tournament. I didn't like the idea that he should have to be thinking of things other than golf at such a time.

"It was a high-powered meeting. IMG were represented by senior executive vice-president Alastair Johnston, Guy Kinnings, the international vice-president, senior vice-president Andrew Pierce and their 'golf talent spotter'. Apart from Guy Kinnings, the other guys flew to Los Angeles from Cleveland specially for the meeting and returned the same night.

"I accompanied Michael and Julie to the meeting, which was amicable. It lasted for two hours and we all went for dinner afterwards. Michael was assured that IMG recognised their shortcomings. They would be rectified, and IMG would match any offer from another company.

"It meant Michael had to choose between two very good offers. Masters were offering a more intimate and personal management style with close involvement and assistance from John Bredenkamp himself.

"I believed that Masters would be more aggressive in seeking business opportunities for Michael but it was important that Michael's priority was to ensure continuing success as a professional. Nothing should be allowed to distract him from that goal."

Collins' worry that Campbell would be distracted by the business meeting in the middle proved to be unfounded. The following morning Campbell went out and shot six under par!

Andrew Collins is as loyal to Campbell as is Grant Duncan. The change of management companies had been a difficult decision for both Campbell and Collins and it was one which was not really resolved until Michael had departed Los Angeles for his next tournament. Collins was left in his hotel room at Loews Santa Monica Beach Hotel drafting a long, handwritten letter to Campbell setting out the pros and cons of Michael's requirements as a professional golfer and balancing these against business and legal issues.

While Masters International now look after Michael Campbell worldwide, Andrew Collins, Grant Duncan and Tom Campbell, who is Michael's New Zealand business manager, take care of things in New Zealand. Contracts such as the one Campbell has signed with Nike still cross Collins' desk.

Within a short time of signing Campbell as a client, Masters International, who don't take any of the player's on-course earnings, arranged a lucrative sponsorship with Nike for Campbell and another of the company's clients, Nick Price.

Andrew Collins knows how important management companies are to sportsmen in arranging schedules and travel, as well as endorsements and business opportunities.

Just as important for Michael Campbell is having people such as Andrew Collins, Grant Duncan and Tom Campbell around to keep an eye on things for him.

While Andrew Collins became involved with Michael Campbell just prior to him turning professional at the end of 1992, Maori Golf Foundation director Vic Pirihi was a part of his early development.

Watching a poised and sartorially-elegant Michael Campbell mingle with guests during his wedding reception at Double Bay's Ritz Carlton Hotel, Pirihi had to pinch himself to make sure he wasn't dreaming.

Pirihi was thinking back to when he first met Campbell in Taupo at the 1988 New Zealand amateur championships. "Michael was only 18 and full of the joys of youth. He was belligerent, over-confident, had long hair, and wore an earring. I have to say we didn't hit it off at first. He arrived on the Sunday and on Tuesday I kicked him out after a noisy night in the unit he was sharing with Martin Phillips and Mark Oliver.

"I didn't see him again till Friday night when Michael and his mates came looking for Martin Tumata, who had made the semi-finals which were to be played the following day. They wanted Martin to go out with them but I wasn't having any of that.

"It was about six months later at Titirangi when we got together again. We had an amicable meeting which ended with me agreeing to give him the full support of the Maori Golf Foundation.

"Over the next few years Michael just got better and better. It was due to good coaching and his own self-discipline. He had lost a bit of weight and physically began to look good."

That Pirihi is a fine golfer himself was demonstrated in 1988 at Taupo where he took Australian Paul Moloney, now a solid professional golfer, to the 23rd hole before losing.

Pirihi reached the final of the 1991 Maori tournament where he came up against Michael Campbell. "Michael beat me and I told him he was the best Maori golfer since Walter Godfrey. I suggested that once he got himself a short game to go with his superb long game he would be even better. Walter Godfrey had a fantastic short game with real feel. Michael now has that touch."

The Maori Golf Foundation was happy to invest in Michael Campbell. Through its programme with Maxfli it ensured Michael had clubs, balls, gloves, and, on most of his overseas trips, financial assistance.

It was through Vic Pirihi and the foundation that Michael Campbell met Bill Gladstone from Pickering Clothing, one of the foundation's sponsors. Gladstone made sure that Campbell was one of the best-dressed amateur golfers in the southern hemisphere, and when he turned professional there was no smarter rookie on tour. When the time came for Campbell to move on to bigger things with Nike he went with Gladstone's blessing and best wishes.

These days Pirihi doesn't see Campbell too often, but eagerly follows his progress wherever in the world he happens to be playing.

Greg Turner, Frank Nobilo, Simon Owen and Grant Waite have all played cameo roles on the international stage in New Zealand golf's recent history, but for many years the name Bob Charles was synonymous with New Zealand in the golfing world, and still is with those who follow the United States senior tour.

Charles hasn't had much chance to watch Michael Campbell play in the flesh, seeing Campbell hit a ball for the first time at The Grange in 1992.

"I've only ever played a few practice holes with him, at Turnberry in 1994," Charles said. "I've seen a lot more of him on television than I have in person but I love the way he swings the golf club. Michael Campbell has a golf swing which I envy. Even when he isn't at his best Michael has great timing and rhythm; that is what makes him so different.

"If I could swing it half as good as he does I would still be winning tournaments on the regular tour.

"Providing he keeps his head on his shoulders, and I have no doubt he will do that, Michael has a great future."

There is a school of thought that today's players are under far more pressure than their predecessors. Charles isn't sure that is the case, though he acknowledges it is more difficult off course for the player of today.

"The money in the game, and golf itself, is much bigger than it was 35 years ago. Whether the amount of prizemoney on offer creates more pressure, who knows?

"I felt pressure when I left New Zealand in December 1960. In my pocket was an air ticket and a thousand pounds. When that money was used up that was it. I would have to go home.

"I had no sponsorship. I was on my own. That is pressure. Today players have good amateur careers which opens sponsorship doors for them. They are offered guarantees to keep them out there playing for a living. Unfortunately, in some cases that is only prolonging the agony.

"The biggest difference between when I started out and when Michael began his professional career is the scrutiny players are put under, the huge media attention they get wherever they are playing in the world.

"When I set out as a pro, New Zealand didn't even have black and white television. When I won the British Open there wasn't even a press tent. The after-round interview at the Open consisted of six guys from the leading newspapers asking 'how did you do it?' Now the interrogation of players is intense, and not just at Major championships. They are put under the microscope wherever they play.

"Today's golfers are better equipped to handle such a situation than we were. In my day the reporters talked about golf. Good golf, bad golf, birdies and bogeys. To get into your personal life was unheard of.

"From what I've seen of Michael Campbell so far he carries himself well when dealing with the media. I've also been impressed with the way he handles himself on the course.

"I am very much a traditionalist on a golf course. I have great admiration for a player who doesn't display his highs or lows. It is important that a player can control his emotions at all times in public. Michael does that.

"We had our characters, but they kept their emotions to themselves while playing. Tennis has had its share of bad-tempered players and there have been times when I haven't been impressed with what I've seen on the football field. These days when I watch cricket I have a chuckle at the players' antics. Thank goodness golfers don't go round hugging and kissing each other.

"I was a great fan of Bjorn Borg. Next to Ben Hogan, Borg was the great unemotional sportsman. There is a big difference between having a smile on your face after a good shot and displaying all your other emotions. The way he carries himself on course Michael Campbell is a credit to those around him."

When Michael Campbell shot to prominence at St Andrews,

some of the world's top players were already aware of his potential.

Australia's Steve Elkington, the 1995 USPGA champion, was one of the first to begin singing Campbell's praises after playing with him at the Australian Masters during Campbell's rookie year on the Australia-New Zealand tour.

"I wasn't a bit surprised by the way Michael played at St Andrews. I have been telling everyone since I played with him at the Australian Masters that he is going to be a sensational player. What he has done hasn't surprised me at all.

"Ernie Els and Michael Campbell are the same type. I think Michael was better off starting out on the European Tour. I'm not saying it is easier but the shot making isn't so demanding, and Europe is a little more relaxed than America.

"Michael has a great swing and I think it will hold up for him."

Sam Torrance has had a close-up view of Campbell during his rise up the rankings and says the New Zealander is getting better all the time. During Campbell's 65 at St Andrews, Torrance was on the course and rates it one of the best rounds of golf seen in a Major championship.

"Conditions were tough. I know. I was playing in them as well. To score as Michael did must make it one of the best rounds ever. It was unbelievable. I couldn't keep my eyes off the scoreboard. Every time I looked his score just kept getting better. Amazing."

South Africa's Ernie Els is eight months younger than Michael Campbell, but after winning the 1994 United States Open, as well as capturing the World Matchplay and World Championship titles, is well-established among golfing's elite.

When, at 24, Ernie Els became this century's seventh golfer born outside America to win the United States Open, he was the youngest player to win the championship since 22-year-old Jerry Pate finished first in 1976, and only the eighth champion in his twenties since Jack Nicklaus beat Arnold Palmer in 1962.

The reason Els reached the top of the golfing mountain earlier than Campbell can be found in their early development. Campbell was 14 when his father Thomas first asked coach Dennis Sullivan to have a look at him.

In contrast Els, the son of a low-handicap amateur, was starting to win tournaments at that time. "I wasn't any good at all till I was 13.

That was when I won a pretty good junior tournament in South Africa," said Els. Then I went to the Junior World Championships in San Diego and won the 13 to 14 year age group."

A year later Ernie Els, at 14, lowered his handicap to scratch. Campbell was still playing at a nine-hole course which had no bunkers.

It was in 1992 that Els first surfaced in professional golf, winning six tournaments in South Africa. That same year he lit up the leaderboard at the British Open, as Campbell was to do three years later, with an opening round 66. Els finished fifth in 1992, seven strokes behind Nick Faldo, but had laid the foundation for his Major championship win in 1994. Maybe Campbell has done the same with his third placing at St Andrews.

Els is looked upon as the leader of a new generation of golf stars, but is delighted that his right to such a position is being challenged by players such as Michael Campbell, Robert Allenby, Lucas Parsons and Phil Mickelson.

"We need young players coming through. Greg Norman has turned 40 and Nick Price is almost there. It is great to see players like Michael Campbell, Robert Allenby and Retief Goosens appearing on the scene.

"It is only a matter of time before Michael wins some Major tournaments. Michael Campbell is a coming force in world golf. He has a terrific swing which can take him right to the top. Just as importantly, Michael has the temperament. Some players let a bad round or tournament eat at them which leads to a drop in confidence. Michael doesn't allow that to happen. When he leaves the course he leaves golf behind and gets on with life. That will stand him in good stead."

Within weeks of making everyone take notice of him at St Andrews, Campbell was in America for the United States PGA championship, being treated as an equal by all the top players.

Playing a practice round with Greg Norman, Jack Nicklaus and Vijay Singh gave the American media a close up look at Campbell in the flesh. They liked what they saw.

So did Jack Nicklaus. He had been impressed by what he had seen of Campbell on television during the British Open. Playing alongside the New Zealander only confirmed Nicklaus' impressions.

"I saw during the practice round that Michael is a fine young player," Nicklaus said. "He hits the ball a long way. Actually, he surprised me in how far he could hit it. Michael showed at the British Open how well he can play the game. There is no question Michael Campbell has a bright future in golf."

Asked if he had given Campbell any advice during their 18 holes together, Nicklaus, a professional for 34 years and with 18 Majors to his credit, laughed and said he was too busy admiring how far the younger man was hitting the ball.

"I was trying to get a lesson myself."

Of the likelihood that Campbell will probably switch his attention full time to the United States tour in the near future, Nicklaus said that would be America's gain. "I think Michael is at the stage in his career where it isn't too early for him to do anything. He is a bright, intelligent golfer who would be a great asset on the US Tour."

16

Fit for Masters

While on one side of the Tasman Michael Campbell's family prepared for their 1995 Christmas celebrations, and on the other his wife to be, Julie, planned their January wedding in Sydney, Campbell, flitting between both countries, struggled to quell the turmoil which was bubbling inside him.

The injury to his left wrist, diagnosed as a tendon strain when it happened during the second round of the AMP Air New Zealand Open at The Grange, was beginning to cause him real concern.

A seemingly endless stream of doctors kept coming up with a different diagnosis on each visit. Rest would be prescribed one day, the next another specialist would be suggesting surgery might be the best plan of attack. One thing was certain. Michael Campbell wouldn't be swinging a golf club for a few weeks. Holding anything in his left hand without supporting his wrist was difficult enough without thinking of trying to hit a golf ball.

Eventually, agreement among the medical experts was reached. In layman's terms the sheath which holds the tendons together in his wrist had come away. Time, it was suggested, would allow the sheath to re-attach itself and there was no reason it shouldn't be as good as new – with a bit of luck. The final diagnosis was made by an Auckland specialist and that night when Campbell returned to his parents' Titahi Bay home he was more on edge than I had ever seen him. We had planned to work on this book for a few hours, and while we did manage to talk for a while it was obvious Michael's mind was elsewhere. He was also shattered emotionally because the enormity of the situation should the sheath not heal had begun to hit him.

He knew he would be receiving an invitation to compete at the US Masters at Augusta in April, thanks to his third placing at St Andrews and fifth placing on the European order of merit. The mere thought of playing at Augusta made Campbell's nerves tingle. Now there was also apprehension. What happened if he wasn't fit in time? Would he get another chance if he didn't play in 1996? How long would the injury take to heal? No one had been able to tell him that. Maybe he wouldn't be able to play golf in 1996, never mind be ready in time for the Masters.

Campbell returned to Australia where he saw another specialist who was to make a support for the wrist, ready for when he resumed golf. That artificial aid proved to be no help, but at the time Campbell was prepared to try anything. At one point he tried a poultice used by horse trainers to clear tendon problems in their animals!

Then it was time for him and Julie to head back to Wellington for Christmas. Throughout the celebrations Campbell put on a brave face, but the injury and its ramifications were never far from his mind.

"I was devastated at that time, absolutely devastated. You try to remain positive but it isn't easy. How long would it be before I could play again? Would I play again? I was thinking good things and bad things, mostly bad things.

"When something like that happens you feel so vulnerable. I don't think I have ever been more nervous. People were suggesting different scenarios. Three months, six months, 12 months . . . I had just finished a fantastic year, and to be forced off the course like that was nerve-wracking.

"During those weeks away from golf I tried to keep busy but it was hard to keep my mind on what I was doing. It was at that time I went to the United States for meetings with Nike over a sponsorship deal.

"Besides Nike I had also signed a contract with Black Hawk. I thought, 'These people will be expecting me to be playing. Not sitting at home watching tournaments on television.'

"It is a fact of life that golfers have to take breaks through injury, but I was feeling it harder because it was the first time it had happened to me. When I had been sidelined in the past it was through illness –

the appendicitis for instance at the Australian amateur – which isn't the same. Once the appendix was taken out I knew how long it would be before I could play again. There was no uncertainty.

"I had the wedding to keep me occupied after Christmas. Once that was over, however, I couldn't wait to get back to playing again. We hadn't planned a honeymoon because I had been scheduled to play the Malaysian Masters in Kuala Lumpur, but it soon became apparent I wouldn't be playing in that tournament."

Campbell was advised by his doctor to also withdraw from Singapore's Johnnie Walker Classic and the Heineken Classic at The Vines in Perth. The Australian Masters at Huntingdale was pencilled in as his first tournament back, but there was still that little matter of swinging a club again before anything could be planned for certain.

The familiar surroundings of Manor Park provided the setting for the start of Michael Campbell's return to golf. He had been away only seven weeks but to Campbell it seemed a lifetime. That Saturday morning Michael and Julie arrived at Manor Park with caddy Max Cunningham to see Mal Tongue, who had suggested some minor adjustments might need to be made to Campbell's swing to take the stress off his wrist.

It was the club's season-opening day. Campbell had been invited to lunch with the members and to have honorary life membership bestowed upon him in recognition of his achievements as both amateur and professional.

While waiting for the proceedings to begin, Campbell couldn't keep still. He paced up and down the pro shop, then fidgeted through the light lunch which followed the presentation. Finally it was time to head for the practice fairway, with Campbell admitting he was apprehensive at the thought of picking up a club after such a layoff.

There were four people present – Julie, Mal Tongue, Max Cunningham and myself – when Michael Campbell hit his first ball for seven weeks. We've talked about it since and agree that the moment is etched into our minds.

Max Cunningham, who needed to know of any adjustments made to the swing so he could keep an eye on it during tournaments, stood behind Campbell. Mal Tongue was to the side, while Julie and myself were sitting on the bank chatting.

As Campbell swung the club face through the ball he shouted in agony and dropped the club onto the ground. No one spoke till Mal Tongue said calmly, "Okay. We are going to have to make some slight changes," and began to set Campbell up for another swing.

Julie turned to me and said, with more hope than conviction, "Mal doesn't seem too concerned, does he?"

Actually, Tongue was as stunned as the rest of us. He told me afterwards that he was shocked when Michael shouted and dropped the club. "I thought, 'I won't be going to the Masters this year.' It was as if I was watching what was happening from afar. The moment seemed frozen."

Max Cunningham, who tried to look unconcerned but failed, admits that he thought he might be looking for another job.

I don't know exactly what I was thinking at the time, being too busy watching the reaction of the others. I do know I felt for Michael Campbell. He looked so distraught and bewildered. It seemed his world was about to fall apart. Seven weeks' rest and he still couldn't hit a golf ball.

That was when Mal Tongue took charge. When Greg Turner had sustained a similar injury he had asked Tongue to modify his swing. That exercise, which proved to be a success, prepared Tongue for what was happening now.

What unfolded over the next two hours was astonishing. Had I not been there it would have been hard to believe. By the time the session ended Michael Campbell was hitting the ball straight down the fairway and laughing as each shot was completed without pain. The only sign there had been an injury was a brace Tongue had attached to Campbell's right arm to help him adjust the way he was swinging.

Fellow professional Stu Thompson arrived to practice and watched with interest as Campbell continued hitting balls. Andrew Collins, Campbell's lawyer, turned up and was delighted to see how well things were going, at first blissfully unaware of how the session had begun and, when told, pleased he had missed the drama.

The following four days were spent practising, and a relieved Campbell emerged from the five-day work-out thrilled with his new swing. Once again he had lived up to his tag as The Adaptable Man.

"Technically I was swinging better than at any time in my life after Mal made the changes. My swing hadn't been that good technically, despite my results, in 1995. Mal had noticed one or two glitches early in the year, but we adopted the policy of 'if it's not broken don't fix it'. Once it broke we set about fixing it. The adjustments aren't drastic but they have taken a lot of stress off my wrist.

"I didn't know what to think after that first swing. The pain which shot up my arm was awful. The negative thoughts came rushing back, but Mal stayed composed and soon had me convinced that we would get it right."

The Australian Masters was still a couple of weeks away. That time was spent working on the new swing, but while Campbell's confidence grew each day he knew there was no substitute for playing in tournaments.

Stepping on to the Huntingdale course nine weeks after withdrawing at The Grange, Michael Campbell was nervous. Even a practice round with Stephen Scahill and Marcus Wheelhouse which was, Campbell said, like being back at the Tower Tournament during his amateur days, couldn't relax him.

"There is a huge difference between hitting balls on the practice ground or playing rounds which mean nothing and going out to play competitively. Once I was under the cosh out on the course I was nervous and it showed over the opening holes.

"I played with John Daly for the first two rounds. On the first day I was two over after three holes, simply because I wasn't confident within myself. That is unusual for me.

"Over the first eight holes I was just pleased to get through without a recurrence of the injury. I was waiting for the pain on each shot, but it never came. Walking away from the eighth green I told myself that everything was fine. That the worst was over. It worked because over the next ten holes I was the Michael Campbell I used to know. I played the back nine in four under for a two-under round. That helped my confidence start to creep back.

"It was such a relief to get through four rounds without any problems from the injury. I had the odd twinge, usually when I slipped back towards my old swing. When that happened there was a sensation a bit like an electric shock. It soon reminded me that I had a different swing now.

"I felt I had adapted pretty well, but it was going to be a while before the new swing became second nature. That was something I had to accept. For years I had been swinging one way, and you can't just change it completely overnight. There is obviously a tendency in the early stages of anything new to revert to the old."

Campbell was two under the card at the end of four rounds, finishing a creditable 19th. Most players would have been quite happy to do that well after a nine-week break. Campbell thought he could have finished higher.

"I should have been happy, but I knew it could have been better. The biggest problem that week was my short game. You soon lose your touch around the greens when you aren't playing competitively, and I had learned early on as a pro that was the area where you win golf tournaments.

"That was the only minor negative though. The rest was all positive. I was playing again. There had been no problems with my wrist. My ball striking was pretty good and I could still score well with my adjusted swing. It was good to be back."

Following the Australian Masters, Michael Campbell turned his attention towards the United States. On his schedule before the US Masters were four tournaments he would be playing in under foreign player exemptions, the Doral Ryder Open in Miami, the Honda Classic in Fort Lauderdale, the Bay Hill in Orlando, and the Tournament Players Championship at the Sawgrass course in Jacksonville.

While he enjoys playing on the European Tour, it is almost inevitable that Campbell will finish up full time in the United States. What better way was there to, as he puts it, dip his toe in to test the water, than prepare for the Masters in America.

The venture didn't get off to the best of starts when Campbell missed the cut in the Doral Ryder Open. When he sat down after that tournament and analysed the two rounds he played Campbell wasn't too downhearted.

"It was the same problem as at the Australian Masters. My short game just wasn't up to scratch. To be honest it was horrible. The important thing was, I could identify the problem and work on it. I was hitting the ball well but round the greens . . . it was woeful."

After missing the cut at the Doral, Michael Campbell spent every spare moment before the Honda Classic working on his short game. The result was dramatic.

An opening round four-under-par 68 put him back in the spotlight. European journalists, and those Americans who travelled to the British Open, knew his background inside out. Those covering the US Tour, however, had to start from scratch and Michael Campbell again found himself explaining his Maori heritage, how Maori were the indigenous people of New Zealand, that his ancestors travelled from Scotland to New Zealand and that one of them, Logan Campbell, became mayor of Auckland. The journalists, used to American players staying home apart from travelling to the really big tournaments overseas, were also fascinated by the fact that Campbell had played in 41 events during 1995 and had played eight tournaments in seven countries over an eight-week stretch.

Leading the Honda Classic after 18 holes was US Tour rookie Tim Herron, who played the round of his life for a ten-under-par 62. Herron was never headed during the rest of the tournament. After four rounds he was 17 under the card on 271, four shots clear of Mark McCumber. If he couldn't win the tournament himself, Campbell was pleased Herron won. The pair had got to know each other in Australia when Herron played the Australia-New Zealand Tour and had become firm friends.

Campbell moved into equal third place at the halfway mark by shooting 69 in the second round. A third round 68 took him to 11 under for the tournament and into second place with one round to play.

Before that round, Max Cunningham was approached on the practice ground by one of the greats of golf, Johnny Miller, who wanted to know more about Michael Campbell. "Johnny is part of the NBC commentary team and he wanted to know about Mike's background and what his strengths were.

"While we were talking Mike carried on practising. Johnny Miller hardly took his eyes off him. Before he left Miller turned to me and said 'He's got one of the finest golf swings I've ever seen.' That is praise!"

A final round 74 pushed Campbell down the leaderboard. He had to settle for equal seventh placing, but being in contention had renewed his confidence. "It was nice to get up there again. I began to feel a confidence that had been missing and was really looking forward to going to Orlando for the Bay Hill.

"Unfortunately, I played terribly there and missed the cut, despite being in a good frame of mind beforehand. The problem at Bay Hill was that I was inching back towards my old way of swinging. I was getting caught between the new and the old. There is enough to think about on the golf course without worrying about that sort of thing.

"I think it was also taking me time to adjust to the kind of exposure I had been receiving since arriving in the United States. Three times I had done live television interviews of up to half an hour.

"Then there was instructional work for the television series Inside the PGA Tour. I was asked to demonstrate bunker play. Not bad for someone who started out on a course which didn't have bunkers!

"Jim Nance and Gary McCord also recorded one of their New Breed television series with me."

After Bay Hill Campbell took a week off. Rather than head straight for the practice ground he spent a few days fishing and accepted an invitation from Nick Price to go jet skiing.

The Tournament Players' Championship on the Sawgrass course was Michael Campbell's last port of call before the Masters. After an opening 70 Campbell had to claw his way back over the cut line during the last couple of holes during his second round 73, posting a gutsy birdie on the 18th to qualify for weekend play. Shooting 69 on Saturday moved him up a few places but a 77 on Sunday undid the good work.

Mal Tongue arrived in Sawgrass during the TPC. Campbell had set aside the week before the Masters to fine-tune his game with the coach, and it was a bonus that Tongue could see him in action competitively. Campbell says it didn't take Tongue long to notice that something wasn't quite right.

"After watching me play one round he said that I wasn't myself. I was hanging my head and letting my shoulders droop, even after a good shot or making a birdie. What he said made me think. I realised that I was a little uncomfortable in America, a bit intimidated. It was strange.

"I think I was putting too much pressure on myself. I was trying to earn enough money on the US Tour to qualify for a card to play there full time. At the same time I was thinking ahead about what would be necessary to retain my European Tour card. It all added up to extra pressure.

"There is quite a difference between the American and European circuits. I call America the land of convenience, though I still love Europe and the players who are on that tour

"It is easier to play in the States, where the players are treated better. The quantity of quality players is higher in America than Europe and there are so many things to consider. I'll have to make a decision which continent to concentrate on eventually but when I arrived in America I should have just put it all out of my mind, though that is easier said than done.

"The 77 at the TPC also hit me hard mentally. That was something I knew I had to work on. It was imperative that I put rounds like that behind me and looked ahead, rather than back.

"From the time I started playing golf I had been able to leave bad rounds on the course, not let them get to me. Now I was having to tell myself to do something which had always come naturally."

The week prior to Augusta was spent at John Bredenkamp's Florida home where Michael Campbell enjoyed a diet of practice and fishing. Then it was time to move on to Augusta where Campbell was to achieve another of his life's ambitions – to play in the US Masters.

As is the case with St Andrews and other Scottish venues on the British Open roster, Augusta's population swells during Masters week. A place which for 51 weeks of the year appears almost sleepy suddenly bursts into life when the alarm clock which signifies the arrival of the Masters circus rings.

Hotels, filled to capacity with those fortunate enough to obtain the hard-to-come-by admission tickets, hold no attraction for golfers. Even that most accommodating breed of sportsmen would find being in such a golfing goldfish bowl off the course as well as on it too much to bear.

Masters International had rented a large house for Campbell's party which included his father Thomas, coach Mal Tongue, sports psychologist Michael Martin, lawyer and friend Andrew Collins, and members of his management team including manager Andrew Ramsey.

Only 15 minutes from the course, the house was perfect. Campbell could come and go as he pleased, which was something to be grateful for as he discovered on his first night in Augusta.

Following their normal tournament routine, the Campbells

headed off to a restaurant where they discovered there was a 90-minute wait for a table. A member of the restaurant staff recognised Campbell and, this being Augusta where for one week a year golfers are treated like God, they were soon being shown to a table. Campbell wasn't going to take chances for the rest of the week, however.

"Next day we stocked up with food. We stayed in the house when not at the golf course. Augusta during Masters week is like a zoo and the players avoid going out if possible.

"It isn't that you are being anti-social. It is nice to be recognised and that people want to talk to you, but it can just become too much when every person in town is a golf fan."

Michael Campbell was introduced to the Augusta National golf course on Sunday, April 7, and wondered what all the fuss was about. "There was hardly anyone around that day. Most of the players were finishing a tournament elsewhere. No more than ten of the guys who would be teeing off on Thursday were out on the course.

"A few club members were on the course and about ten people were watching what was going on. No one else was allowed on the course that day so what I was experiencing was nothing like what I had been seeing on television over the years.

"I had been thinking back to the days when I would get up and watch the Masters before going to school. I couldn't wait to get to the course. Sunday at Augusta National is nothing like you expect. You think, 'What's the big deal about this place?' Then you go back on Monday and it hits you full blast.

"Instead of thirty or forty people there are 40,000 to 50,000, and that is just for a practice day. I was pleased I had gone to the course on Sunday. It sort of eased me into it.

"On the Monday I had a round with Ernie Els, Lee Janzen and Brian Henninger. The following day Sandy Lyle, Ian Baker-Finch and myself played nine holes, while on Wednesday I was paired with Colin Montgomerie for the par-three tournament which was a lot of fun.

"At the TPC Ben Crenshaw had suggested we have a practice round together at Augusta and I was delighted at the prospect of playing with the defending champion. Unfortunately, there was a communication problem. I thought we were meant to be playing on Monday, while Ben thought it was Tuesday. By the time we realised the mistake I had another commitment for Tuesday.

"The practice rounds were invaluable. Augusta is all about placing the ball. You need to know where to be on the fairways and greens, though even if you put it in the right spot it doesn't guarantee results. The greens are particularly hard to read. Gary Player has played in 39 Masters tournaments and still has problems. He told me that the 16th green is the most difficult he has ever come across."

Going into the Masters, Campbell was struggling mentally. Such a frame of mind is particularly unhelpful when putting and that was the area of Campbell's game which most contributed to him missing the cut. Over the two rounds Campbell had 70 putts.

"On those greens you have to think twice about every putt. A two-footer you would just knock in anywhere else requires plenty of thought or you can finish up ten feet past the hole. On the 16th in the second round I had a 30 foot uphill putt which finished up three feet past the hole. The second putt lipped out and finished up further away than it started and I ended up four putting.

"Watching the Masters on television you can't see the undulations in the greens. They are amazing.

"I learnt a lot during the week at Augusta and came away with more respect for the golf course. The front nine, which you don't really get to see on television, is a lot more difficult than the back nine."

In the days leading up to the tournament, Campbell tried to play down the fact that this was the US Masters. It was something special, he acknowledged, but was trying not to put too much pressure on himself.

Once the pairings were announced for the opening round there was no chance of Campbell staying out of the spotlight. Partnering Campbell on his debut at Augusta would be Jack Nicklaus, playing in his 37th Masters and a six-time winner of the tournament. Experienced commentators said someone playing in their first Masters, as Campbell was, could have done without being paired with Nicklaus.

"This is Jack's house, his home. Campbell will face enormous pressure," Steve Hersey, long-time golf editor of USA Today, said. "There will be huge galleries following Jack and, of course, you know what is going to happen every time Jack putts out? The crowd is going to run to the next tee and the marshals will have a hell of a time holding them back while Campbell putts out."

Hersey's fears about the galleries proved unfounded. Campbell wasn't troubled. Those who did rush off to the next vantage point were obscured by those who had staked their claim to a spot at a particular green for the entire day.

Playing with Jack Nicklaus was a different experience, however. Julie Campbell, outside the ropes, won't forget that day. "It was overwhelming. Very moving. When he appeared, Jack Nicklaus got a standing ovation and that is how it was for the whole round. Just to be part of it was an emotional experience."

Inside the ropes it was nerve-wracking for Michael, even though he had tried to prepare himself for the moment. Was he intimidated by the great man's presence?

"Yes and no. It is hard to explain how I felt. I was nervous enough with it being my first Masters, and here I was playing in front of the biggest gallery on the course with a living legend. I hit my first drive 280 yards, which settled me down a little. We both made par on the first, and after we hit our tee shots at the second Jack started chatting to me.

"I really appreciated the way he treated me throughout the round. He told me stories about past Masters and how the course had changed over the years. He would point to a bunker and say that it wasn't there in 1964. Jack pointed out a number of changes that had taken place during the time he had been playing Augusta National.

"It was quite entertaining and helped me settle down. The crowds are different to those in Europe. They are very vocal, even more so when Jack Nicklaus is around, and you are clapped onto every tee, whoever you are. I was fortunate to play with Jack Nicklaus and Gary Player, who between them had played in 76 Masters and won nine titles."

Campbell again showed his fighting qualities to finish with a one-over 73, when the first round could easily have got away from him after a potentially soul-destroying trio of bogeys between the fourth and sixth holes.

In the second round Campbell couldn't find his putting touch. Even though he birdied his final two holes he had to settle for a 76 which meant he missed the cut.

Campbell could take consolation from the fact that missing the cut in a first appearance at the Masters is commonplace. Among those who missed out along with him were defending champion Ben Crenshaw and Tom Watson, who has eight Majors to his name, including two Masters. In 1995 fellow New Zealander Frank Nobilo opened with a horror 80 and failed to make it to weekend play. A year later Nobilo returned, played solidly and finished strongly for fourth behind winner Nick Faldo.

"It was good to see Frank come back into form, and great to see a New Zealander finish so high up in a Major championship again. For a small country we don't do too badly in what is truly a world game."

While pleased for Nobilo, Campbell couldn't believe what was happening as he watched on television Greg Norman's demise. "My heart went out to Greg. I had some idea how he was feeling. I had been in the same position at the British Open, though I was only two shots ahead starting the last round.

"Had Greg been leading by two then I believe he would have gone on to win it. He was attacking during the first three rounds but seemed to change his game plan in the fourth because of the six-stroke lead he had.

"In a way it puts what happened to me at St Andrews in perspective. It was only my second Open whereas Greg had played 16 times in the Masters. It shows you can't take anything for granted.

"Playing with Nick Faldo didn't help him either. Faldo is like a bulldog. He just won't let go even when there seems to be no chance of winning. That is why he has won six Majors.

"The thing that struck me was how both Nick and Greg handled themselves at the end. It was very emotional and both came out of it with credit."

It was only after his part in the Masters was finished that Campbell realised how much it had taken out of him.

"On the Saturday I went to the practice ground with Mal to hit some balls. The guys who were playing over the weekend were there practising and I suddenly felt relieved that I wasn't going out there again. That the tournament was over for me.

"A huge weight had been lifted off my shoulders and, according to those who had been around me leading up to the Masters, I returned to my normal self.

"Apparently I had been difficult to live with, really crabby with people I care about. Mal had been with me in the days leading up to the tournament and said I had been unbearable.

"Ever since I had received the invitation three months earlier my mind had been on the Masters. I didn't realise it at the time but the injury, a new swing, and a lack of self-confidence in tournaments leading up to the Masters all took their toll."

During the Masters, Michael and Julie Campbell met up with friends from the European Tour. They began to realise how much they were missing the familiar atmosphere of Europe. Playing in the United States had been a great experience, but Michael now couldn't wait to get back to Europe to consolidate on what he had achieved the previous year.

This time he would be going as a seasoned campaigner rather than a rookie. Michael Campbell's rookie years were over and a new chapter of his career was just beginning.